# Perspectives on Peter Maxwell Davies

For Helen, Lewis and Harriet

# Perspectives on
# Peter Maxwell Davies

*Edited by*
RICHARD McGREGOR

## Ashgate

**Aldershot • Burlington USA • Singapore • Sydney**

Published by

Ashgate Publishing Ltd
Gower House, Croft Road,
Aldershot, Hampshire GU11 3HR
England

Ashgate Publishing Company
131 Main Street
Burlington, VT 05401–5600
USA

Ashgate website: http://www.ashgate.com

ISBN 1 84014 298 7

**British Library Cataloguing-in-Publication Data**
Perspectives on Peter Maxwell Davies
    1. Davies, Peter Maxwell, 1934– —Criticism and interpretation.  I. McGregor,
    Richard
    780.9'2

**US Library of Congress Cataloging-in-Publication Data**
The Library of Congress control number is pre-assigned as: 00–107423

This volume is printed on acid-free paper.

Typeset in Great Britain by The Midlands Book Typesetting Company, Loughborough, Leics.
Printed and bound in Great Britain by MPG Books Ltd, Bodmin, Cornwall.

# Contents

# Contributors

**Michael Burden** is Director of the New Chamber Opera which he founded with Gary Cooper in 1990. He has been a lecturer in music at New College Oxford since 1989 and since 1995 Fellow in Music and Lecturer in Opera Studies at the university. He has directed some twenty productions of the New Chamber Opera including recently Britten's *Curlew River* and, with Lynn Meskell, Slade's *Salad Days* – combining them with research interests in theatre music of the seventeenth, eighteenth and twentieth centuries. His volume *A Woman Scorned: Responses to the Dido Myth* was published in 1999.

**Joel Lester** is Dean of Mannes College of Music in New York City. An accomplished scholar, violinist, and administrator, he has authored seven books on music, including texts on harmony and twentieth-century music, an award-winning monograph on eighteenth-century compositional theory, and a forthcoming study of Bach's solo-violin works. He was violinist for twenty-two years in the Da Capo Chamber Players, winners of the Walter W. Naumburg Chamber Music Award in 1973. He is Professor Emeritus of The City College and Graduate School of the City University of New York, and has also taught at Eastman and Juilliard.

**Richard McGregor** currently lectures in music at St Martin's College, based in Lancaster. He has a particular interest in the sketch materials for the music of Peter Maxwell Davies and is presently working on an article focusing on the composer's script. He is also a composer and recent works include *I am the Rose of Sharon* for soprano, SSA and strings, and '*...Greeks bearing gifts*' for two pianos.

**Peter Owens** read music at Royal Holloway College and subsequently undertook Ph.D. research at King's College, London, on the works of Peter Maxwell Davies. Between these studies he taught music at Queen Elizabeth's School, Faversham, and directed musical holiday courses in France. Since 1987 he has pursued a career in music publishing and is now a director and Head of Publishing at Peters Edition Ltd.

**David Roberts** is currently an editor of *Early Music* magazine. His ground-breaking articles for *Contact* on the music of Peter Maxwell Davies led to a doctoral dissertation at Birmingham University which has since become an essential source document for all those writing on the composer's music.

**John Warnaby** was born in Neath, South Wales, in 1941. He did not achieve any notable educational success until, as a mature student, he obtained a First Class honours degree with the Open University, after studying part time while working with the British Steel Corporation. Subsequently, he obtained a Major British Academy Award from the Department of Education and Science, enabling him to pursue full-time research at the Open University. He completed his D.Phil. degree in 1990, the title of his doctoral dissertation being 'The Music of Peter Maxwell Davies, based on the Writings of George Mackay Brown'. He currently works as a music critic and as a part-time tutor with the University of Wales Extra-Mural Department.

**Arnold Whittall** is Emeritus Professor of Music Theory and Analysis, King's College, London. His main publications are in the field of twentieth-century music and music theory. They include *Music Since the First World War* (1977/ 1988), now revised and extended as *Musical Composition in the Twentieth Century, The Music of Britten and Tippett, Jonathan Harvey: A Handbook*, and substantial articles on Peter Maxwell Davies, Birtwistle, Maw and Dillon.

# Foreword

*Peter Maxwell Davies*

It is a disquieting experience to realize that not only do performing musicians spend many hours practising the music you have written, but that composition students and others spend possibly even more hours studying your full scores. As a composer one forgets, in time, the fine detail of composition processes which produced past work, and it is only the most recently completed music, and that under construction, which is truly alive and present: it must be left to scholars to recreate, slowly and painstakingly, earlier creative procedures.

Creation takes place, as it were, in a hot crucible, very fast, and becomes quasi-intuitive. The danger of analysis is that it can, perhaps, sometimes suggest much more considered and methodical slow work than the reality – and it is important to understand that any commentator is bound to emphasize structural features the composer takes for granted, when presented with musical ideas more or less complete. A huge amount of composition occurs before anything filters through into consciousness. This, however, does not imply that a composer need not study scores in the ways suggested in these essays – particularly in a period when the very basis of musical expression has been the subject of so much debate and controversy. In my apprentice years I needed to read scores with this kind of X-ray intensity, helped by the writings of Schoenberg, Boulez, Schenker, Ratz and others, as well as learning from detailed discussion with my teachers Petrassi and Sessions, and with a whole host of musicians encountered at the Dartington summer schools, and elsewhere – from Aaron Copland and Luigi Nono to Hans Keller and Charles Rosen, and not forgetting my everyday encounters with fellow students Alexander Goehr and Harrison Birtwistle.

The more deeply one studies analysis, the more the results of insights gained become second nature. Analysis, far from being academic in any pejorative sense, can become an inspiration on the lifelong quest for the right expression of personal creative ideals. Moreover, if more performing musicians took the trouble to study the structure of music to any depth, one would be spared so many unsyntactical, ungrammatical 'interpretations', where, for example, a transitional tonic within a development becomes a point of arrival, and cross-phrasing and extensions are routinely misunderstood and confused.

I am extremely grateful to Richard McGregor and his team for these detailed, devoted studies. They have undertaken tasks for which I would never have the inclination or patience, and from which I have learned much. I trust that they will lead to increased and more understanding pleasure and insight into my work, on the part not only of composers and performers, but of interested parties generally.

# Acknowledgements

In the preparation of this volume I have received much support and encouragement from a variety of sources and I would like to record my appreciation here.

I am indebted to all those who contributed to this volume for their work and the helpful way in which they responded to my requests. In the early stages I was grateful to Raymond Monelle for his support and the enthusiasm he shared with me for the project. I have enjoyed discussing many aspects of the music with Peter Owens who has also been most helpful from the earliest stages.

My own contributions to this volume have been made much more focused as a result of the access to sketch material still in the possession of the composer. Max has been most gracious in his encouragement, co-operation, and the giving of his time, and this helped me enormously. My sincere thanks are also due to Judy Arnold for providing access to pre-concert talks from the collection of tapes which she has made over the years, as well as for arranging the provision of study-score material.

I have appreciated the help and assistance of Andrew Cross at Salford Archives, and the staff of the Scottish Music Information Centre while the sketches were in their care. When subsequently the sketches were transferred there I was given every assistance by the British Library staff, and especially Arthur Searle and Chris Banks. Arthur Searle's handlist to the sketches has been invaluable.

In the preparation of this text for publication both Rachel Lynch and Ruth Peters of Ashgate Press have been very supportive and accommodating. My sanity has been preserved by research funding from St Martin's College Lancaster. Typesetting and the reading of my editorial markings must merit some sort of prize for Karen Cumpsty, secretary to the Music section at St Martin's. Justin Doyle has set the musical examples to be found in the text.

Reproduction of the musical examples is by kind permission of Boosey and Hawkes Music Publishers Ltd, Schott and Co. Ltd, and Oxford University Press, as follows:

*Veni Sancte Spiritus* © Copyright 1964 by Boosey and Hawkes Music Publishers Ltd.

*Alma Redemptoris Mater* © Copyright 1965 Schott and Co. Ltd. Reproduced by permission.

*Ave Gracia Plena* © Oxford University Press 1965. Reproduced by permission.

*Worldes Blis* © Copyright 1975 by Boosey and Hawkes Music Publishers Ltd.

*Ave Maria Stella* © Copyright 1976 by Boosey and Hawkes Music Publishers Ltd.

*Hymn to Saint Magnus* © Copyright 1978 by Boosey and Hawkes Music Publishers Ltd.

*Vesalii Icones* © Copyright 1978 by Boosey and Hawkes Music Publishers Ltd.

Trumpet Concerto © Copyright 1988 by Boosey and Hawkes Music Publishers Ltd.

*Strathclyde Concerto No. 1* © Copyright 1988 by Boosey and Hawkes Music Publishers Ltd.

*Strathclyde Concerto No. 3* © Copyright 1992 by Boosey and Hawkes Music Publishers Ltd.

Symphony No. 5 © Copyright 1994 by Boosey and Hawkes Music Publishers Ltd.

*The Beltane Fire* © Copyright 1995 by Boosey and Hawkes Music Publishers Ltd.

Symphony No. 6 © Copyright 1996 by Boosey and Hawkes Music Publishers Ltd.

Permission to cite the diagram from John MacQueen's *Numerology* (© University of Edinburgh Press 1985) has been received from the publisher. The expanded version of the *Ave Maris Stella* discussion, originally published in *Analytical Approaches to Twentieth-Century Music* by Joel Lester: Copyright © 1989 by Joel Lester, is reprinted by permission of W.W. Norton and Company Inc. Extracts from the sketches appear by kind permission of the composer.

My special thanks go to my family for their forbearance and to my colleague Gerry Doyle for his help through the whole period of research and preparation.

Richard McGregor

# Introduction

For all the fact that Peter Maxwell Davies and Harrison Birtwistle will have achieved their sixty-sixth years by the time this book comes to print and, critics aside, have achieved their positions in the musical establishment comparable to Britten and Tippett at roughly the same age, it is astonishing that so little has been written about their work.

In the 1970s it seemed likely that a large body of analytical writing on these two composers was about to be generated and, as far as Davies's music was concerned, a great deal of interest was sparked by David Roberts's clear exposition of the composer's compositional technique in the contemporary music magazine *Contact* of 1978.

The 1980s came and went with comparatively little discussion of the important new works being written. We should be grateful that some doctoral theses were completed in this period – most notably David Roberts's own thesis which has become a standard reference work for all those wishing to understand the composer's technical methodology over the first twenty years of his output. David Roberts established a terminology for categorizing the composer's procedures and his work has directly influenced that of Peter Owens who has contributed to this volume.

During the 1980s *Tempo* magazine carried a few articles on Davies's new works, but the majority of references to the composer's output came in the form of first performance and/or recording reviews, to which John Warnaby contributed often after 1983. Warnaby's own doctoral thesis with the Open University appeared in 1990 – a study of the works based on the writings of George Mackay Brown.

The only two substantive volumes to have appeared up to 1990 were the book, published in 1981, by Paul Griffiths, the first in a series of volumes devoted to the work of contemporary composers, and, two years previously, the compilation of previously published *Tempo* articles edited by Stephen Pruslin under the title *Studies from Two Decades*.

In terms of a comprehensive thoroughgoing presentation of Davies's actual techniques of composition available in the public domain one has to go back to the article which Stephen Arnold wrote in 1975 for the volume *British Music Now*, edited by Lewis Foreman, in which he explored the techniques of set transformation found in the opera *Taverner* and associated works.

Only in the mid-1990s have we begun to see an increase in analytical writing about Davies's techniques with the work of Peter Owens which concentrates on the period 1965 to 1978, Arnold Whittall's perceptive interpretations of Davies's works and their context, and my own work on the music of the 1980/90s including the sketch material.

The bibliography included with this volume does not pretend to be comprehensive. A list of articles, reviews and certain American theses will be found in Carolyn Smith's *Bio-bibliography*, which unfortunately does not include some *Tempo* articles, David Roberts's *Contact* articles and British theses (details of which are found in Bartlett and Sarnaker's 'Register of Dissertations and Theses on Music in Britain and Ireland', *Research Chronicle* 25 [1992] published by The Royal Musical Association). Needless to say this somewhat devalues the usefulness of the book. Similar reservations attach to Colin Bayliss's book *The Music of Sir Peter Maxwell Davies* (London: Highgate 1991). A comprehensive listing of all *Tempo* articles referring to Davies's music will be found at the website <http://www.maxopus.com>.

Clearly this present volume is, by any measure, overdue, and I am grateful to all those who have contributed. The genesis of this project came at the LANMAC Conference (held at Lancaster University) in 1994, and a chance conversation with Raymond Monelle about the desirability of a serious study of Davies's music. Early discussion with the composer's agent suggested several routes but in the end Judy Arnold decided to go forward on the webpage, which has become a useful tool for all those inclined to find out about the composer and his music. Raymond Monelle and I therefore began the project as joint editors but after some time pressure of other commitments obliged Dr Monelle to pull out of editing the volume.

Initial discussions centred on the possibility of having a consistent language in which to express the technical elements of Davies's style, drawing on the work of Roberts and Owens, but in the end it seemed better to have a variety of approaches reflecting differing points of view. In fact interpretation of the sketches might be hindered by having to translate Davies's terminology into another format. Therefore this volume demonstrates a variety of approaches to Davies's music which, it is hoped, will both complement and contrast with each other sufficiently to allow the reader to appreciate the different levels on which the composer's music operates. If a greater understanding and appreciation of Davies's style and compositional imperatives is realized then this volume will have achieved its primary purpose.

One aspect of Davies's terminology requires a short explanation here. Some of the sketch material utilizes an alphabet which Davies devised as a teenager. It would not be appropriate to explore this alphabet in the present volume, but I intend to publish separately concerning this aspect of the composer's compositional procedure. Suffice to say that in general the annotations fall

within four categories and none of these is found exclusively in the sketches in
the alphabet code – in other words each is sometimes found in normal script
(albeit perhaps in German and occasionally in Greek). Each work is different –
there is no absolute norm. The annotations can be found as follows: set labels (for
example, 'O.T./N.T.' or 'Mars'); details of orchestration; structural comments;
general comments, usually relating to the work. Some reference to the
annotations will be found in my articles in this volume.

   As a final comment it is important to note that I had hoped to include an article
written specifically for this volume by David Roberts. For various reasons this
proved to be impossible and so I have edited a version of Roberts's discussion of
*Alma Redemptoris Mater*, the fourth chapter of his thesis, with some additions
from David Roberts himself. I hope that the link with the latter part of my article
on the 1980s compositional processes will prove of interest.

# Alma Redemptoris Mater

*David Roberts*

## Author's note

The following article is the fourth chapter of my 1985 Ph.D. dissertation with a number of minor editorial emendations. Its academic origins will be plain to the reader in the general severity of its style and the somewhat puritanical conclusion: were I rewriting it from scratch I should attempt to make it more amiable: I hope the reader will not be discouraged. I have added a few endnotes to explain terms and notational conventions defined earlier in the thesis. But perhaps the most important theoretical issue addressed in the preceding chapters is that of hierarchical levels of serial structure. To make sense of what follows it is necessary to begin with a summary of that theory.

From early in his compositional career Peter Maxwell Davies used pitch-class sets in ways that extend Schönbergian practice. Although he employed twelve-note sets in his early works, he rapidly abandoned these in favour of sets having greater or fewer than twelve elements. More significantly, he rarely composed with sets as isolated units to be strung together on an *ad hoc* basis, but used instead *sets of sets*. A number of compositional possibilities flow from this way of thinking, and Davies makes ingeniously varied use of them. He quickly realized the potential of using not merely *sets of sets* but *sets of sets of sets*, and so on and so on. To bring some order to the description of these hierarchical levels of serial structure I adopt the following terminology. Relationships between individual notes and the sets of which they are members are said to belong to the *primary serial level*; the grouping of primary-level sets to form sets of sets constitutes *the second serial level*; the grouping of second-level sets to form sets of sets of sets constitutes the *third serial level*; and so on. Davies frequently also makes use of a level of serial structure inferior to the primary level, generally in the form of decorations of individual pitch classes: this is the *sub-primary level*.

Sets are labelled as follows.[1] Given a set-type S, then $S_t$ is the set-form in prime aspect that has pitch-class number t as its first element; $S_tR$ is the set-form in retrograde aspect that has t as its final element; $SI_t$ is the set-form in inverted aspect that has t as its first element; $SI_tR$ is the set-form in retrograde-inverted aspect that has t as its final element. The subscript t is the *transposition number* of the set-form. Transposition numbers run from 0 to 11, though here the numbers 10 and 11 are represented by the symbols T and E respectively. This shorthand was a convenience to me at the time; now I find it distracting, and apologize to the reader. Sets belonging to higher levels of serial structure are indicated by a preliminary superscript: thus $^2S_t$ is a second-level set-form; $^3S_tR$ is a third-level set-form in retrograde.

*

Davies's habit of 'borrowing' pre-existing material – particularly from the medieval and Renaissance periods – for use as the basis of original works is well known and much commented on. The three-movement sextet *Alma Redemptoris Mater* (1957) for flute, oboe, two clarinets, bassoon and horn is the earliest of his published compositions to incorporate material from a medieval source. The identity of that source raises some interesting questions upon which I shall comment at the end of this article.

**The set**

With the notable exception of the music played by the oboe in the third movement, and the less important exception of some sub-primary decorations, all the pitch-class material of the sextet is drawn from a ten-element set-type, S (Ex. 1.1).

Ex. 1.1:   *Alma Redemptoris Mater* – ten element set [S]

---

[1]    In discussing pitch-class sets I have found it helpful to draw a distinction between set-types, set-forms and set-statements. A *set-type* is the most abstract conception of a set: we might thus say that Schoenberg's Fourth String Quartet employs one set-type only. A *set-form* is one stage less abstract, consisting of a set-type manifested as a particular configuration of pitch classes: we might thus say that Schoenberg's Fourth String Quartet employs all 48 set-forms produced by the operations of inversion, retrogression and transposition. A *set-statement* is a concrete realization of a set-form in terms of specific pitches: we might thus say that Schoenberg's Fourth String Quartet employs several hundred set-statements.

An important difference between composition with conventional twelve-note sets and with sets using fewer than twelve pitch classes is that (with exceptions) set-forms of the latter type may be differentiated (or associated) not only by the order of their elements but also by their pitch-class content. A particular feature of the set-type used in *Alma Redemptoris Mater* is the identity with respect to pitch-class content of set-forms that stand in the relation $S_t$:$SI_{t+1}$. Set-forms so related are, moreover, strongly linked through mutual permutation of discrete dyads (Ex. 1.2).

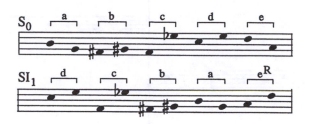

Ex. 1.2: *Alma Redemptoris Mater* – $S_t$ and $SI_{t+1}$

Twelve set-forms are employed in the work and these are displayed in Ex. 1.3. These are either primes with even transposition numbers or inversions with odd transposition numbers. No retrograde or retrograde-inverted forms are used (though there are instances where two- and three-element cells within set-forms are reversed). It is more usual to find Davies confining himself to primes and retrogrades only in a work, and the restriction to just two aspects is characteristic.

## First movement

### Second-level structure

The second-level serial organization of the first movement, summarized in Ex. 1.4, may be generated by the following algorithm:

1. Partition each prime and inverted set-form thus: (0 1 2 3 4 5) (6 7 8 9).
2. Call the two resulting segments 'the long segment' and 'the short segment' respectively.
3. In each statement superpose the long and short segments as independent counterpointed lines.
4. Beginning with $S_6$ as statement 1, form a concatenated succession of set statements in prime aspect thus:

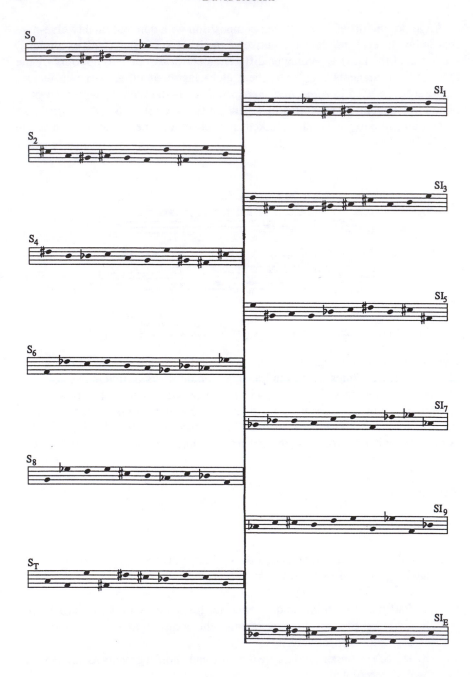

Ex. 1.3: *Alma Redemptoris Mater* – twelve set forms

- for statements 2, 4, 6 and succeeding even-numbered statements choose the set-form starting with the last pitch class of the long segment of the preceding statement
- for statements 3, 5, 7 and succeeding odd-numbered statements choose the set-form starting with the last pitch class of the short segment of the preceding statement.

5. Continue to the point where the process begins to repeat itself (this occurs at statement 10).
6. Complete the first statement of the second cycle (so ending the succession as it began, with a statement of $S_6$).

These ten statements correspond fairly exactly to the ten sections indicated in the score by double bars.

7. Group the ten statements in pairs: (1,2) (3,4) (5,6) (7,8) (9,10).
8. Superimpose on the statements of the symmetrically-positioned second and fourth groups, i.e. statements (3,4), (7,8), their inversional partners from the $S_t:SI_{t+1}$ pairs.

This device for organizing second-level structure is unrepresentative of Davies's more usual practice in that, unlike the transposition square and transposition cycle,[2] the number of primary-level sets generated by the algorithm depends on the interval structure of the set itself. Like them, however, it is a process that can be applied to any set.

A feature of the second-level structure that has an important formal implication is the interlocking succession of paired sections (these are indicated in Ex. 1.4 by braces above the staves). Each of the pairs of sections is realized compositionally as statement-variation. Since the realization also develops material linearly by establishing links between contiguous sections, it follows that the interrelationships among sections is quite complex. See Ex. 1.5. for a detailed analysis of the realization of the first two sections.

---

[2]    A *transposition square* is formed by taking the pitch classes of a set in order and using them to determine the transposition levels of a succession of set-forms. Thus a seven-element set would give rise to seven set-forms, which can be set out as a 7 x 7 square array that is symmetrical about one diagonal axis. A *transposition cycle* is formed by taking a set and repeatedly transposing it by a constant interval (the *transposition constant* or tc): the cycle concludes when a further transposition would reproduce the initial set-form. Where tc = 1, 5, 7 or E, a cycle of twelve sets results; tc = 2 or T gives cycles of six sets; tc = 3 or 9 gives cycles of four; tc = 4 or 8 gives cycles of three; tc = 6 gives a cycle of two; and (not trivially!) tc = 0 gives a cycle of one.

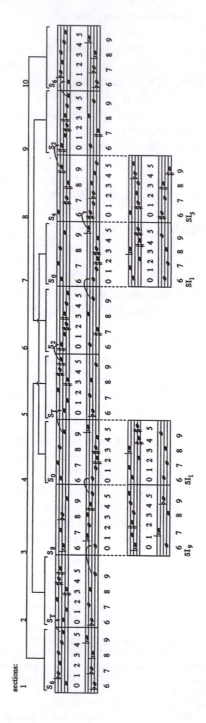

Ex. 1.4:   *Alma Redemptoris Mater* – paired sections

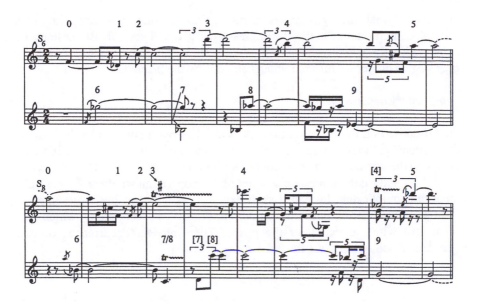

Ex. 1.5:   *Alma Redemptoris Mater* – first movement bars 1–17

## Interfusion and fragmentation

The (0 1 2 3 4 5) (6 7 8 9) partitioning preserves all five shared dyads in the $S_t{:}S_{t+1}$ pairs; furthermore, the long segment of the prime and the short segment of the inversion begin with the same dyad (vic 8), as do the short segment of the prime and the long segment of the inversion (vic 4). Hence in the four sections that use $S_t{:}S_{t+1}$ pairing, there is available to the composer the opportunity of employing one of his most characteristic compositional principles: this can be called *interfusion*. Interfusion consists of co-ordinating two or more serial lines – often realized as contrapuntal voices – so that they coincide at the same pitch or collection of pitches at the same moment or at slightly staggered time-intervals. In this way the distinctness of the separate lines is compromised: their identities are momentarily confused. The principle is most often used in slower tempi where the aural image is blurred by continual long *crescendi* and *diminuendi*.[3] On the opposite side of the coin and equally characteristic is *fragmentation*: the division

---

[3]    The characteristic sound-image of Davies's music of the 1950s and 1960s has been memorably captured in words by John Harbinson:

The result is a language with fractured diatonic melodies, slow suspended harmonic motion, and a unified surface, which through structuring of dynamics, often sounds like a tape played backwards, or music in an overresonant church.

Harbinson, 'Peter Maxwell Davies "Taverner"', *Perspectives of New Music* 11/1 (Fall–Winter 1972), p. 233.

of a single serial line by means of phrasing, instrumentation, overlapping, and other shaping resources so that the impression is given of several distinct lines. In combination these two techniques produce a shifting, ambiguous surface which may sustain numerous different interpretations by the listener.

*Sub-primary decoration*

Superimposed on the serial framework is an elaborate network of sub-primary decorations. Although these may be of interest to the analyst, I do not propose to deal with them in detail: their manner of derivation is untypical of Davies's work as a whole and a comprehensive account of their operation would be excessively long and complicated. Instead, I shall examine, as a reasonably representative example, the interrelationships among a family of decorations which are associated with element 0 of the prime. There are six occurrences of this decoration (see Appendix 1 for Ex. 1.6):

- Bar 11, section 2 (Ex. 1.6(b))
  $A^5$–$F^4$ ($S_T$:0–1) is elaborated by the interpolation of $G^4$–$C\#^5$: these pitches are an echo of the $G^4$–$C\#^5$–$F^4$–$A^5$ of bar 7 (Ex. 1.6(a)).[4] In this earlier place $G^4$–$C\#^5$–$F^4$ decorates $B^5$–$A^5$ ($S_6$:4–5): this figure, sometimes modified, appears at the appropriate transpositional level at the equivalent position in each set-statement.

- Bar 18, section 3 (Ex. 1.6(c))
  $G^4$ ($S_8$:0) is elaborated by $G^4$–$C\#^5$–$F^4$–$E^5$–$F\#^5$, an echo of bars 11–12.

- Bar 25, section 4 (Ex. 1.6(d))
  $B^3$ ($S_8$:0) is elaborated by $B^3$–$F^4$–$A^3$–$A\flat^4$, a transposition of the first four pitches of the decorative figure of bar 18.

- Bar 32, section 5 (Ex. 1.6(e))
  $A^3$–$F^3$ ($S_T$:0–1) is elaborated as a variant of bar 11.

- Bar 40, section 7 (Ex. 1.6(g))
  $B^3$ ($S_0$:0) is elaborated by a variant of bar 25, where $B^3$–$F^4$–$A^5$–$A\flat^5$ is itself elaborated in a way that harks back to bars 36–7 (Ex. 1.6(f)). In this earlier place $D^4$–$F\#^4$ ($S_2$:6–7) is elaborated by a 'chromatic' infilling with octave displacements.

---

[4]    Pitches are here labelled according to the system of the Acoustical Society of America. The superscript following each note name indicates the octave register in which it appears. Middle C is the first note of the fourth register and is labelled $C^4$; the B above that is the last note of the fourth register and is labelled $B^4$; $C^3$ is an octave below middle C, and so on. [Editor's note: I have retained this system in the present article as it reflects this author's thesis even though it differs from that used by Peter Owens whose work can be viewed as a development of that begun by David Roberts.]

- Bar 46, section 8 (Ex. 1.6(h))
  $E\flat^6$ ($S_4$:0) is elaborated by $A^6$–$A\flat^5$–$F^5$–$A\flat^5$, a reordering of the last three pitches of the decoration of bar 40 transposed up an octave.

What is striking about this example is the diversity of the elaborative criteria: transposition, non-transposition in a transposed context, echo, and omission, which are employed cumulatively and in various combinations.

*Durational organization*

Because of the complexity of the fragmentation and decoration it is difficult to see whether there is a systematic basis for the durational organization of the movement (or indeed the work as a whole). It is tantalizing to find that the lengths of the ten sections run:

$$9, 8, 7, 6, 5, 4, 6, 6, 5, 6 \text{ x measure}$$

that is to say, what begins as an incremental duration string tails off into no particular pattern (though a case may be made for subdividing the seventh section $3 + 2 + 1 = 6$).

**Third movement**

Since the structure of the second movement is more complex than that of the third, and in a sense dependent on it, I shall deal with the two movements in reverse order.
    The third movement comprises three superposed layers of material:

- a single statement of the third-level structure $^3S_0$
- sub-primary decorations of $^3S_0$
- the material played by the oboe, none of which is derived from S.

The following discussion should be read in conjunction with Ex. 1.7 (see Appendix 2).

*Higher-level structure*

In the discussion of the first movement, Ex. 1.3 was treated simply as a repertoire of set-forms: their disposition in the chart was of no importance. For the second and third movements, however, its layout has a particular significance, for when read from top to bottom it indicates the organization by means of two interlocking transposition cycles, each with tc = 2, of the second serial level. The two transposition cycles, $^2S_0$ and $^2SI_1$, are interleaved to form the third-level structure $^3S_0$:

$$^3S_0 = S_0 \quad S_2 \quad S_4 \quad S_6 \quad S_8 \quad S_T \quad (=^2S_0)$$
$$SI_1 \quad SI_3 \quad SI_5 \quad SI_7 \quad SI_9 \quad SI_E \quad (=^2SI_1)$$

Such an ordering, by bringing the $S_t:S_{t+1}$ pairs into adjacency, provides an opportunity for the exploitation of their associative properties. It is thus particularly ironic that Davies imposes a system of partitioning and permutation (described below) on the component elements of $^3S_0$ so that their capacity to form associations is considerably reduced.

The texture of the movement is contrapuntal: each primary-level set-statement is realized as a single line (which may, however, be shared among several instruments). The number of lines heard at one time gradually increases from one to five and then reduces again to one, forming a roughly symmetrical design (though it is far from obvious that this design is the result of a simple algorithm, described below). The aspect of set-statements is differentiated through instrumentation: primes ($=^2S_0$) are assigned to flute and bassoon and inversions ($=^2SI_1$) to horn and clarinets. In addition to their latter role, the clarinets play all but one of the sub-primary decorations (the other is given to the flute).

*Partitioning and permutation*

Although there are several instances of interfused lines in the movement, the invariant dyads of the $S_t:SI_{t+1}$ pairs do not provide the opportunity for such extensive use of interfusion as might have been expected, since the dyadic pattern is disrupted by a scheme of partitioning and systematic permutation:

Primes are partitioned (0 1 2) (3 4 5) (6 7) (8 9)
Inversions are partitioned (0 1) (2 3) (4 5 6) (7 8 9)

Thus of a potential five invariant dyads, three only survive (Ex. 1.8).

Ex. 1.8:   *Alma Redemptoris Mater* – invariant dyads

The partitioning is realized compositionally through the insertion of rests between segments and through the permutation of the segments. If the four segments of the prime are labelled W,X,Y,Z, and those of the inversion are labelled w,x,y,z, then the pattern of permutation appears as follows:

| | | | | |
|---|---|---|---|---|
| $S_0$ | W | X | Y | Z |
| $SI_1$ | w | x | y | z |
| $S_2$ | W | X | Z | Y |
| $SI_3$ | w | x | z | y |
| $S_4$ | W | Y | X | Z |
| $SI_5$ | w | y | x | z |
| $S_6$ | W | Y | Z | X |
| $SI_7$ | w | y | z | x |
| $S_8$ | W | Z | X | Y |
| $SI_9$ | w | z | x | y |
| $S_T$ | W | Z | Y | X |
| $SI_E$ | w | z | y | x |

Ex. 1.9: *Alma Redemptoris Mater* – permutation patterns, third movement

That is, the pattern of permutation is the same for both members of each $S_t:SI_{t+1}$ pair (though it should not be forgotten that the elements being permutated are different for primes and inversions), and is derived through permutating segments X, Y, and Z (and x, y, and z) in all 3 x 2 x 1 = 6 ways. Unlike the permutation patterns of slightly later works such as *Prolation* and the String Quartet, this is not based on a change-ringing pattern, since permutated elements sometimes move more than one position at a time. The effect of the permutation on $^3S_0$ is shown in Ex. 1.10.

*The symmetrical design*

The temporal disposition of the set-statements of $^3S_0$ is determined by the following algorithm:

1. Align the first segment – always W (or w) – of each statement with segment y (or Y) of its preceding statement.
2. Align the succeeding segments of the two statements one-to-one.

The first part of the algorithm ensures the coincidence of segments Y and w of the $S_t:SI_{t+1}$ pairs, these segments being identical (and thus providing opportunities for interfusion). Since set-forms in the relation $SI_t:S_{t+1}$ have no segment in common there is of necessity no such motivic connection between their respective segments y and WI which also coincide. The result of the application of the algorithm – which results in the symmetrical design remarked on above – is schematized in Ex. 1.11.

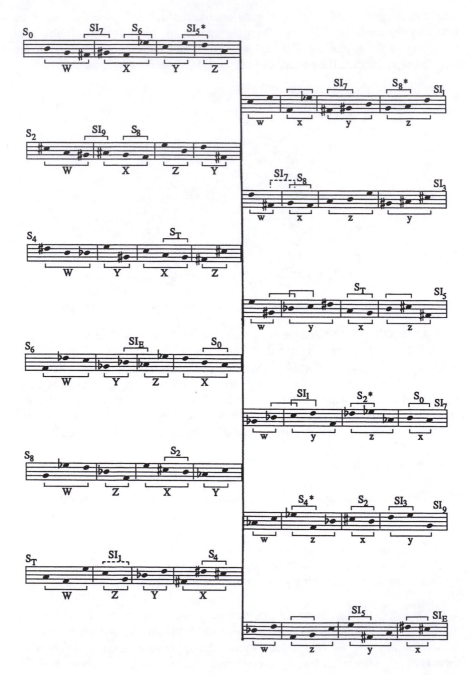

Ex. 1.10:   *Alma Redemptoris Mater* – permutation of $^3S_0$

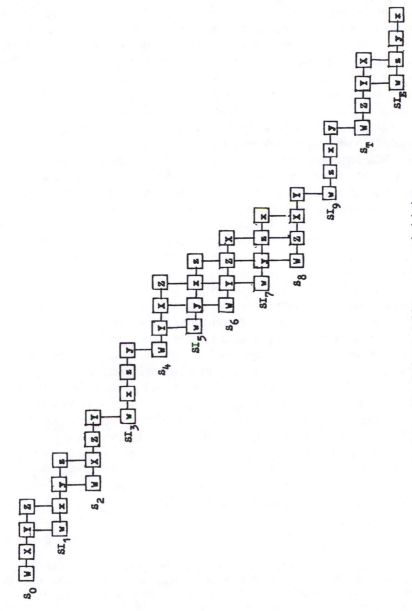

Ex. 1.11:   *Alma Redemptoris Mater* – symmetrical design

## Sub-primary decoration

Superimposed on these long-drawn melodic lines are the quick sub-primary decorations of the clarinets. These are ornaments of a type encountered frequently in later works: they have indeed appeared in less developed form in the pieces which preceded *Alma Redemptoris Mater*. From their overall character I shall call them 'melismas'. In general, a melisma derives from primary-level material but treats it in a relatively unrestrained way: elements may be freely permuted, omitted, and repeated, and occasionally pitch classes that are not members of the set-form from which the decoration is drawn may be included. In the movement presently under discussion it is best to regard the free permutation as being applied to set-forms drawn from Ex. 1.10, that is, to set-forms which have already undergone systematic permutation. Despite these possibilities for obfuscation, the identity of the set-form which is the source of the melisma is usually clear. The element of fantasy in their treatment reflects the relatively low position of such decorations in the serial hierarchy.

The first note of a melisma is usually at the same pitch as a primary-level note sounding at the time. Here they are somewhat unusual, for not only do they fulfil this condition but in addition the last note of each is normally at the same pitch as the next element in the primary-level set. In other words the melisma acts as an elaboration of a dyad. With just two exceptions the interval decorated is sic 2 – the scalar interval class that appears most frequently in the unpermutated set.[5]

All occurrences of sic 2 in the set-forms of Ex. 1.10 are marked with a solid brace (the two anomalies by a dotted brace): the accompanying set-form designations indicate the serial derivation of the melismas. As the chart shows, every sic 2 in the primes and the majority in the inversions are decorated. In most cases, when sic 2 is ordered as vic 2, it is decorated by a melisma derived from an inverted set-form; when it is ordered as vic T, the melisma is derived from a prime set-form. Presumably these choices are made because the vector interval class formed between the first and last elements of unpermutated primes and inversions are vic T and vic 2 respectively. The five asterisked melismas in Ex. 1.10 are the exceptions to this rule and work the other way about, with vic 2 decorated by primes and vic T by inversions – consequently all these melismas end with pitches alien to the set-form from which they derive.

---

[5]     A *scalar interval class* (sic) is a measure of the distance between two pitch classes: the scalar interval class between the two pitch classes numbers n and m is the smaller of the two numbers (m – n) and (n – m) (modulo 12). There are seven scalar interval classes: sic 0, ... sic 6. A *vector interval class* (vic), as well as measuring the distance between two pitch classes, indicates their order: the vector interval class between two pitch-class numbers n and m which appear in that order is the number (n – m) (modulo 12). There are twelve vector interval classes, vic 0, ... vic 11.

## The oboe material

The oboe material is not drawn from set-type S but from the Sarum plainchant antiphon *Alma Redemptoris Mater* (Ex. 1.12)[6] (*Liber Usualis*, p. 273). The oboe line consists of a quotation of the pitch classes of the melisma on the word 'Alma' followed by a restatement of its first three pitch classes (Ex. 1.13).

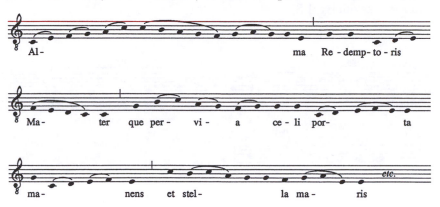

Ex. 1.12:   Sarum Antiphon *Alma Redemptoris Mater*

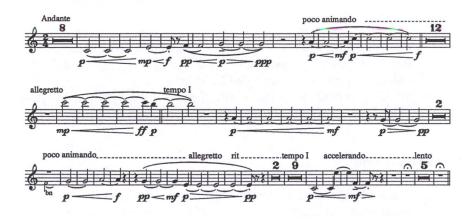

Ex. 1.13:   *Alma Redemptoris Mater* – third movement, oboe

---

    [6]    After *John Dunstable: Complete Works*, ed. Manfred F. Bukofzer, *Musica Britannica*, vol. 8, rev. Margaret Bent, Ian Bent, and Brian Trowell (London: Stainer and Bell, 2nd rev. edn, 1970), p. 161.

In the light of Davies's later practice, it is natural to seek some systematic means of transforming the plainchant into the set, but I have had no success in finding one. It is perhaps more productive to observe that the set and the opening of the plainchant are unified by four ordered trichords held in common – one of these is the same as the final isolated trichord of the oboe (Ex. 1.14). These correspond to the four trichordal divisions of the partitioning of S and SI in this movement (compare this with Ex. 1.8).

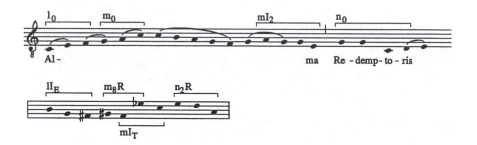

Ex. 1.14:   *Alma Redemptoris Mater* – set trichords

The juxtaposition of the oboe line and the material derived from S seems to have been carried out with an eye to interfusion and harmonic interaction. For example

- the opening $C^4$–$E^4$ of bars 9–13 interfuses with $S_0$:6–7 and $SI_1$:0–1
- the $C^6$ of bars 38–42 combines with the interfused $S_4$:6–7 and $SI_5$:0–1 ($E^4$–$G\#^4$) of bar 40 to form a (0,4,8) trichord
- the $E^4$ of bars 65–9 combines with the interfused $S_8$:6–7 and $SI_5$:0–1 ($A\flat^3$–$C^4$) of bar 66 to form another (0,4,8) trichord.

## Second movement

The discussion of the second movement should be read against the analysis of the movement shown in Ex. 1.15 (see Appendix 3). The movement is divided into three sections (indicated in the score by double bars), each of which comprises a single statement of $^3S_0$.

The second section, bars 16–27, is organized according to the scheme already presented in Ex. 1.11, and is in effect a condensed reworking of the third movement (excluding the material derived directly from the plainchant). The condensation is achieved through more rapid presentation of material, verticalization, elision and omission. Inversions lose their segment w (elided with segment Y of the primes) and are assigned to the 'quasi cadenza' horn part. The component segments of the primes are stated as verticals by the remaining instruments. $S_T$ disappears altogether.

The outer sections are organized on a different basis. In essence the first section, bars 1–15, groups the six $S_t$:$SI_{t+1}$ pairs into units and within those units associates by means of instrumentation, contour, rhythm, and so on, the W,X,Y,Z,w,x,y,z segments that are similar in pitch-class content. Segments Y and w are invariably amalgamated into a vertical. The other segments are treated with a certain freedom, but tend toward the following scheme:

W   is paired with   y
X    is paired with   x
Z    is paired with   z

and in each case the paired segments have two pitch classes in common (Ex. 1.16).

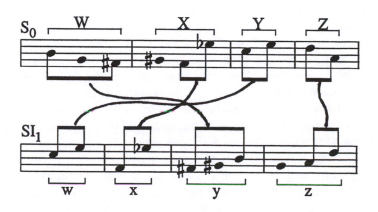

Ex. 1.16:   *Alma Redemptoris Mater* – pitch-class correspondence

The third section, bars 28–45, is a reworking of the first. The six amalgamated (Y + w) verticals are extracted from their proper places and placed at the end. The remaining paired segments appear in a more condensed form than in the first section, with a great deal of elision: for example, X and x are always combined so that the two notes of x are assigned to one instrument and the additional note that converts x into X is assigned to a second.

Decoration in this movement is restricted to non-serial mordents, trills, and single grace notes fixed at a distance of scalar interval 11 or 13 from the note they decorate.

### *Alma Redemptoris Mater* and its source

It is surely incontrovertible that the oboe part of the third movement is 'based on' a piece of Sarum plainchant. But is this the sole 'borrowing' made in the sextet? It has been stated frequently by various commentators (including, among the more dependable, Robert Henderson, Roger Smalley, Bayan Northcott, Stephen Arnold and Paul Griffiths)[7] that the work is based on a motet by Dunstable. This I believe either to be erroneous or else to be true in such a weak sense as to be of virtually no value. To disprove the idea absolutely is scarcely possible, particularly in view of Davies's capacity to work extreme transformations of musical material, but, for the reasons I shall now outline, the weight of evidence is against it.

As I have shown, the work is constructed almost entirely from a ten-element chromatic pitch-class set: this surely can have little if anything to do with Dunstable. The only material of any importance that does not derive from the set is the oboe line of the third movement. My demonstration that this is based on a Sarum plainchant does not immediately exclude the possibility that it is also based on Dunstable, for it could be a borrowing at second remove: that is, Dunstable might have borrowed the plainchant for a *cantus firmus* tenor and Davies might then have borrowed the tenor. The long durational values of the line make this a tempting proposition, though it should be noted that the problems of representing those durational proportions in fifteenth-century mensural notation are very great – if these durations derive from a medieval model then they have almost certainly been modified.

Since there is some ambiguity in the matter of precisely which Dunstable motet is intended by the writers mentioned above, it is as well to examine the likely candidates. There are two motets to the words of the antiphon *Alma Redemptoris Mater* in the *Dunstable Complete Works* (*Musica Brittanica*, vol. 8). One of these (no. 60), ascribed by the editors to Leonel Power, makes no use of the plainchant. The other (no. 40) is interpreted by Reese[8] as using an elaborately paraphrased version of the plainchant as a *cantus firmus* in the discant; the editors of the *Complete Works* are unenthusiastic about this view and remark that 'the resemblances [between the chant and the discant] are quite possibly unintentional' (p. 195): in any event there is no question of Davies's oboe line being derived from either the discant or any other part of the motet. A third motet included in the *Complete Works* (though the editors favour an

---

7    See Henderson, 'Peter Maxwell Davies', *Musical Times* 102 (October 1961), p. 625; Smalley, 'Some Recent Works of Peter Maxwell Davies', *Tempo* 84 (Spring 1968), p. 3; Northcott, 'Peter Maxwell Davies', *Music and Musicians* 17/8 (April 1969), p. 39; Arnold, 'Peter Maxwell Davies' *British Music Now*, ed. Lewis Foreman (London: Paul Elek, 1975), p. 72; Griffiths, *Peter Maxwell Davies* (London: Robson Books, 1982), pp. 27–8.

8    Reese, *Music in the Middle Ages* (London: J.M. Dent and Sons, 1941), pp. 418–20.

ascription to Forest), *Ascendit Christus* (no. 61), certainly does employ as its tenor the plainchant melody antiphon *Alma Redemptoris Mater* but in a transposed, decorated, rhythmically active version that is clearly not the progenitor of the oboe line. Hence the one manifest borrowing in Davies's work has only an indirect link with any of the three candidate pieces.

Of the authors mentioned above, only Griffiths produces any coherent argument in favour of the Dunstable connection, when he claims that there are formal and proportional links between the sextet and no. 40 of the *Dunstable Complete Works*. I reproduce the whole of what Griffiths has to say on the matter:

> [Dunstable's] antiphon is in three sections, triple counterpoint enclosing a central duo, and Davies's piece is similarly in three movements, two *andantes* around a *presto*. Just as Dunstable's duo is made up of phrases of nine, eight and ten dotted minims (in modern notation), so Davies's *presto* follows a pattern of even contraction and expansion in having sections of fifteen, twelve and eighteen 2/4 bars (the duple measure is used throughout the piece, … making rhythmic designs quite clear). Moreover, the similarities between the first and last phrases of the Dunstable duo are mirrored in the Davies *presto*. [9]

To say that X is based on Y must surely mean that a singular feature, a feature that somehow marks out Y as being Y, is incorporated into X. A claim that the sextet is 'based on' the motet, simply on the grounds that the latter is in three sections and the former is in three movements, would, in the absence of further, more substantial evidence, be taken seriously by few people: tripartite structures are simply too common in western music for such an assertion to be of any value. In much the same way, the argument concerning the triple division of both the duo of the motet and the second movement of the sextet would be more convincing if, on the one hand, there were any structural resemblances between the outer sections of the motet and the outer movements of the sextet or, on the other, the similarities between the first and last phrases of the duo amounted to much more than that both begin on C and end on G (seeing that in the sextet the last section of the second movement is demonstrably a variant of the first).

The most substantial point that Griffiths puts forward is the comparison between the proportions of the duo and of the second movement. Incidentally, his argument is not affected in any important respect by his having made an error in counting: Dunstable's duo is, in point of fact, made up of phrases not of nine, eight and ten breves (modern dotted minims) in length, but of ten, nine and eleven.[10] It is true that the structural proportions of many of Dunstable's works

---

9     Griffiths, *op. cit.*, p. 27.
10     Strictly speaking, Griffiths is also incorrect in saying that the outer sections of the motet are in 'triple counterpoint': in fact they merely contain counterpoint in three parts.

are particularly interesting[11] and it seems not unlikely that such proportions
might be of interest to a modern composer of a serialist turn of mind. The
question is, if such a composer were to base a work on this motet, would it be
anything like the sextet? The 10, 9, 11 structure is indeed of significance within
the motet, but only as part of a larger scheme, as the three diagrams in Ex. 1.17
make clear[12] (the figures represent semibreves in the original). Were such a
nested system of proportions observable in the sextet, that would be far stronger
evidence in favour of the supposition that its structure was based on that of the
motet: since there is no such system, the case that the proportional relationships
between the parts of Davies's work are modelled on those of Dunstable's is left
in a rather weak state.

From all this I conclude that most of the writers who cite the Dunstable motet
as the source of the work have not done so because each has made such a
discovery for himself. (Griffiths, to give credit where it is due, has not accepted
the idea blindly, though he has not perhaps been sufficiently critical). That a
writer may relay an untested assertion is of course unremarkable: what is
interesting in this case is the persistence of the notion. It persists, I suggest,
because it forms part of a mythology that has grown up around Davies's music.
A mythology may encompass both true and false information, but what matters
to the culture that cherishes it is not its value as information, but its value as a
tool for the imagination. Once the suggestion has been implanted in a listener's
mind that the sextet is based on a motet by Dunstable, he or she may perceive the
work in a frame that he or she is unlikely to have invented for him- or herself, as
we may judge from the reaction of Northcott, who writes that the work is:

> ... based upon a motet of John Dunstable ... it is a keen and knowledgeable
> ear that can trace Dunstable's tenor, even through the opening phrase – yet
> the major thirds that suffuse the textures seem not only a refraction of
> Dunstable's sweetness, but mark the appearance of Davies' characteristic
> harmonic ambience, a curious sense that there is a diatonic centre in even
> the most dissonant progressions. [13]

As an objective description of events in the score this account is indefensible:
there is no Dunstable tenor in the opening phrase of the sextet (least of all there)
or anywhere else. Major thirds do indeed play an important role in the work –
though it is doubtful whether they can legitimately be said to 'suffuse' its
textures – but their function within the context of its serial construction is so
utterly different from that of major thirds within the harmonic language of the

---

[11]     See particularly Trowell, 'Proportion in the Music of Dunstable', *Proceedings of the Royal Musical Association* 105 (1978–9), p. 108.

[12]     The analysis of proportions in these examples, though indebted to Trowell's work, is my own.

[13]     Northcott, *op. cit.*, p. 39.

**Figure 4.2**

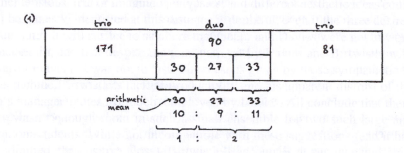

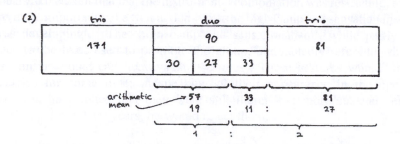

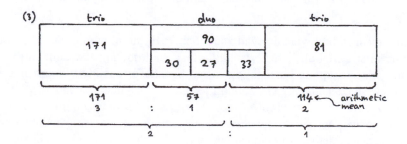

Ex. 1.17: *Alma Redemptoris Mater* motet – structural proportions

early fifteenth century as scarcely to tolerate comparison. Yet I accept this author's account as a genuine record of his listening experience, and I refuse to say that his mode of listening is an inappropriate one. However, this case should demonstrate that in seeking to understand the response of listeners to Davies's works – to explain for example why they may receive 'a curious sense that there is a diatonic centre in even the most dissonant progressions' – it is not sufficient to examine the music alone: it is necessary also to take into account the titles, programme notes, and other extrinsic phenomena that contribute to the mythology.

It is natural to wonder how the idea concerning the Dunstable motet arose in the first place. I have been unable to trace its origins. The composer's programme note makes no mention of Dunstable,[14] but I do not exclude the possibility that it may have originated in some utterance of Davies. Even if that were the case, my comments on the mythology still stand. In any event there is a world of difference between the composer's saying 'this work is based on a Dunstable motet', and the same pronouncement on the lips of a critic or analyst. The composer is in the uniquely privileged position of being sure of his meaning. For a commentator to relay such an item of information as a fact – except as a fact about what the composer has said (and none of the writers cited above gives a source for his information) without verifying it for him- or herself – can only promote mystification and charlatanry.

---

[14] Davies's programme note, supplied by Schott and Co., the publishers of the work, cites only the plainchant as a source.

# 2

# *Worldes Blis* and its satellites

*Peter Owens*

Whatever else one may question about the developing aesthetic of Davies's now considerable œuvre – its modernistic or anti-modernistic tendencies, or the composer's 'aspiration to classicism'[1] – there is no doubt as to the fluency by which it has consistently been characterized. Stephen Pruslin, writing in 1977, already noted 'a virtuoso compositional technique ... capable of producing *From Stone to Thorn*, directly into full score without prior sketches, in three days',[2] and it is clear that Davies himself valued the acquisition of such a technique from the earliest stages of his artistic formation:

> It would be a travesty to say that Bach, Mozart or Beethoven did not 'know' ... what they were about when they penned those flights of inspiration which thrill us so much ... each note is governed by an inner logic which makes it just right, and once heard, it appears to be, of course, the only entirely satisfactory choice in that position.
>
> It is glib to ask a young contemporary composer to achieve just that. Before he could, he would have to amass a tremendous technique of composition at his finger-tips – a 'contemporary' technique, for it would be useless to repeat outworn formulae. Only then could he subconsciously order his material to suit the expression, and do those 'unpredictable' things, which are, however, always ultimately justifiable from every point of view, and not least from the 'analytical' or 'scientific'.[3]

Pruslin's 'pragmatic definition' of Davies's success at such technical mastery should, however, be qualified: although the whereabouts of sketches relating to *From Stone to Thorn* may not be documented,[4] the work could not have been

---

[1]    Matters addressed in Whittall's 'Cross-Currents and Convergencies: Britten, Maxwell Davies and the Sense of Place', *Tempo* 204 (April 1998), pp. 5–11.

[2]    Nel mezzo del cammin – In mid flight', *Peter Maxwell Davies: Studies from Two Decades*, Tempo Booklet No. 2, selected and introduced by Stephen Pruslin, p. 2.

[3]    From a letter, in response to an article by Ernest Gold, *The Score,* (March 1956), p. 84.

[4]    None have been identified in the British Library's collection; Colin Bayliss's *The Music of Sir Peter Maxwell Davies: An Annotated Catalogue*, (Highgate Publications, 1991), locates the MS in private ownership, though enquiries via Judy Arnold have shed no further light on the matter.

written without 'precompositional charts' as I and other writers would understand them.[5] Ex. 2.3 offers a reconstruction of the single matrix of pitch-class material from which the work is realized, itself the result of typical generative processes:[6]

(a)    $N_A$ (Ex. 2.3, line 1: $\alpha$–$\zeta$) is produced by segmenting phrases from the plainsong *Victimae Paschali Laudes* (see Ex. 2.18), verse 1, 'Victimae ... oves' producing segments $\alpha$–$\zeta$,[7] and verse 4, 'Scimus Christum surrexisse ... Amen' producing segments $\gamma$–$\zeta$. With the identical $\gamma$ segments overlapped, each is subjected to 'first-only sieving'[8] (preserving only the first occurrence of each pitch) and transposition by –5, –4, –3, –2, –1 and 0 semitones respectively.

(b)    $P_C$ is produced from the *Dies Irae* plainsong whose three-phrase incipit ('Dies ... Sibylla') gives segments $\alpha$–$\gamma$ by first-only sieving. Segments $\delta$–$\zeta$ invert segments $\alpha$–$\gamma$ respectively, the initial transpositional levels ($\delta$ on c′, $\varepsilon$ on d′, $\zeta$ on f′) being fixed so that the tessitura of each inversion remains identical to that of its prime. All six segments of the set are subsequently transposed by +7, +6, +5, +4, +3 and +2 semitones respectively to give $P_C$ as shown at the foot of Ex. 2.3.

(c)    $N_A$ is transformed into $P_C$ in ten subunits, mapping the segments of one set to those of the other ($[N_A \Rightarrow P_C]$, the prototype for Ex. 2.3 which in its 'un-modified' form does not feature in the work). Only for segment $\beta$ is there a corresponding one-to-one mapping of individual elements. Though segments $\varepsilon$ and $\zeta$ of both sets likewise have five elements each, these are mapped so as to preserve maximum invariance, thus:

$N_A\varepsilon$:1    2    3    4    5          $\zeta$:1    2    3    4    5
       ↓    ↙    ↓    ↓    ↓↘          ↘    ↓    ↓    ↓    ↓↘
$P_C\varepsilon$:1         2    3    4    5   $\zeta$:    1    2    3    4    5

Ex. 2.1: *From Stone to Thorn* = $N_A\varepsilon$, $P_C\varepsilon$ mapping

---

[5]    See, for example, McGregor's 'The Maxwell Davies Sketch Material in the British Library', *Tempo* 196 (April 1996), pp. 9–19, or Jones's '"Preliminary Workings": the precompositional process in Maxwell Davies's Third Symphony', *Tempo* 204, (April 1998), pp. 14–22.

[6]    Nomenclature and description of sets and precompositional processes is in line with the development of David Roberts's terminology expounded in my article 'Revelation and Fallacy', *Music Analysis* 13 2/3, (Blackwell, October 1994), pp. 161–202.

[7]    The process thus far generates a set identical to one in *Stone Litany*, cf. 'Revelation and Fallacy', p. 167, Ex. 4b.

[8]    Likewise generating a set found in *Stone Litany*, cf. 'Revelation and Fallacy', p. 167 Ex. 4a.

The mappings of $N_A\gamma$: 2 to $P_C\gamma$: 4 (a′ to a′) and $N_A\delta$: 3 to $P_C\delta$: 2 (f′ to f′) similarly give rise to invariance throughout all ten subunits for the transformation of these elements. The melodic contours of the subunits are otherwise determined by registral 'expansion' of the terminal sets,[9] so that $N_A\alpha$: 1 falls to $P_C\alpha$: 1 (a″ to c″) in ten semitone steps; $N_A\alpha$: 3 rises to $P_C\alpha$: 3 (c″ to a″) in ten semitone steps; $N_A\beta$: 1 falls to $P_C\beta$: 1 (f‴ to b′) in ten wholetone steps, etc. (These registral locations are not explicit in Ex. 2.3,[10] where pitch classes are shown 'in close position' and to avoid leger lines.)

(d)     A self-transposed variant is created, $z[N_A \Rightarrow P_B]$, by transposing successive subunits of $[N_A \Rightarrow P_C]$ to begin on a sieving of $N_A\alpha$–$\gamma$ (the stemmed notes of Ex. 2.3).

Realizations of subunits in the transformation process of Ex. 2.3 are relatively easy to trace in the outer sections of *From Stone to Thorn* (the opening to rehearsal letter **K**; **O** to the end), for example, subunit 1 on clarinet, opening to **A**; subunit 2 followed by 3R, voice, **A–B**; 4, voice, **C–D**, 5R, 6, harpsichord, **D–E**; 7$\zeta$, clarinet, **F–G**; 8, clarinet, **G–G**$^{+7}$; 9, voice, **I–J**; 10, voice, **J–K**; then on glockenspiel: 1, **O–P**; 2, **P–Q**; 3R, **Q–R**; 4, **R–S**; 5R, **S–T**; 6R, 7R, **T–U**; 8, **U–V**; 9R, **V–W**; 10, on harpsichord, **Y–end**. $P_C$, independent of $z[N_A \Rightarrow P_B]$, is also to be found, for example, in retrograde on harpsichord (right hand) from the opening to rehearsal letter **A** (with a left-hand accompaniment deriving from its prime form).

Material in the work's central section, however, derives from a variant reading of $z[N_A \Rightarrow P_B]$, realizing segments from subunits in the transformation process in diagonal sequence parallel to the dotted line shown in Ex. 2.3, thus:

Clarinet, **K–L**: 1$\zeta$; 1$\epsilon$, 2$\zeta$; 1$\delta$, 2$\epsilon$, 3$\zeta$. **L–M**: 1$\gamma$, 2$\delta$, 3$\epsilon$, 4$\zeta$. **M–N**: 1$\beta$, 2$\gamma$, 3$\delta$ 4$\epsilon$, 4$\zeta$ [*sic*]; 1$\alpha$, 2$\beta$, 3$\gamma$. **N–O**: 4$\delta$, 5$\epsilon$, 6$\zeta$; 2$\alpha$, 3$\beta$, 4$\gamma$, 5$\delta$.

Harpsichord, **K–L**: 10$\alpha$; 10$\beta$, 9$\alpha$; 10$\gamma$, 9$\beta$, 8$\alpha$. Voice, **L–M**: 10$\delta$, 9$\gamma$, 8$\beta$, 7$\alpha$; 10$\epsilon$, 9$\delta$, 8$\gamma$, 7$\beta$, 6$\alpha$. **M–N**: 10$\zeta$, 9$\epsilon$, 8$\delta$, 7$\gamma$, 6$\beta$, 5$\alpha$. **N–O**: 9$\zeta$, 8$\epsilon$, 7$\delta$, 6$\gamma$, 5$\beta$, 4$\alpha$; 8$\zeta$, 7$\epsilon$, 6$\delta$, 5$\gamma$, 4$\beta$, 3$\alpha$.

Ex. 2.2: *From Stone to Thorn* – $z[N_A \Rightarrow P_B]$

Though I cannot offer a paradigm for rhythmic organization in the work, the 'surface presence' of isorhythmic features[11] – cf. variants of the time-signature

---

[9]     Cf. 'Revelation and Fallacy', p. 165, Ex. 1.

[10]    A registral paradigm for Ex. 2.3 has proved extremely difficult to reconstruct: realizations throughout *From Stone to Thorn* are characterized by wide leaps, though I cannot ascertain with any certainty which are determined precompositionally.

[11]    Comparable to those noted in *Hymn to St Magnus, Sonata Seconda*, 'Revelation and Fallacy', p. 177, Ex. 14.

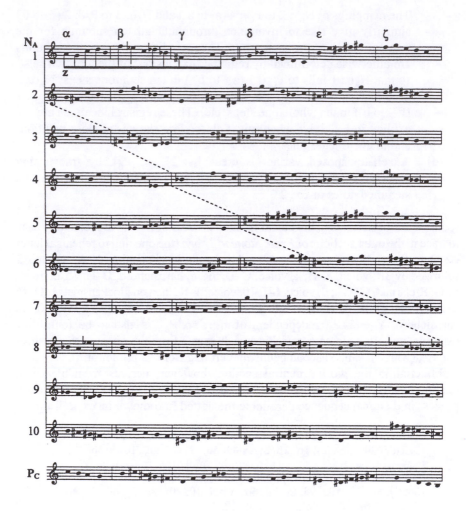

Ex. 2.3: z[$N_A$⇒$P_B$] underlying *From Stone to Thorn*

sequence 6/8, 5/8, 5/8, 3/4, 4/8, 4/8, 3/16, 3/8 from the opening which recur at rehearsal letters **D–E, E–F, G–G$^{+7}$, J–K, O–P, R–S** – suggests that some precompositional numerical workings underlie this aspect of the music. Not that these observations undermine Pruslin's essential remarks concerning the consequences of Davies's technique (rather, they define more precisely its nature): that it facilitates speed to meet urgency of communication in thoroughly wrought compositions, allows flexibility through control, and supports concretely 'dramatic' (as well as abstractly 'symphonic') creations.

Though it would appear that *From Stone to Thorn* inhabits and explores its own microcosm of compositional material,[12] Davies's fluency benefits elsewhere from his readiness to develop material generated for one work in the context of another, sometimes as simple redeployment, or else invoking new technical procedures to increase the potential of ideas already worked with. To some extent, this *modus operandi* illuminates the situation encountered when examining sources of his works at the British Library. For certain pieces there are copious precompositional charts, summarizing a basic stock of transposed, transformed and permuted material along with its associated means of durational organization, while for others there is apparently little more than a first short-score draft. These latter often turn out to be 'satellites' of other works: ideas which have 'spun off' and developed an 'orbit' of their own. Such nomenclature is without implication for the status of the pieces as more generally perceived in Davies's œuvre, so that, for instance, sketches reveal *Blind Man's Buff* as quite a major 'planet', though critical assessment has generally accorded it relatively little importance. In some cases the composer has commented explicitly on works which, as it were, reflect the light of another – such as the three instrumental solos, *The Kestrel paced around the Sun*, *The Door of the Sun* and the *Seven Brightnesses* (for flute, viola and clarinet respectively) written 'around' the First Symphony, or the Piano Sonata 'taking off' from the Second Symphony – though sometimes his remarks may seem to point away from true illumination in this respect. The remainder of this article will consider *Worldes Blis* and two of its satellites, with a view to illustrating some of the very different approaches that may be taken to identical material in the context of each work and the consequent greatly contrasting results.

*Worldes Blis*, written between 1966 and 1969, was, according to the composer's programme note, a conscious attempt to maintain:

> the basic architectural principles employed in my earlier large-scale orchestral music [a 'consciously integrated and balanced style of composition'] but exploring unashamedly ... the acceptance and integration

---

[12]     Transformations between sets derived from the *Dies Irae* and *Victimae Paschali Laudes* plainchants certainly feature in other works, though in detail these can be quite distinct from Ex. 2.3 (cf. for example, *Stone Litany*, 'Revelation and Fallacy', p. 191 Ex. 24). The existence of additional works based on Ex. 2.3 cannot be discounted, however.

into my continuing creation of the Antichrist which had confronted me within my own self [explicit in the shattering experience of a 'sequence of violent and dramatic works' including *Eight Songs for a Mad King, Revelation and Fall* and *Missa Super l'Homme Armé*].[13]

Its reassertion of rational musical argument, and reintegration of form and content is apparent in the composer's handling of his material on all levels, though this is coupled with an assimilation of dramatic possibilities way beyond those of *Prolation,* the Sinfonia of 1962 or even the second of the *Taverner Fantasias* (itself a satellite of a theatrical work).

Whatever the eponymous thirteenth-century monody may have to do with the composition, there is a deep sense in which *Worldes Blis* is *about* its first five notes: exploring their potential for organic growth and examining relationships among the resultant material. This germinal set is labelled $S_G$ in Ex. 2.5, from which its expansion to $+W_G$, of fundamental importance in the work, can be understood thus (in line with the composer's sketches):[14]

(a)　$S_G$ is succeeded by its retrograde-inverted, retrograde, and inverted forms respectively, with each set transposed to begin on the last pitch of its predecessor ($S_G$, $SI_A R$, $S_{Ab}R$, $SI_{Ab}$).

(b)　The order of $SI_{Ab}$: 2–5 is reversed in the permutation $SI_{Ab}{}^P$, motivically recalling $SI_A R$: 1–4.[15]

(c)　$S_{Ab}R$: 3–5 are transposed up two octaves, creating a motivic reference to $S_G$ across $+W_G$: 8–12 (and preserving the retrograde contour of $S_G$: 1–3 in $+W_G$: 11–13).

$+W_G$ is a seventeen-element set from which pitch classes B and F are absent. A reduced variant, $-W_G$, is created by first-only sieving (the result can be seen in the top line of Ex. 2.9, where registral adjustment of the final element to gb″ has also been implemented for motivic balance between the $S_G$ and its 5-note complement). Though Davies produced a wealth of precompositional material from manipulations of $+W_G$ and $-W_G$ for deployment in *Worldes Blis,* it will be helpful now to outline only a selection of it to inform consideration of the work's

---

13　Reproduced in Griffiths, *Peter Maxwell Davies* (London, Robson Books, 1982), pp. 149–52.

14　Most of the sketches for *Worldes Blis* are in private ownership (with facsimiles available at the British Library): I am grateful to Karl Renner and Stephen Pruslin for allowing access to material in their possession. David Roberts, 'Techniques of Composition in the Music of Peter Maxwell Davies' (Ph.D., Birmingham University, 1985) pp. 319–25 independently uncovered many of the techniques deployed in the work, without having had sight of sketch material, and his labelling of sets and processes fundamentally affects this account, distinguished essentially by attention to pitch – not only pitch-class – manipulations.

15　Cf. 'Revelation and Fallacy', p. 169, Ex. 8a.

large-scale structure, a summary of which is given below to assist orientation in the comments which follow ((Ex. 2.4):[16]

| 2 | | 201 | 212 |
|---|---|---|---|
| **Introduction** | **First Cantus** | **Interruption** | **Second Cantus** |
| $^3 + W_G$: 1–4 on two harps | $z[+W_G \Rightarrow +WI_A]$ on trombones–trumpets | $^3 -W_G$ on trumpets $^3 +W_G$ on strings (synoptic realizations) | $z[-W_G \Rightarrow -WI_A]$ on strings |

— — — — — — — — — 'Extended Upbeat' — — — — — — — —

| 286 | 382 | 482 | 515 | 585 |
|---|---|---|---|---|
| **Antecedent/ Consequent Material** | **Development 1** | **Development 2** | **Development 3** | **Development 4** |
| $z[+WI_A \Rightarrow +W_G]^3$ bars 286–322 $z[+W_G \Rightarrow +WI_A]^{(0)}$ bars 323–46 $z[+W_G \Rightarrow +WI_A]^9$ bars 347–81 | $z[+W_G \Rightarrow WI_A]^{3,0,9}$ oscillatory transposition, on harps $[+W_G \Rightarrow +WI_A]$ (first appearance) as accompaniment | $W_E$: 1–6 (sustained organ chord) $z[-W_G \Rightarrow -WI_A]$ on trombones and bassoons 'Death' chord introduced | $W_G$: 1–6 (sustained organ chord) $[+WI_A \Rightarrow +W_G]$ on trumpets and reeds *Dies Irae* introduced | $W_{Bb}$: 1–6 (reiterated on violins) $[+W_G \Rightarrow +WI_A]$ on brass and wind (subunits 1, 3, 2, 4, 5, 7, 6, 8, etc.) $[-WI_A \Rightarrow Ave]$ (first full realization) in organ, left-hand |

| 623 | 638 | | | 730 |
|---|---|---|---|---|
| **Ant/Con Reprise** | **Coda** | | | **Cadence** |
| Terminal sets (reduced) replace earlier transformations.<br><br>'Death' chord highlighted in the texture | $^3 + W_G R$ fully realized $z[+W_G \Rightarrow +WI_A]$ on trombones–trumpets $[Ave \Rightarrow Dies\ Irae]$ (first realization) on violins *Worldes blis* monody (modally adjusted) appears on bells | | | $-WI_A$ vertical-ized on bass and strings Bells reiterate generative sets: *Ave, Dies Irae,* $-W_c$ Ends on 'Death' chord |

Ex.2. 4: *Worldes Blis* – structural summary

---

So as not to overload discussion with detail that might distract from the essential points, certain niceties are glossed here.

Beyond the derivation of $+W_G$ from $S_G$, Ex. 2.5 shows the beginning of $^3+W_G$, a 'third-level' hierarchical grouping of sets to be understood thus:

(a)     $+W_G$ and $+WI_A$ share identical pitch-class content (a property clearly resulting from the sets' concatenated embodiment of $S_G$ in its particular transposed and inverted forms). Pairing of $+W_G$ (a 'primary' set) with its transposed inversion represents serial organization on a second hierarchical level.

(b)     Transposition cycles, descending in semitone steps, are initiated for $+W_G$ and $+WI_A$ (i.e. the pairing is organized on a yet higher level) with elements aligned as shown, and prime and inverted set forms alternated. The cycle is continued beyond a full chromatic rotation – a total of 28 primary sets – to the point where $+W_{Gb}$ and $+WI_{Ab}$ 'coalesce' (indicated by the double-bar in Ex. 2.5), stopping short of a further, permuted realization of $S_G$.

(c)     Duplication of pitches and pitch classes in the alignment of sets is a consistent feature of $^3+W_G$, indicated by broken lines in the example, as is the closely contiguous repetition of dyads, connected by broken slurs in the example.

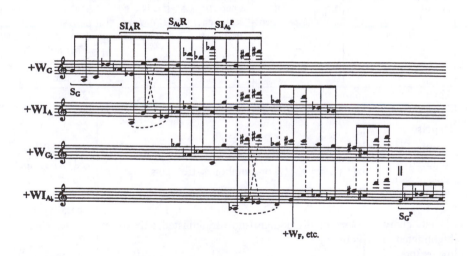

Ex. 2.5: *Worldes Blis* – $^3+W_G$ (incipit)

The harp duet, with which *Worldes Blis* opens, initiates a realization of $^3+W_G$ presenting its first four sets (i.e. the material shown in Ex. 2.5) which end with a re-ordering of $S_G$. The entire cycle (as described above) is not fully deployed, however, until the long climactic coda to the work – during which the *Worldes Blis* monody makes its entry on bells – where a complete retrograde presentation, beginning on organ pedals, tuba and low reeds, slowly rises through the texture, culminating in $S_GR$ (on clarinets, violas and cellos, bars 726–9). Between these symmetrically balanced poles, however, there are more fragmented realizations (characteristic features of which are the sieving out of repeated dyads, and the verticalization of precompositionally 'successive' elements) one of which accounts for the exhilarating outburst between the two large spans conceived by the composer as an 'extended "upbeat"' in the work (bars 201–11), very much an example of what David Roberts terms 'synoptic paraphrase':

> In synoptic paraphrase, it is as if Davies, having realized a passage with his set-chart in front of him, put it aside and wrote, relying largely on intuition, a variant of that passage – ignoring its serial pedigree, emphasizing its strong gestures, and eliminating its weak ones. And as if, having done that, he wrote variant on the variant, and so on. I call this 'synoptic' paraphrase to draw attention to the often quite drastic condensation that material undergoes.[17]

Material before and after this interjection is concerned with 'transformation'. After the harps' juxtaposition of prime and inverted set forms, what follows might be regarded as a systematic exploration of what happens *between* these forms. The transformation of $+W_G$ to $+WI_A$ is conceptualized in terms of the intervallic span that separates corresponding elements from each set, registrally aligned so that $d''$, as element 10 and 15 of both sets, is invariant. The progress of element 2, from a to $g'''$, is thus accomplished in eighteen whole-tone steps, determining the eighteen stages of the process $[+W_G \Rightarrow +WI_A]$. The open-headed notes of Ex. 2.6 show a self-transposed variant of this transformation, $z[+W_G \Rightarrow +WI_A]$, in which subunits 1 to 17 have been transposed to begin on successive elements of $+W_G$. This variant dominates the outer sections of the work: there is no deployment of its prototype $[+W_G \Rightarrow +WI_A]$ until the first of what Davies identifies as 'four development sections ... the first strictly a "predevelopment" in which material is prepared for subsequent development processes', where it accompanies foreground material for the two harps, not heard since the work's opening.

In the work's 'extended "upbeat"' a full, linear realization of $z[+W_G \Rightarrow +WI_A]$ (with even-numbered subunits in retrograde) forms the First Cantus (bars 3–200), passing from timpani to trombones to trumpets and respecting the

---

[17]    Roberts, *op. cit.*, p. 73.

Ex. 2.6: *Worldes Blis – z* [+W$_G$ ⇒ +WI$_A$] $^{(3,0,9)}$

durations – determined by intervallically dependent ratios – indicated numerically in Ex. 2.6. In the Second Cantus (bars 212–85) the prime-to-inversion transformation is recapitulated, as it were, in the form of $z[-W_G \Rightarrow -WI_A]$ – a process based on the sieved set, likewise accomplished in eighteen subunits, the first seventeen of which are transposed to begin on successive elements of $+W_G$ – as a long melody on strings (now with odd-numbered subunits in retrograde). A final realization of the complete $z[+W_G \Rightarrow +WI_A]$ (with odd-numbered subunits in retrograde) forms the duration-controlling line in the work's coda, once more alloted to trombones and trumpets.

The remaining sections of *Worldes Blis* are generally constructed from less strictly linear realizations of the transformation processes so far outlined – with subunits superimposed, fragmented contrapuntally, or verticalized into sustained chords (cf. for example, the realization of $+WI_AR$ which accounts for the woodwind flourish of bars 344–6, beneath which violins and viola I present $z[+W_G \Rightarrow +WI_A]$: 17, and lower strings $z[+W_G \Rightarrow +WI_A]$: 16R). What the composer identifies as 'Antecedent/Consequent' material – characterized respectively by high jagged string lines accompanied by woodblock and claves, and 'heavy brass' with 'deep violent percussion' – consists of a three-fold reworking of $z[+W_G \Rightarrow +WI_A]$ (first transforming inversion to prime, i.e. Ex. 2.6 subunits 18 to 1, followed twice by the opposite process). In the first, bars 286–322, all subunits are transposed up by a minor third (or, more accurately, vector interval class 3) – cf. $+WI_CR$ on violins, bars 286–9, and $+W_{Bb}$ on piccolo, bars 315–23 – while in the third, bars 347–81, all subunits are transposed down by a minor third (vic 9) – cf. $+W_ER$ on trumpets, bars 347–9 and $+WI_{F\#}$ on violins, bars 364–82. These variants, $z[+W_G \Rightarrow +WI_A]^3$ and $z[+W_G \Rightarrow +WI_A]^9$ respectively, are shown in the filled noteheads of Ex. 2.6.

As a counter to this large-scale descent by minor thirds in the Antecedent/Consequent material, the transformations in Development Sections 2, 3 and 4 all take place against the background of a sustained or reiterated chord, the roots of which *rise* successively by vic 3:

| | |
|---|---|
| f♯–c–e′–ab′–bb′ (organ, bars 482–514) | $W_E$: 2, 6, 1, $5^3$, 4 |
| a′–c″–eb″–g″–b″–db‴ (organ, bars 515–584) | $W_G$: 2, 3, 6, 1, $5^3$, 4 |
| c‴–eb‴–fb‴–gb‴–ab‴–bb‴ (violins, bars 585–622) | $W_{Bb}$: 2, 3, 4, 6, $5^9$, 1 |

that is, the chords are verticalizations of the first six elements of $+W_t$ or $-W_t$ sets (element 7 distinguishes the full set from its sieved variant), very much respecting relative register, as precompositionally determined, though omitting element 3 from the first verticalization, and modifying element 5 in each, twice by transposition of vic 3, and finally of vic 9. This 'minor-third' transposition of complete transformation processes, independent sets and ultimately their individual elements represents a form-building principle in the work, distilled in the harp duet of Development Section 1.

Ex. 2.7 shows the opening of this passage in which elements of subunits in $z[+W_G \Rightarrow +WI_A]$ are shifted by vector interval class 3, 0 or 9 as indicated, with Harp One taking all odd-numbered subunits, overlaid by Harp Two with the even-numbered subunits. Though the realization of subunit one is anomalous, systematic rotations are applied of: vics. 3, 0, 9, 0 (pattern X); vics. 0, 9, 0, 3 (pattern Y); and vics. 9, 0, 3, 0 (pattern Z); to create what David Roberts has termed 'oscillatory transposition'.[18] For the realization of all eighteen subunits in the transformation process, patterns X, Y and Z are themselves applied in six-fold rotation (X, Y, Z; X, Y, Z; etc.), following which the entire transformation process is repeated twice more, subsequent realizations beginning with patterns Y and Z respectively (that is, from bar 418: Y, Z, X; Y, Z, X; etc. and from bar 449: Z, X, Y; Z, X, Y; etc.). The treatment of subunit one is also significantly freer on these repetitions in comparison to the strict realizations applied to subunits two to eighteen. Of stronger aural impact than the process described is the doubling of selected intervals as they occur in the two-voiced counterpoint: by horns (taking perfect fourths and fifths), timpani and xylophone (doubling tritones) and pizzicato strings (reinforcing major and minor thirds and sixths).

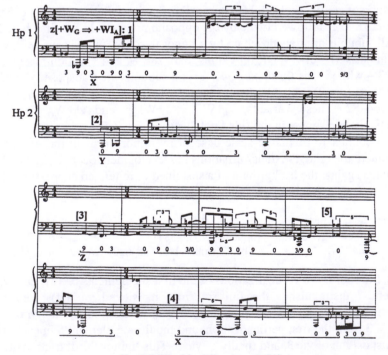

Ex. 2.7: *Worldes Blis* – bars 382ff.

---

[18]     *Ibid.*

It is after this mid-point of the work that material of potentially extra-musical significance begins to interact with what has grown from manipulations of $S_G$. The so-called Death chord (d-f#-e′-g#′) – with its associations from the opera *Taverner* – is sounded on horns at the beginning of Development Section 2, after which its characteristic superimposed thirds are highlighted – by doubling – in occurrences within autonomously generated counterpoint (similar to the treatment of the harp lines noted above). This technique is especially clear in the reprise of the Antecedent/Consequent material, in which the transformation processes of the 'exposition' are reduced to permutations of their terminal sets (+$WI_C$: 16, 17, 14, 15, 12, 13, 10, 11, 9, 7, 8, 5, 6, 3, 4, 1, 2 on violins, bars 623– 6; –$W_G$: 3, 2, 1, 5, 4, 7, 6, 8–10 on violins, bars 630–2; –$W_G$: 1, 3, 2, 4–7, 9, 10 on trombone 2, bars 634–6). The 'Death' chord emerges, for example, on oboes and flutes, bars 623–6 (f′-a′-g″-b″) and powerfully dominates the end of the section, in variants sustained on wind, bars 634–7 (e–g–f#′–a′), strings, bars 636–637 (F#–A#–g#–b#) and brass (*ffff*, bells raised), bar 637 (D–F#–e–g#).

In Development Section 3 another 'deathly image', the incipit of the *Dies Irae* plainsong, appears in retrograde on violins in bar 551 (f#″, a′, g#″, a′), while Development Section 4 unfolds a completely new transformation process in twelve subunits of –$WI_A$. to a set $M_{Gb}$, realized as a long melodic line in the left-hand organ part. This new set, as revealed in Ex. 2.8, turns out to be a sieving of Davies's carol *Ave plena gracia,* an appeal to the Virgin for divine consolation in respect of the earthly pessimism expressed by the text of the *Worldes Blis* monody 'Thou pray for us unto thy Son, In heaven bliss that we may wone, Maria'.[19] The set is also prominent in the dramatic conclusion to the Antecedent/ Consequent reprise, realized *fff* on trombone 1, doubled by whooping horns in bars 634–6. A fuller reading of the significance of textual and dramatic associations of material assimilated as Davies's 'Motet for Orchestra' reaches its conclusion should also note the transformation (in seven subunits) of $M_{Gb}$ to the *Dies Irae* incipit[20] on unison violins at the start of the Coda (bars 638–71, with odd-numbered subunits in retrograde) and the superimposition of the *Ave plena gracia-* and *Dies Irae*-derived sets, on first and second violins respectively, at its end (bar 725, last note, to bar 729).

---

[19]    My earlier relating of $M_{Gb}$ to the *Worldes Blis* monody – the 'fallacy' in 'Revelation and Fallacy', p. 170, Ex. 9a – highlights little more than the similarity of mode between Davies's carol and his distorted presentation of the medieval monody on handbells in the work's Coda (bars 665ff.).

[20]    Specifically, set $K_{Gb}$, see 'Revelation and Fallacy', p. 168, Ex. 7.

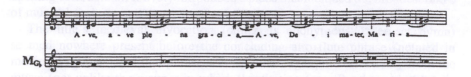

Ex. 2.8: *Worldes Blis*: Sieving of $M_{Gb}$ from *Ave plena gracia*

For the work's concluding cadential gesture, $M_{Gb}$, the *Dies Irae* incipit, and $-W_C$ are sounded repeatedly, *prestissimo,* on glockenspiel, handbells and tubular bells, over a progressive verticalization of $-WI_A$ on brass and strings, brought to silence by the finally resonating 'Death' chord – at once a comprehensive summary of the material with which the work has been concerned and a forcefully dramatic apotheosis.

After the first performance of *Worldes Blis,* the composer recalls that he:

> withdrew the work, feeling that it was too short, having only explored a fraction of its form-building potentialities. Later I realized that it was not so much incomplete as germinal, in that its methods lead directly into later large works such as *Hymn to St Magnus* and *Stone Litany*. Moreover, bearing in mind that ultimately one's music and one's life are inseparably interrelated, I had in its form defined, in a way which made immediate and instinctive sense, the future environment in which I was to compose, when the music, as it were, materialized into a physical landscape ... Orkney's wildest island seems to be a natural extension and a living out of the territory explored and cartographed in *Worldes Blis*.[21]

Technical and poetic considerations may therefore underlie the deployment of material from *Worldes Blis* in Davies's first large-scale Orcadian composition, the *Hymn to St Magnus* of 1972, whose very opening – $S_C$ played pizzicato on viola – suggests that the work is picking up where its predecessor left off (compare with the concluding repetitions of $-W_C$ noted above). In his programme note, Davies records that:

> Saint Magnus was martyred on the island of Egilsay on 16 April, 1117 during a dispute with his cousin, Earl Hakon, over the just division of the Earldom of Orkney ... This work was written in total isolation in a remote part of Orkney. The central parts of the work are permeated by the violence of the martyrdom and the violence of the sea.[22]

---

21    Programme note reproduced in Griffiths, *op. cit.,* p. 150.
22    Sleeve note to the recording by The Fires of London (Decca, 1976) DSLO 12.

Between an opening Dedication and a concluding Eulogy, *Hymn to St Magnus* comprises two movements entitled Sonata, of which the second accounts for over two-thirds of the work's duration. Though precompositional sketches have not been available for perusal,[23] I have illustrated elsewhere how the opening movement unfolds a transformation of $S_C$ to a 5-note 'scanning' of a phrase from the original twelfth-century hymn *Nobilis humilis*, $(G_{Db})$,[24] and this process is deployed for a second time – though in the opposite direction (that is, $[G_{Db} \Rightarrow S_C]$) in the flute line of Movement IV. It would be possible to outline a formal plan of the two central Sonatas illustrating a rhetorical discipline in the presentation of the musical 'argument' every bit as thorough as that which I have attempted to highlight in the construction of *Worldes Blis*. This would not be concerned with further manipulations of set S, however, but with the development of a 5-note collection sieved from the *Dies Irae* incipit $(H_F)$. My earlier article also outlines the means by which this is expanded into a 625-note square whose pitches and assigned durations account for the 'enormous interlocking isorhythmic structures of great complexity' to which Davies draws attention in his own remarks.[25]

Material taken over from *Worldes Blis* provides a more static background against which the drama of the Second Sonata – a huge two-voiced canon with the second voice entering a third of the way through, and reproducing rhythmic values at the proportion of 3:2 until final unison alignment – is played out.

A sequence of 100 'chords' (10 unisons and 90 dyads) is developed from $-W_G$ (Ex. 2. 9) labelled $^2W_G{}^{(P)}$, since +/− distinctions are irrelevant in the *Hymn*, which uses only the sieved set), and this is repeated five times in accompaniment to the leading canonic voice, as may be apprehended from Ex. 2.10. Systematic permutation, fundamental to the genesis of $^2W_G{}^{(P)}$, plays little part in *Worldes Blis* though we have already noted the re-ordering of elements in the linear set realizations of bars 623–37 and of subunits from $[+W_G \Rightarrow +WI_A]$ – exchanged in alternating pairs – in Development Section 4. More germane is the writing for timpani concluding the Antecedent/Consequent material (on exposition, bars 347–71, and reprise, bars 633–7), an illustration of which is given in Ex. 2.11: – $W_t$ or $-WI_t$ sets are partitioned into five-note segments and their elements successively reordered according to a plain-hunt bell-ringing pattern until a retrograde statement of the initial set is produced.

---

[23]    No charts are included with Add Ms 71407, a pencil full score held at the British Library: enquiries of the composer have produced nothing further.

[24]    'Revelation and Fallacy', p. 171, Ex. 10.

[25]    'Revelation and Fallacy', pp. 173–6, Exx. 12–14.

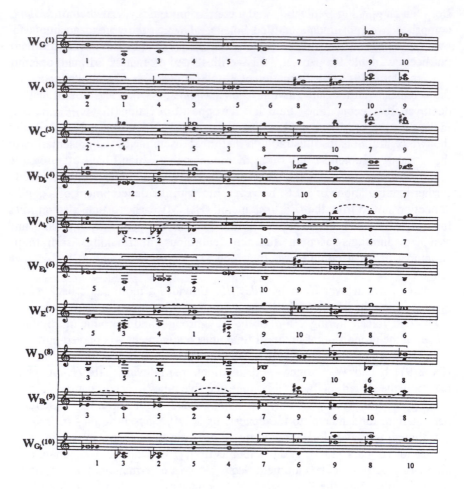

Ex. 2.9: *Hymn to St Magnus* – chart $^2W_G^{(P)}$

| L | W | I2 | S2 | |
|---|---|---|---|---|
| $H_F$ Squares **1:** A–E (125 notes) | $H_F$ Squares **2:** A–E (125 notes) | $H_F$ Squares **3:** A–E (125 notes) | $H_F$ Squares **4:** A–E (125 notes) | $H_F$ Squares **5:** A–E (125 notes) |
| Flute/Clarinet | Marimba | Flute/Clarinet | Viola | Flute/Clarinet |
| ${}^2W_G{}^{(P)}$ (100 chords) | ${}^2W_G{}^{(P)}$ (100 chords) | ${}^2W_G{}^{(P)}$ (100 chords) | ${}^2W_G{}^{(P)}$ (100 chords) | ${}^2W_G{}^{(P)}$ (100 chords) |
| Viola/Cello | Piano | Celesta | Flute | Piano |

| $S^{+1}$ | A2 | | $P2^{-1}$ | $X2^{-1}$ |
|---|---|---|---|---|
| $H_F$ Squares **1:** A–E (125 notes) | $H_F$ Squares **2:** A–E (125 notes) | $H_F$ Squares **3:** A–E (125 notes) | $H_F$ Squares **4:** A–E (125 notes) | $H_F$ Squares **5:** A–E (125 notes) |
| Cello | Glockenspiel | Clarinet | Vlc/Vla | Cello |

Ex. 2.10: *Hymn to St Magnus* – 100 'chord' sequence

Plain-hunt permutation of $-WI_{Eb}$:6–10

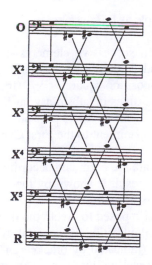

Ex. 2.11: *Worldes Blis* – bars 347ff.

In *Hymn to St Magnus,* this pattern is applied, symmetrically, to full ten-element sets, continuing until one further permutation would return the elements to prime order (Ex. 2.12):

| | | | | | | | | | | |
|---|---|---|---|---|---|---|---|---|---|---|
| $W_t^1$ | 1 | 2 | 3 | 4 | 5 | 6 | 7 | 8 | 9 | 10 |
| $W_t^2$ | 2 | 1 | 4 | 3 | 5 | 6 | 8 | 7 | 10 | 9 |
| $W_t^3$ | 2 | 4 | 1 | 5 | 3 | 8 | 6 | 10 | 7 | 9 |
| $W_t^4$ | 4 | 2 | 5 | 1 | 3 | 8 | 10 | 6 | 9 | 7 |
| $W_t^5$ | 4 | 5 | 2 | 3 | 1 | 10 | 8 | 9 | 6 | 7 |
| $W_t^6$ | 5 | 4 | 3 | 2 | 1 | 10 | 9 | 8 | 7 | 6 |
| $W_t^7$ | 5 | 3 | 4 | 1 | 2 | 9 | 10 | 7 | 8 | 6 |
| $W_t^8$ | 3 | 5 | 1 | 4 | 2 | 9 | 7 | 10 | 6 | 8 |
| $W_t^9$ | 3 | 1 | 5 | 2 | 4 | 7 | 9 | 6 | 10 | 8 |
| $W_t^{10}$ | 1 | 3 | 2 | 5 | 4 | 7 | 6 | 9 | 8 | 10 |
| $[W_t^1]$ | [1] | [2] | [3] | [4] | [5] | [6] | [7] | [8] | [9] | [10] |

Ex. 2.12: *Hymn to St Magnus* – set permutations

The dyadic square of Ex. 2.9 develops this principle as follows:[26]

(a)   (–)$W_G$ is transposed to begin on its ten successive elements: these transpositions are shown in the open-headed notes of Ex. 2.9 and create what David Roberts has termed a 'transposition square', $^2W_G$. (In this form the square is deployed a number of times in subsidiary layers of *Worldes Blis,* e.g. a four-fold realization, with alternate transpositions in retrograde, in the lower strings' accompaniment to the First Cantus, bars 19–200).

(b)   Elements of sets in the transposition square are permuted according to the plain-hunt pattern set out above (the result is shown by the filled note-heads of Ex. 2.9, with order-numbers beneath).

(c)   Permuted and un-permuted sets are superimposed to create the dyadic square, $^2W_G^{(P)}$. Attention is drawn to the duplication of identical dyads within the even-numbered permutations (indicated by brackets in Ex. 2.9), and pitches common between consecutive dyads (connected by dotted slurs) in the remainder.

---

26   Roberts, *op. cit.,* pp. 273–4, also describes this process.

In their simplest deployment rows from the dyadic square are presented in succession, each reads left to right, and a five-fold repetition of this realization accounts for the accompaniment to the Second Sonata's canon outlined above. The fourth presentation on solo flute is interesting in its use of special techniques to manage 'chords' on an essentially melodic instrument: simultaneous humming and playing, rapid alternation of notes by trilling and *tremolando*, and 'arpeggiation' in which notes are realized in simple melodic succession, the second preceded by an *acciaccatura* from the first. The opening realization on viola and cello is similarly coloured by all manner of string effects, in contrast to which the central statement on celesta has not even rhythmic articulation to obfuscate the chordal sequence.

The two presentations of $^2W_G^{(P)}$ on piano, however, are embedded in a complex instrumental part which also carries decorative 'melismatic'[27] material and percussive clusters, not always distinct in terms of register, articulation or dynamics. The second occasion on which the piano is assigned the dyadic square in the Sonata it simultaneously initiates other realizations of $^2W_G^{(P)}$ which are of particular interest. No longer is the material treated as ten successive horizontal rows, but as a two-dimensional matrix through which a variety of paths can be traced.

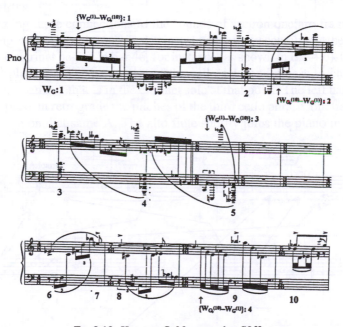

Ex. 2.13: *Hymn to St Magnus* – bar S2ff.

---

[27]    As defined by Roberts, *op. cit.*, p. 186: 'a melisma derives from primary-level material [an ordered set] but treats it in a relatively unrestrained way: elements may be freely permuted, omitted, and repeated, and occasionally pitch classes that are not members of the set-form from which the decoration is drawn may be included'.

Ex. 2.13 shows the beginnings of these realizations – between elements of $W_G$ – for comparison with the diagram below, which summarizes how the pattern is continued (Ex. 2.14). This tracing of vertical, diagonal and meandering paths is very much an anticipation of Davies's approach to handling material organized according to the properties of Magic Squares (beginning with *Ave Maris Stella* of 1976), and coupled with the harmonic enrichment afforded by the superimposition of parallel rows of dyads (A3–$^{3}$-B3$^{+2}$), gives a sense of the vast array of material which the composer is able to generate by relatively simple means. Matrices of this kind would seem both to satisfy Davies's desire that

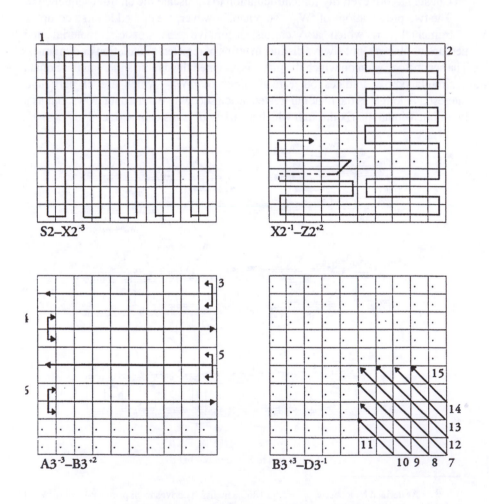

Ex. 2.14: *Hymn to St Magnus* – set reading patterns

each note should be 'governed by an inner logic', and to give free reign to his creative fantasy. The turbulent seascape evoked as the Second Sonata's two-voiced canon approaches its inexorable conclusion amply demonstrates the power of the latter.

Following the climax of the Second Sonata, 'spilling over' into the *fff* improvized gong cadenza of Movement Four ('Sancti Magni Hymnus Alias'), $^2W_G^{(P)}$ comes to the musical foreground: first in the opening declamation for solo clarinet (realizing elements 1–5 from $W_t$ sets 1–10 of Ex. 2.9, with retrogrades and freer permutations)[28]; and finally as the basis for the long vocal melody to which Davies sets the text of the original twelfth-century hymn *Nobilis humilis*. Dyadic lines of Ex. 2.9 are realized right to left from bottom to top (that is, ending with a statement of $W_GR$). Somewhat in the manner of the flute's realization in the Second Sonata, 'simultaneous' elements are presented in melodic succession, and this monodic summary of material contrapuntally generated is a technique found elsewhere in Davies's works at analogous structural points: the concluding vocal lines of *Revelation and Fall* and *Stone Litany*, for example, where the instrumental accompaniments likewise evaporate pitched material away to ethereal textures.

Deployment of $^2W_G^{(P)}$ has been identified by David Roberts in *Tenebrae Super Gesualdo*, completed by Davies in the same year as *Hymn to St Magnus*.[29] $S_G$ also powerfully announces its presence at the opening of *Hymnos,* for clarinet and piano, of 1967, and that work proves to be constructed from smaller-scale realizations of $z[+W_G \Rightarrow +WI_A]$, $z[-W_G \Rightarrow -WI_A]$ and $^3+W_G$ from *Worldes Blis*.[30] In complementary manner, *Stedman caters* – nominally 'a revision of an unperformed 1958 work, made in 1968 for the Pierrot Players [which] became, however, in the course of its revision, a complete recomposition'[31] – turns out to be based largely on the primitive (un-transposed) transformation $[+W_G \Rightarrow +WI_A]$ though it is tempting to link the work's title – a change-ringing pattern of bells – with the operations taken up and developed in *Hymn to St Magnus*.[32] It is 'oscillatory transposition' of $z[+W_G \Rightarrow +WI_A]^{3,0,9}$, however, that accounts for the opening cello line of *Vesalii Icones*, as illustrated in Ex. 2.15a (which should be compared to the harp parts of Ex. 2.7),[33] and the obfuscating power of this technique is likely to be one reason why *Vesalii Icones* has not previously been noted as a *Worldes Blis* satellite.

---

[28]     At the start of this melody three notes in the printed score differ from those in the MS (*op. cit.*), presumably by copyist's error: note 1, b″ not g″; note 8, e♮″ not e♭″; note 9, d♭ ′not d♮′.

[29]     Roberts, *op. cit.*, p. 274.

[30]     *Ibid.*, pp. 326-8 (though $^3+W_G$ is not identified: cf. *Hymnos*, piano, bars 1ff. with Ex. 2.5).

[31]     Composer's programme note, reproduced in Griffiths, *op. cit.*, p. 136.

[32]     See Roberts, *op. cit.*, p. 328.

[33]     Taylor, 'Vesalii Icones', *Peter Maxwell Davies: Studies from Two Decades*, p. 62 offers an analysis of this line in terms of whole-tone scales.

(a)

(b): 'Agony in the Garden', bar 8 ff

(c): 'Christ prepared for Death', bar 297 ff, 'synthesizing' $X_B$ and $X_BR$

(d): 'Christ prepared for Death', bar 325 ff, 'paraphrasing' bar 297 ff

(e): 'The Death of Christ', bar 344 ff, $z[+W_G \Rightarrow +WI_A]^3$: 18R / $+WI_CR$

Ex. 2.15: *Vesalii Icones* – extracts

Another is the composer's programme note:

> the music is not an attempt to 'illustrate' in a traditional way, the
> movements or 'moods' of the dancer but works out its own inter-
> relationships, between my own present 'style' and the fragments of Good
> Friday plainsong used, my motet, *Ecce Manus Tradentis,* and the work I
> wrote for the Fires of London at the beginning of 1968, [*Missa Super*]

*L'Homme Armé* each of which is in itself full of musical quotes and cross-references.[34]

From this reading it might be appropriate to understand what Davies calls 'my own present "style"' as meaning 'material present in *Worldes Blis*', with the other references cited serving, in this set of dances based on Vesalius's anatomical drawings and the fourteen Stations of the Cross, rather like the *objets trouvés* in *Eight Songs for a Mad King* 'musical objects borrowed from many sources, functioning as musical "stage props"'.[35]

Understandably, critical comments about *Vesalii Icones* have often focused on the work's referential elements – its juxtapositions of stylistic parodies and quotations – considered, for example, by Steve Sweeney-Turner for their dialectical or deconstructive significance,[36] or prompting Stephen Walsh's observation on Davies's music-theatre works of this period that 'the musical intrusions often display more virtuosity than stylistic coherence'.[37] Nor is it possible here to restore the balance, as it were, with a more objective account of compositional technique in those parts of the work where parody is of lesser importance. For whereas *Worldes Blis* shapes practically its entire structure from a 'rationalized' sequence of procedures applied to a germinal set, $S_G$, and *Hymn to St Magnus* subjects one fragment of derivative material to additional manipulation, which then accounts for large- and small-scale features of the composition, *Vesalii Icones* selects material from the precompositional charts of *Worldes Blis* in a way that would make reconstruction of the relevant generative processes utterly impossible from this work alone. This situation mitigates Michael Taylor's decision in 1970 to offer 'not an attempt at a systematic analysis of the piece, but rather some guidelines and suggestions which will, I hope, make apparent the richly allusive quality of the score'.[38] What follows here is essentially in the same vein.

After the opening cello line of Ex. 2.15a ('Agony in the Garden', bars 1–4) two further extended phrases are produced by oscillatory transposition of subunits from $z[+W_G \Rightarrow +WI_A]^{3,\,0,\,9}$ (Ex. 2.6): bars 4-6, subunit 2R (9, 0, 3, 0, etc.); bar 7, subunit 3 (3, 0, 9, 0, etc. – the pitch-class sequence given in the upper line of Ex. 2.16a). It is a feature of *Vesalii Icones* that material generated by one process in this way takes on an identity of its own – for reference, the phrases can be labelled $X_{Bb}$, $Y_E$ and $Z_{Eb}$ respectively – to become the starting point for subsequent 'development'. Following the three melodic statements, for example,

---

[34]   Griffiths, *op. cit.*, p. 153.

[35]   The composer's programme note, reproduced in Griffiths, *op. cit.*, p. 148.

[36]   Sweeney-Turner, 'Resurrecting the Antichrist: Maxwell Davies and Parody – Dialectics or Deconstruction?', *Tempo* 191 (December 1994), pp. 14–20.

[37]   Walsh, 'Davies, Peter Maxwell', *The New Grove Dictionary of Music and Musicians*, vol. 5, p. 277.

[38]   Taylor, *op. cit.*, p. 62.

each phrase is worked into a short canon of which Ex. 2.15b gives the upper voices of the first, realizing $X_{Bb}$ on flute and $X_BR$ on basset clarinet. This contrapuntal material, in its turn, generates a new melodic line – the sequence traced by dotted lines in Ex. 2.15b – in movement nine, 'Christ Prepared for Death', as clarified in Ex. 2.15c (bars 307–15 similarly 'synthesize' $Y_ER$ and $Y_{Bb}$, and bars 316–24, $Z_{Eb}$ and $Z_{Cb}R$), later 'paraphrased' at greater speed, starting at bar 325, reproduced in Ex. 2.15d (bars 329–34 likewise rework the Y- and Z-canonically derived lines, more and more 'synoptically').

In movement 11, 'The Death of Christ', later subunits of $z[+W_G \Rightarrow +WI_A]$ have clear realizations, no longer featuring oscillatory transposition, but consistently transposed by vic 3: $z[+W_G \Rightarrow +WI_A]^3$: 18R, bars 344–50; $z[+W_G \Rightarrow +WI_A]^3$: 17, bars 351–8; $z[+W_G \Rightarrow +WI_A]^3$: 16R, bars 359–67; $z[+W_G \Rightarrow +WI_A]^3$: 15, bars 368–77. As Ex. 2.15e illustrates, however, individual elements of the subunits are subject to apparently freer variation, and the solo cello line simultaneously embodies both the sets' melodic realization and their melismatic decoration.

As a final illustration of techniques applied to *Worldes Blis*-derived material in the work, Ex. 2.16 shows a new transformation process taking $Z_{Eb}$, the third cello phrase of movement 1, as its starting point:

(a)   For ease of reference, $ZI_{Eb}R$ is termed $V_{Cb}$.

(b)   A simple transformation process, in five subunits, maps corresponding elements of $V_{Cb}$ to those of $VI_{Cb}$, filling out the intervals between them in whole-tone steps. Note that the terminal sets are registrally modified to reduce these intervals, and that steps are omitted in the transformation of elements five and seven as shown. The substitution of e´ for d´ as element three of $VI_{Cb}$ is a freer variation, perhaps unintentional.

(c)   A self-transposed variant, $z[V_{Cb} \Rightarrow VI_{Db}]$, is produced by transposing successive subunits to begin on a sieving of $V_{Cb}$ (the stemmed notes of Ex. 2.16b). Register and duration here are as shown in the composer's sketch.[39]

---

[39]   A separate leaf included with Add Ms 71258.

(a): $z[+W_G \Rightarrow +WI_A]^{3.0.9}$: $3 / Z_{E_b}$

$ZI_{E_b}R = V_G$

(b): $[V_G \Rightarrow VI_G]$         (c): $z[V_G \Rightarrow VI_D]$

Ex. 2.16: *Vesalii Icones* – basis of xylophone part, 'The Betrayal of Judas', bars 42ff.

Subunits 1–4 of the transformation are realized on xylophone in movement 2, 'The Betrayal of Judas' (beginning in bars 42, 48, 55 and 61 respectively) with modifications to register and to pitch class (subunit 3, element 10, A not G♯; subunit 4, element 14, F not A), but entirely respecting the identical rhythmic articulation of successive subunits.[40]

---

[40]    Cf. Taylor's discussion of this passage, *op. cit.*, p. 64. This transformation process is actually of quite a rare type progressing, paradigmatically, by 'a given interval [whole tones] throughout'; Ex. 2.3 and Ex. 2.5 illustrate Davies's more common technique of transforming 'by a series of intervals' – semitones, tones, minor thirds – to use the terminology of his article 'Sets or Series', *The Listener* 79 22 (February 1968), p. 250.

At some future time, analysis or sketch material may elucidate further techniques at work in *Vesalii Icones* – notably in the predominant cello lines of movements 2, 3, 4, 5, 7, 10 and 12. Movement 13, 'The Entombment of Christ' is a clear reprise of the 'X, Y, Z' canons from movement 1;[41] the remaining movements – 6, 8 and 14 – exploit parody and pastiche, as has long been noted, though additional technical explanation would still seem merited. Concerning No. 8, 'St Veronica Wipes His Face', Davies wrote:

> The raw material from *Ecce Manus* is ... bent to resemble a Schenker analysis, but instead of stripping off layers of music to expose ultimately a 'common' skeleton below, the 'skeleton' is heard first and levels are added ... but when it would just about become clear to a perceptive ear that the analysis concerned is of the scherzo of the Fifth Symphony of Beethoven, the flute twists the *Ecce Manus* fragment into a resemblance of the scherzo of the Ninth – it is a related but false image. [42]

The point seems previously to have been missed – for example, in Steve Sweeney-Turner's comment that 'With the 7 in the *Urlinie*, and the VII–VI in the *Bassbrechung*, this [is] obviously no "pure" *Ursatz*'[43] – that Davies's reference to Schenker and Beethoven here is exact. An analysis of the *Scherzo* from the Fifth Symphony is included in *Der freie Satz* as an example of 'reaching-over' (*Übergreifen*).[44] An upper line, Eb-D-C-B-[C], is 'reached-over' by an F (above the D) falling to Eb, beneath which the bass descends from I to V via a 'fourth-progression' through flattened VII and VI, before returning to I. Precisely these lines are assigned to flute, cello and clarinet respectively in bars 263–8, repeated in bars 269–74 and again in bars 273–9 (the final I of the second realization 'dove-tailing' into the opening I of the third). Only in the final realization, however, are VII and VI of the bass line (on clarinet) flattened: the preceding statements descend via B♮ and A♮, giving a sense that the 'true' Schenkerian *Ursatz* emerges as the goal of a compositional process. Complementary to this process is the superimposition of a 'middle-ground' analysis – on glockenspiel and xylophone – in bars 268–72, repeated in bars 273ff., where 'foreground' figures are finally added on piano. The 'authentic' relationship of these higher structural levels to the Beethoven original is illustrated in Ex. 2.17. In striking contrast, the flute's reference to the *Scherzo* of the Ninth Symphony in bars 278–80 is based on simple allusion to the melodic contour and rhythm of its opening theme.

---

[41]   As detailed by Taylor, *op. cit.*, p. 67.
[42]   Griffiths, *op. cit.*, p. 154.
[43]   Sweeney-Turner, *op. cit.*, p. 15.
[44]   Schenker, *Der freie Satz* (Universal Edition, 1935); available in English as *Free Composition*, translated and edited by Ernst Oster (Longman Inc., New York, 1979), Fig. 41 (1).

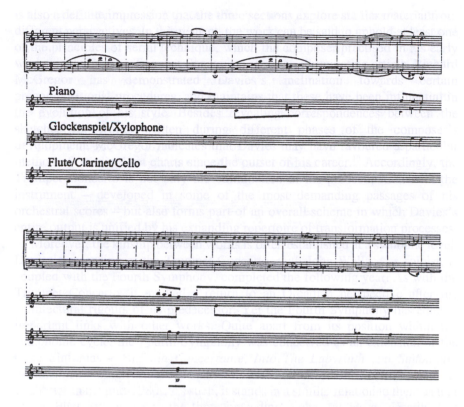

Ex. 2.17: *Scherzo* of Beethoven's Fifth Symphony, after Schenker, and *Vesalii Icones* no. 8
'St Veronica wipes His Face'

In the play of 'distinguishing the false from the real' with which Davies has said
*Vesalii Icones* is ultimately concerned, critics stand in danger of taking another
remark in the composer's programme note, 'in No. 6 ... the dancer plays ... a
garbled Victorian hymn', at face value (though the same music, occurring in
*Missa Super l'Homme Armé* is identified as 'pseudo-Victorian').[45] Any mis-
understanding is a tribute to the composer's skill for stylistic pastiche, since bars
236a ff. actually present a melody derived by selective sieving of the *Victimae
Paschali Laudes* plainsong – further modified by transposition and freer
interpolations as illustrated in Ex. 2.18 – harmonized with a chordal vocabulary
appropriate to the target of his parody (notably 'dominant'-seventh and
diminished-seventh sonorities).

---

45    Composer's programme notes, *op. cit.*, pp. 153 and 146 (cf. Taylor, *op. cit.*).

This harmonic framework then becomes the explicit support of the foxtrot in bars 236b ff., and underlies an entirely new melodic surface in movement 14, 'Resurrection – Antichrist'. Thus, what Sweeney-Turner terms 'perhaps *the classic Davies foxtrot parody*'[46] has its origins in a plainsong for Easter Sunday, and provides yet another example, in the composer's own terms, of 'one of those "unpredictable" things' which proves to be 'ultimately justifiable'.[47] *Vesalii Icones* may apparently draw on an 'inner logic' of a different kind from that operating in *Worldes Blis* (or the other pieces I surveyed here): it is nonetheless a 'logic' equally integral to Davies's technique, and its repercussions are to be felt right up to his most recent music,[48] the particulars of which I leave to the exploration of other commentators.

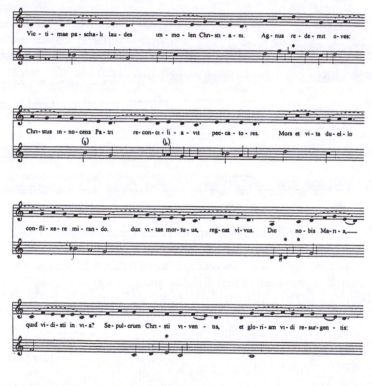

* indicates liberties in strict transposition by vic 5

Ex. 2.18: *Vesalii Icones* – no. 6 melody of 'Victorian hymn' from *Victimae Paschali Laudes*

---

[46]    Sweeney-Turner, *op. cit.*, p. 16.

[47]    Cf. Davies's response to Paul Griffiths's observation, 'No doubt the foxtrot there is related to other things that have been going on in the music – but ... it could almost be any foxtrot.' in Griffiths, *op. cit.*, pp. 113–14.

[48]    For example, in the 'folk-songs' and 'hymn tunes' of his 'final' opera, *The Doctor of Myddfai*.

# 3

# A foxtrot to the crucifixion: the music theatre of Peter Maxwell Davies[1]

*Michael Burden*

## Setting the scene

There is no doubt that the music theatre of Peter Maxwell Davies is some of the most riveting of the later twentieth century. Starting in the 1960s, Davies produced a series of works notable for their originality, power, and dramatic coherence. This discussion will address the music theatre works primarily from a dramatic angle – music in service to drama – but is in no way intended to demote the score: it is an acknowledgement of Davies's authorship of most of his own libretti, and his admission that his ideas and inspirations are 'often theatrical in the first place rather than purely musical'.[2] Indeed, Davies writing on *Eight Songs for a Mad King* said of the music:

> In some ways, I regard the work as a collection of musical objects borrowed from many sources, functioning as musical 'stage props' around which the reciter's part weaves, lighting them from extraordinary angles....[3]

And it is the notion of Davies's theatrical props that is the subject of this article.

The roots of Davies's achievement in the realization of ideals of drama that would become music theatre lay in the 'Manchester Group', or to use the title of their one London concert, 'New Music Group Manchester'.[4] Formed by composers and performers who studied at the Royal Manchester College of

---

[1]    My personal thanks are due to Colin Baldy (George III), Lindsay Bramley (Miss Donnithorne, the Medium), Angus Edwards (cello, *Vesalii Icones*), and Ivan Rockey (clarinet and administrator, the Phoenix Ensemble) for the inspiration they each brought to New Chamber Opera's series of music theatre productions during the early 1990s.

[2]    Milnes, 'Towards Music Theatre', *Opera*, 23/12 (1972), p. 1067.

[3]    Griffiths, *Peter Maxwell Davies* (London: Robson Books, 1982), p. 148.

[4]    Seabrook, *Max: The Life and Music of Peter Maxwell Davies* (London: Gollancz, 1994), p. 42, reports that the only evidence that the group existed is the heading to the programme notes of the group's one London concert at the Arts Council on 9 January 1956.

Music (Davies was there from 1952 to 1956) in the early 1950s, the group championed not only their own new music, but also paid great attention to the output of European composers, such as Webern, Berg and Stravinsky, then not widely known in Britain. Although the group members – amongst them the composers Alexander Goehr and Harrison Birtwistle, and the pianist, John Ogden[5] – developed in different ways with different ideals. This is not to suggest that the members therefore had nothing in common with, or were unsympathetic to, the others' directions, and there can be no doubt of the stimulus provided by the interaction between the members, whether of a positive or negative kind. Davies, Birtwistle and Goehr went on to organize the Wardour Castle Summer School of Music in 1964 and 1965. The second one of these was to be a defining moment in British music theatre, for it culminated in a highly dramatized performance of Schoenberg's *Pierrot Lunaire* by the Melos Ensemble, with Bethany Beardslee as the vocalist, a style of concentrated drama which was to be subsequently reflected in the output of all three composers.

Precisely how Goehr reacted to the Melos performance is difficult to gauge: what is clear is that his three major pieces of music theatre – *Naboth's Vineyard* (1968), *Shadowplay* (1970), *Sonata about Jerusalem* (1971) – appeared in the following years. These were closely related to the work of the producer John Cox and the Music Theatre Ensemble.[6] In the case of Davies and Birtwistle, the response was more precisely connected with Schoenberg's piece, for in 1967 they established a music theatre ensemble of their own, although in Davies's account, it was Birtwistle who was keenest to write music theatre works and who initially got the players together.[7] The group took not only its name, Pierrot Players,[8] from *Pierrot Lunaire*, but also its instrumentation, for the line-up was for voice, piano, flute, clarinet, violin and cello, with the violin doubling viola and various doublings in the wind. A percussionist was added to their number: Schoenberg had in fact excluded percussion, as he already had a number of exotic sounds,[9] including the harmonium, an instrument that would later be an inspiration for Davies.[10] *Pierrot Lunaire* was included in the group's first concert on 30 May 1967, the vocalist Mary Thomas presenting a brilliant, extravagant interpretation. In the rush by musicans to accord iconic status to *Pierrot Lunaire*, it was often forgotten that the work was commissioned by an actress and cabaret artist Albertine Zehme, who had already been declaiming the poems to music by

---

    [5]    The 'inner circle' consisted of Davies, Birtwistle, Goehr, Ogden and the trumpeter Elgar Howarth.

    [6]    See Melanie Daiken, 'Notes on Goehr's Triptych' in Bayan Northcott (ed.), *The Music of Alexander Goehr* (London: Schott and Co, 1980) pp. 40–48.

    [7]    Seabrook, *op. cit.*, p. 100.

    [8]    *Ibid.*, p. 101; in fact, Steve Pruslin, the group's keyboard player, came up with all the names the group would use in future years.

    [9]    See Dunsby, *Pierrot Lunaire* (Cambridge: CUP, 1992), p. 24.

    [10]    See the hymn in *Missa Super L'Homme Armé*.

Vrieslander, and that the performances of Beardslee and Thomas come closer to the intentions of the work's creators than a 'straight' performance.

The Wardour Castle Summer School was a defining moment not only for British music theatre, but also for the relationship between the three composers. Whether tensions, real or imagined jealousies, and different aesthetic ideas could or can be honestly identified at this distance is doubtful, even if the three desired to discuss it.[11] It will suffice to say here that Goehr and Davies were not to work together again, and that despite the joint path set by Davies and Birtwistle with the Pierrot Players, it was not to last. The reasons given by those sympathetic to Davies include Birtwistle's lack of productivity and his apparent distrust of the group's manager James Murdoch, employed by Davies. All conclude that there simply wasn't enough room in such a small ensemble for two such large and inspirational talents. While not incompatible with these suggestions (and it has to be admitted, the positive gloss), Birtwistle's account is at variance with this. He appears to have felt that that the instrumental combination was restricting, but perhaps more importantly, he 'felt at odds with the high camp and sensationalism that was developing'.[12] The 'high camp and sensationalism', while partly a reference to the hype used to promote the group, undoubtedly refers to what Davies himself would call 'extravagant gestures'. These gestures would stay with Davies for some time; in speaking of their appearance in the opera *Resurrection*, he claimed that they were still there, 'but more so, and very differently'.[13] But in later years, he would reject them:

> ... that sort of gesture is OK at that sort of stage in your career and that sort of age, but if you go on making it, it becomes tired, and there's just no point.[14]

This, however, was in the future: Birtwistle may have already tired of them, but Davies at this time was not yet done, and ultimately Birtwistle left. The Pierrot Players felt morally obliged to change the name, and the group took the one suggested by Stephen Pruslin – 'The Fires of London'. During the next decade or so, The Fires – administered successively by James Murdoch, Louise Honeyman and Judy Arnold – performed, toured, gave premieres of Davies's works and commissioned a large number of works from young composers, making the group a powerful force in British contemporary music. Finally, after three major changes of line-up, and a series, both happy and unhappy, of *ad hoc* conductors after Davies stepped down in 1980, the group disbanded after their twentieth

---

[11] There are various accounts of the relationship between the three men; it is Seabrook (*op. cit.*, pp. 119–24) who tells us that Goehr will not discuss the matter, and relates the guarded accounts of the other two.

[12] Hall, *Harrison Birtwistle* (London: Robson Books, 1984), p. 50.

[13] Griffiths, *op. cit.*, p. 130.

[14] *ibid.*, p. 114.

anniversary concert in 1987. Accounts of the difficulties of running The Fires, and of the circumstances of its final years can be found elsewhere,[15] and more need not be said here. It should be added though that whatever the financial and administrative reasons behind the group being disbanded, Davies's own work had, not surprisingly, simply gone in another direction and there seems to have been little reason for him to expend the effort, both financial and emotional, required to maintain a performing ensemble which did not reflect his current enthusiasms.

## Music theatre

> While one must sympathise entirely with today's composers seeking a new name for the medium and jettisoning the excesses of duration, orchestral and choral forces, diversification and diffusiveness associated with late-romantic opera, there is still a slight impression that they are stealing the emperor's clothes while pretending that they do not exist.[16]

So commented Rodney Milnes on the results of a workshop session which preceded the Queen Elizabeth Hall performance of Davies's *Nachspiel*, a workshop during which the composer had talked lucidly and accessibly about his work. Milnes's comment hints at the problems in defining the term 'music theatre', problems which have presented themselves to scholars on one hand, and to composers on the other, many of the latter simply using the term to avoid having their work labelled as 'opera'.

The central preoccupation of any definition is, of course, when is a vocal work not an 'opera', but a piece of music theatre? Or – to quote Milnes again – is 'music theatre little more than opera writ small'? In fact, if it is remembered that it is a question of emphasis (that is to say, a characteristic of music theatre may well be present in opera, but it may not play the same role or be given the same emphasis), then it is relatively easy to identify what the parameters of the genre are, even if it is difficult to draw the definition much tighter. Stripped of all their verbiage, most definitions reach the apparently elastic one, best expressed by Bayan Northcott: 'Anything you can do with an acting space and a handful of musicians.'[17] In that simple expression, Northcott manages to emphasize several of the most important aspects of the genre. The very opening phrase 'anything you can do', if taken to mean 'anything appropriate that is achievable', illustrates its elasticity. It might include dance, mime, *sprechsgesang*, speech, colour transparencies, film, in fact anything by which a theatrical result may be achieved. Northcott's 'acting space' is of equal significance: that he refers to it

---

[15]   Esp. Seabrook, *op. cit.*, pp. 158–63.
[16]   Milnes, *op. cit.*, p. 1069.
[17]   *Ibid.*, p. 1608.

as an *acting* space rather than a *singing* space focuses attention on the dramatic aspect of the performance, while the use of the word 'space' rather than 'stage' conveys precisely the elements of flexibility and of self-defining dramatic context which are the essential ingredients of any piece of music theatre. Similar flexibility is found in Northcott's expression 'a handful of musicians', a phrase which suggests nothing in terms of instrumentation, and makes no assumptions about the players which might be used in each piece. The only thing it does suggest is that the group will be small, having practical advantages: a new work was more likely to have both a first and subsequent performances if it could also be seen to be economical.

This 'smallness' was as much a political statement as it was an aesthetic one, however. A consistent thread of references which runs through criticism and commentary on the genre is the desire that works should be seen to be as unlike opera as possible, a stance which was as much an objection to the opera house and the trappings that went with it, as it was to the works themselves. Some composers found that this stance sat uneasily with the works they desired to produce:

> I cannot, will not, compose a traditional 'opera'; for me the operatic genre is irrelevant today [however] I do not mean at all that I cannot compose a work for the facilities an opera house offers.[18]

Other composers and performers were at pains to point out that the notion of music theatre rested as much in the style of performance and presentation as it did in the composition itself. In writing of *Curlew River*, Benjamin Britten objected to theatrical and operatic effects and wanted the production to be quite unlike opera,[19] while John Cox, writing in the introduction to Goehr's *Naboth's Vineyard*, suggests a more sweeping approach: 'An orchestra pit and all the other conventions of "opera" must be avoided at all costs'.[20] As a comparison between Davies's own earlier miniature opera *Notre Dame des Fleurs* 1966 (rev. 1973) – a lush, indulgent, obscene, yet highly satisfying piece – and any one of his own music theatre works – spare, demanding and troubling – shows, the smugness and exaggerated nature of the first was 'out'.

The task of definition also becomes easier if it ceases to be used as a chronological catch-all term, and its remit is limited to the period during which the works called 'music theatre' by their creators were written. It then becomes apparent that the nature of opera has changed, or more, precisely, the perception of what composers, performers and audiences think of as operatic has shifted. If

---

[18]   György Ligeti quoted in Griffiths, *Modern Music and after* (Oxford: Oxford University Press, 1995), p. 171.
[19]   See Colin Graham's production notes to *Curlew River* (London: Faber Music, 1965).
[20]   Alexander Goehr, *Triptych, 1 Naboth's Vineyard* (London: Schott and Co., 1973), staging note by John Cox.

one sets *Eight Songs for a Mad King* alongside works such as Nicholas Maw's *One Man Show*, or Britten's *Owen Wingrave*, the distinguishing traits of music theatre are obvious. If the definition is stretched to include contemporary works, the differences between the two genres becomes less pronounced. The more dynamic, flexible, and dramatically integrated approach to writing opera found in works as diverse as Birtwistle's *The Second Mrs Kong*, Mark-Antony Turnage's *Greek* and Nicola Lefanu's *Blood Wedding*, suggests that 'opera' has adopted aspects of 'music theatre'.

Thus, to return to Milnes's quotation, it is not so much a question of music theatre 'stealing the emperor's clothes', but that the emperor, having unwittingly loaned his underused finery and having seen its possibilities when tailored on someone else, takes them back again. And the extent to which those 'stealing the clothes' denied they existed, reflects not so much the denial of the clothes themselves, but of the context in which they were worn.

**Davies's music theatre: themes and trends**

The five central pieces in Davies's output are *Revelation and Fall*, *Missa Super L'Homme Armé*, *Eight Songs for a Mad King*, *Vesalii Icones* and perhaps *Miss Donnithorne's Maggot*; followed by *Blind Man's Buff* and *Le Jongleur de Notre Dame*. To return to Davies's own admission that during this period at least, the theatrical images tended to come first and inspire the music, it is clear that they tended to come unbidden. The early theatre piece, *Revelation and Fall* of 1965–6, only started out as a theatrical piece in a 'limited way' – the full theatrical implications of Davies's approach were not immediately clear to him.[21] It might, though, be more accurate to suggest that Davies's theatrical notions had not yet been fully crystallized, the work having been completed in the February before the formative summer school performance of *Pierrot Lunaire* at Wardour Castle. The orchestration is much larger than that of *Pierrot*, requiring sixteen players, and the work only reached its present form after a revision in 1980. The compositional *raison d'être* was the use of the medieval and Renaissance *cantus firmus*, mensural canon, and the 'complexity of rhythmic relationships between the voices'. These old compositional devices had occupied Davies for some years, being freely acknowledged in *Alma Redemptoris Mater* (1957), and Griffiths suggests that these 'rigorous post-Medieval techniques' fuel rather than restrict Davies's 'expressionist violence'.[22] With a text by Georg Trakl, *Revelation and Fall* was first performed at the Conway Hall on 26 February 1968. Its central figure is habited as a nun: Davies specifies a blood-red habit.

---

21    Griffiths, *Maxwell Davies*, pp. 62–4.
22    Griffiths, *Modern Music: The Avant Garde since 1945* (London: Dent, 1981), p. 261.

Here we encounter one of the themes that run through his music theatre pieces – the hypocrisy of an established institution. The colour of the nun's robe can be seen to represent the blood of those killed needlessly in the First World War (the subject of Trakl's text), killing which the established church (represented by the use of a religious figure) conceded as necessary in a 'just war'.

The analysis of such religious posturing is also the subject of Davies's next piece of music theatre, *Missa Super L'Homme Armé*, a work similarly inspired by early music, and it, too, gained theatrical elements as time went by. In this case, Davies used an incomplete composition based on the 'L'homme armé' tune. The piece was premiered in 1968, but the work's text was pre-recorded, using a boy's voice. When it was revised in 1971, the taped voice became a vocalist, adding a further visual dimension to the work's innate theatricality. The central character – a soprano – is a disaffected priest habited as a nun, a piece of cross-dressing that served to emphasize the religious distortion and hypocrisy Davies sought to represent. At the final denouement, it is Judas who is associated with the church through the Victorian hymn played on the harmonium, while the transvestite nun declaims Christ's curse on the betrayer.

After these two works comes *Eight Songs for a Mad King*, a work which, by a somewhat unnecessary sleight of hand, is often referred to as Davies's first music theatre work.[23] The desire to make it so is entirely understandable: it is an extraordinarily intense piece and is probably Davies's greatest work in the field, yet to suggest that it sprang unheralded from Davies's pen offers a construct which clearly has no basis in fact. The text was by the Australian writer, Randolph Stow, whom Davies had previously encountered. Stow and Davies were enchanted on different occasions by the mechanical hand-organ which had belonged to George III: when incarcerated as insane, the King attempted to use it to teach his pet birds to sing. It clearly held inspiration for both artists: Stow wrote the eight songs, the central figure being King George III, much of the text based on the King's ravings as recorded by Fanny Burney, while Davies parodied to great effect in using passages from Handel's *Messiah*, one of George III's favourite works.

Although slightly later, it is helpful to view *Eight Songs* alongside *Miss Donnithorne's Maggot*, also from Stow's pen. A commission from the Adelaide Festival of Arts premiered on 9 March 1974, it too used a central historical figure, Miss Emily Donnithorne, the jilted bride and daughter of a Sydney judge, and one of several possible models for Dickens's Miss Havisham. The central theme is the same – madness leading to death – and the work's structure – a cycle of 'songs' – are recognizably similar. However, differences in the type of madness are reflected in the contrasting vocal writing, for Miss Donnithorne's

---

[23]    The argument goes that because both *Revelation and Fall* and *Missa Super L'Homme Armé* were subsequently revised and theatrical elements added, they were not the 'first'.

madness is rather more gentle. Instead of the great range of bizarre vocal effects, and tortured sounds required in *Eight Songs*, the score of *Miss Donnithorne* is characterized by an almost lyrical quality – although some vocal 'bells and whistles' are present – and the audience is not, despite the crude and frank language, continually shocked by the events. Although there are comic elements in the work,[24] pathos is the over-riding engagement with the audience.

Davies capped the achievement of *Eight Songs* with *Vesalii Icones*, a piece of even greater power, albeit in a less flashy, but perhaps less accessible way. A piece for dancer, cello and ensemble, it takes the fourteen stations of the cross and superimposes on them the anatomical prints of the sixteenth-century anatomical artist Vesalius, the juxtaposition of both images then serves as a starting point for each dance movement. The two cycles of images – the station of the cross leading to the resurrection, and the anatomical images leading to the human skeleton – work in a different way to that which might be expected. The Vesalius prints are arranged so that they progressively show the human flesh being stripped from the body, so that at the resurrection, we are confronted with not a complete man, but the skeleton, 'a stripping down of the human condition'. The dancer is thus exposed as the Anti-Christ, offering not comfort and hope, but destruction, and the audience is shown to have deceived itself in the worship of an interloper. The dancer William Lowther – who premiered the work at the Queen Elizabeth Hall on 9 December 1969 – was intimately involved in the creative process, working on the choreography movement by movement as Davies completed the pieces.[25]

The idea of 'peeling down', or stripping down, or 'revealing a "true" self' also plays a central role in *Blind Man's Buff* from 1972. In it, The Boy King asks of The Jester, 'Who are you?' The Jester responds:

> Jester:              Am I this, or this, or this or that?
> (*The Dancer and Mime strike attitudes and peel off a succession of masks*)
>                      It scares me to think how easily I can be peeled and segmented.
> Boy King:            But you must be something.
> Jester:              As your Majesty commands.[26]

As The Jester and The Boy King sing at the end:

> Stick, stock, stone dead,
> Blind man can't see.
> Every knave will have a slave,
> You or I must be he.[27]

---

[24]   Seabrook, *op. cit.*, p. 148.
[25]   Griffiths, *Maxwell Davies*, pp. 112–3.
[26]   Davies, Peter Maxwell, *Blind Man's Buff* (London: Chester, 1981), p. ii.
[27]   *Ibid.*, p. iii.

A curious work, it is also engages with the problem of seeing clearly – 'Blind men can't see' – and the confusion of identity – 'You or I must be he'; both themes are highlighted by the use of mirrors in the Mirror Dance. In fact during the piece, the King takes on the role of the Jester telling the jokes.

1978 saw the composition of *Le Jongleur de Notre Dame*, which also picked up on these themes of the artist in relation to his surroundings. Here, we return to the use of the church and the religious as a vehicle for Davies's ideas, but without the sinister intentions or the need to see through hypocrisy. The tale – of the Jongleur and Our Lady – is one of piety. The Abbot, against his better judgement, takes in 'even a clown' and accepts him as a novice. For the Virgin's birthday they are all required to present a gift: the monks are commanded to produce items reflecting their skills, but Mark is told that, given his sinful life, he has nothing to offer. Mark, however, sneaks before the statue of the Virgin and performs an offering; she accepts by playing her violin. The Abbot sends him out into the community to develop and communicate his artistic talents. The Jongleur is a mime and the monks are played by the instrumentalists and as characters are represented by those instruments; the Abbot is the only vocalist. While it is true that we are confronted with the smugness of the church, it is not the gross, expressionist hypocrisy of the earlier pieces.

## Moving the frame

One of the key aspects of Davies's music theatre is the 'frame': the dramatic structure which surrounds the piece. The role played by the theatrical frame in all its different guises is often an unconscious one, and Davies's moving of it draws attention to its presence in an audience's consciousness, often in a startling way. Davies dispenses with what might be called the largest frame or the first frame, the proscenium arch. In fact, the space for any music theatre work is best summed up by Davies in the instructions to *Blind Man's Buff*:

> The stage should be a simple platform, with simple lighting ... there is no 'set' as such.[28]

Again, *Pierrot Lunaire* can be pinpointed as a source for such ideas. The first performance required only:

> Dark screens [which] stood on stage and between them was Albertine Zehme in the costume of Columbine. Behind the scenes a handful of musicians conducted by Schoenberg played ...[29]

---

[28]   *Ibid.*, p. ii.
[29]   Stuckenschmidt, *Arnold Schoenberg* (London: Calder, 1955), pp. 60-1.

The audience has had the safe and comfortable shield removed, a shield which would normally put distance between the audience and the performance, and conceals the backstage support. By implication, the technical aspects are, when they still exist, simplified. The audience is thus confronted with the bare minimum on, for all intents and purposes, an empty stage, with its attention focused almost solely on the central character: the nun in *Revelation and Fall*; the King in *Eight Songs*; the dancer in *Vesalii Icones*; Miss Donnithorne in *Miss Donnithorne's Maggot*; the Jongleur in *Le Jongleur de Notre Dame*, and so on.

The 'set' into which musicians are thus integrated is not always essential to the work, even when specified by the composer. *Miss Donnithorne's Maggot* is the only one of Davies's music theatre pieces that requires a major structure:

> There should ideally be a set consisting of a huge wedding cake in an advanced state of decay, the instrumentalists being integrated into the set. The mezzo-soprano soloist, Miss Donnithorne, must be dressed in a period wedding gown with veil, also in a state of decay. Additionally she tears little cakes (made of cardboard or paper, to make a lot of noise) or bits from the cake forming the set, in No. 2. In No. 8 she takes confetti from pockets in her dress and throws it about.[30]

After *Miss Donnithorne*, 'set' is in fact a misleading term, for they are not so much 'set' requirements, but 'prop' requirements. To paraphrase Davies's own comment that 'musical objects act as stage props', it can be seen that the stage supports the central notions of the drama.

Such paring away also highlights the position of the band in the drama. For a start, it is nearly always in full view rather than placed in a pit below eye-level. But Davies goes further than that, exhibiting a range of approaches. There is the relatively simple approach found in *Miss Donnithorne's Maggot*, specified by Davies in the score, with the band inside the cake. But although Miss Donnithorne's wedding cake surrounds the musical centre of work, the musicians do not loom larger in the action. Nor do they in *Blind Man's Buff*, where the King is surrounded by the musicians who 'should be dressed brightly as courtiers'.[31] In *Le Jongleur de Notre Dame* however, not only are some of the monks played by instrumentalists, but the violinist is also the Virgin Mary who finally responds to the Jongleur's offering with a violin solo.

In *Eight Songs*, the musicians represent the songbirds of Stow's text, the bullfinches that George III was trying to teach to sing. Davies organizes the score so that the percussionist acts as the King's 'keeper', while the flute, clarinet, violin and cello stand for the bullfinches. In the first production, the musicians, as the bullfinches, were 'caged' in large wooden latticed upright cylinders. Yet,

---

[30]     Davies, Peter Maxwell, *Miss Donnithorne's Maggot* (London: Boosey and Hawkes, 1977), staging note.

[31]     *Blind Man's Buff*, p. ii.

there is the feeling here that the cages kept the King *out* as well as the musicians (as 'songbirds') in, a feeling which conveys all too clearly the isolation of the King in his madness. That it would be dangerous for the musicians to be in the same space as the King becomes apparent in the 7th song, when the King reaches through the bars, snatches the violinist's instrument, and smashes it up. The violin can also be seen to represent the King's voice, an 'instrument' also driven to complete destruction by being used so constantly during the King's ravings that it becomes hoarse and unrecognizable.

Perhaps the most important absorption of an instrument into the narrative is that found in *Vesalii Icones*. Here, the cello offers its own commentary on the stations of the cross, the images that inspire the dancing. The dramatic frame is purely that mapped out and created by the dancer, a frame that is redefined by the solo cello. The space for the drama to be played out therefore becomes that encompassed by the relationship, between the cello and the dancer at any one time. The performer is instructed to be physically removed from the rest of the instrumentalists, and in the eyes of the dancer, can be 'Pilate, Veronica, or even a Flagellator'.[32] On another level – and perhaps more interestingly, given the constant theme of 'stripping down' – Davies suggests that the player can also be viewed as the 'Anatomy Demonstrator'. Such a viewpoint alters the relationship between the instrumentalist, the dancer and the audience, for the cello is in the hands of the one who is 'demonstrating' to the audience (rather than merely commenting upon the action as presented) that the people have been taken in, and have been worshipping the Anti-Christ.

Focusing on the frame of the musical and dramatic material – rather than on what might be described as the 'frame for reception' – there is a tendency towards non-narrative structures. Apart from *Le Jongleur*, the pieces do not tell stories, but are studies of their subjects: for example madness, in both *Eight Songs* and *Miss Donnithorne*; the human condition in *Vesalii Icones*. Thus, as studies, they do not 'progress', but present a view of their subjects from a number of different angles in a manner that might be called 'snapshot'. This is true even for *Vesalii Icones*, which might be thought to progress through the stations of the cross. In fact, Davies himself is very careful to point out that each station is not an interpretation of the subject matter, but is a starting point for what follows in each dance. To convey this, the frame chosen in each piece for the musical material is a form divided up into smaller, separate (when not self-contained), units: eight songs in *Eight Songs*; Prelude–Miss Donnithorne's Maggot–Recitative–Her Dump–Nocturne–Her Rant–Recitative–Her Reel in *Miss Donnithorne*; the stations of the cross in *Vesalii Icones*; and the Overture–Mirror Dance–Wedding Dance–Recitative Dramatico in *Blind Man's Buff*.

---

[32]     Griffiths, *Peter Maxwell Davies*, p. 153.

Davies's music theatre then, is characterized by lack of a conventional theatrical frame on one hand, and its replacement by a frame which, in each case, is generated from within each individual piece. There can be no assumptions about what each frame might be, and it can also vary from realization to realization. Furthermore, the technique described above as 'snapshot' suggests that there is a 'circumpolar' frame to the action, in which one central point is occupied by the main character – the King, Miss Donnithorne – who is then viewed from a number of different, but discreet, angles.

## Ritual, revelation and fall

The shocking, disturbing, and sometimes outrageous nature of much music theatre of the 1960s and 1970s sometimes disguises the extent to which the works rely on ritual, and often on a traditional framework upon which that ritual is hung. Noh theatre, the Punch and Judy story, the mummer's plays and puppet theatre, for example, offer specific models for Britten's *Curlew River*, Birtwistle's *Punch and Judy*, his *Down by the Greenwood Side*, and Goehr's *Shadowplay*. Davies draws on some of these models, his type of ritual being codified through its extraction from these models, and the ultimate success of Davies's works depends on the audience's grasp of the ritual involved.

Davies has claimed that 'ritual' is central to his music theatre. In *Vesalii Icones*, the audience will not recognize the Christ they know in the figure they watch, but the inclusion of Judas accompanied by the parodied hymn on the harmonium immediately gives the clue. In fact, the point of *Vesalii Icones* is that the ritual of the resurrection is inverted: man is made whole, but is destroyed by the risen figure – the risen figure here is the Anti-Christ. Furthermore, the ritual of the stations of the cross is the backbone of the work: comprehension of the nature of that ritual is essential to Davies's structure. And the importance of the Anti-Christ figure should not be underestimated. It is not simply the Devil, a figure which would be relatively easy to portray, but the other side of Christ.

One of the central metaphors of Davies's ritual is that of the journey. The journey is not – as it is in, say, Britten's *Curlew River* – part of the 'plot', but is a wholly spiritual one, and one which is undertaken by the audience as often as it is by the characters in the acting space. Of the first five of Davies's music theatre works – three are studies of religion, and two are studies of madness – each of the central characters is undergoing a transformation or journey. In both the portraits of madness – *Eight Songs* and *Miss Donnithorne* – the central characters are journeying towards death. Both in different ways revisit the past, and both challenge the audience's own comfortable position. In *Eight Songs*, we are left wondering not only about the nature of the King's madness, but about our own perceptions. Are we watching a mad king? Or is the madman believing he is king? To what extent are we his subjects, and therefore the focus for his concern? When this is coupled with the ludicrous, comic and frightening portrayal of the central character, the audience is forced to examine its own ideals and reactions. It becomes disconcertingly clear as the piece proceeds that, as Paul Griffiths puts it, 'we are not only voyeurs, but voyeurs at our own potential extremity'.[33] In *Miss Donnithorne*, we are disconcertingly drawn into the action by her opening speech:

> Your Excellency, Your Honour, Your Worship, ladies and gentlemen
> people of Sydney, most of all the deserving poor,
> Miss Donnithorne begs the favour of your presence
> at her nuptial feast and ball.
> May it choke you one and all.[34]

Both these portraits of madness – the King's violent and aggressive, Miss Donnithorne's comparatively gentle – end in death, the journey through life being thus completed. And at both deaths, the central characters are ready to face their destiny. The King has been hit so hard by events that there is nothing left but death. At the end of *Miss Donnithorne*, she calls:

> I come! I come. O heart, I am faithful as you are.
> I am perilous as pear-flower that falls at a touch,
> I am virgin. O chevalier,
> I come.[35]

She is aware that she moves towards her end, and in fact welcomes it, believing that the lover who jilted her at the altar, is waiting.

Death is also the end of the journey in *Blind Man's Buff*. The dramatic label 'masque' that Davies uses for *Blind Man's Buff* suggests – intentionally or unintentionally – reference to the English theatre form. Its characters were also sometimes masked, but the form was used to convey complex political allegories and messages. It was also a Court form with the King at the centre of both the allegory and the action: the masque was almost the only occasion on which a monarch could take part in Court theatricals. We are not left to interpret the 'allegory' for ourselves: the King tells us that 'things are not what they seem'. Indeed, that Davies inverts this ritual is the essence of the piece. The King entertains the Jester, and instead of being confirmed on the throne and having his greatness honoured (as one would in a masque), he abdicates and dies when presented with the 'unmasked' mime and dancer who prove to be a Prince and Princess, and who can be seen as his Royal successors.

---

[33] *Ibid.*, p. 65.
[34] *Miss Donnithorne*, p. iv.
[35] *Ibid.*, p. vii.

*Le Jongleur de Notre Dame* is also entitled 'masque' by Davies, and is clearly an allegory about musical talents – they should be shared and employed:

> But, Brother Mark, she thinks you do wrong to hide your talents inside our community, where only she appreciates them, and she now commands you, with her blessing, to go out into the world, and forsake the cloister, and take your gift among men....[36]

Although the mystery play is often cited as its model (a play in which monks and a group of religious adherents act out a biblical story), the ritual here is that of a morality, a presentation which aims to teach through the acting out of a fable. In *Le Jongleur*, it is possible to distinguish good from bad, or at least between the unchallenged self-satisfied offerings of the monks, and the heartfelt offering of the Jongleur. There is no death here, and in fact, we are given hope. The Jongleur leaves the monastery to spread his talents in the community, a move inspired by the Abbot's interpretation of the Virgin Mary's response to the Jongleur's performance.

Not unexpectedly, the most powerful moment in such ritualized music theatre is what might be described as the 'moment of revelation', the moment at which the drama snaps into focus. The fact that the image itself might be still blurred is irrelevant. If it is, then that is Davies's intention. And this is the nature of that revelation which is the defining moment of each work. In some pieces of music theatre it is the foxtrot, a dance form memorably parodied by Davies and employed by him in a number of contexts in the 1960s and 1970s. In fact the employment of the foxtrot became such a Davies hallmark that it became known as his 'Widwaf' technique ('When in doubt write a foxtrot'), but whatever doubts might be expressed about its use in some contexts, to dismiss it with such a soundbite is to ignore its revelatory nature. In fact, such a defining moment is inevitable, since the snapshot technique requires that all the images presented to the audience must, at some point, be brought together. The foxtrot makes an appearance in *Missa Super L'Homme Armé*, *Eight Songs*, and *Vesalii Icones*. *Missa Super L'Homme Armé* and *Vesalii Icones* employ it in similar circumstances, that is at the exposure of the Anti-Christ. In the first, it accompanies Christ's recognition of the traitor Judas, where the nun – visibly a man impersonating a religious female – is instructed to 'fox-trot out, perhaps pulling off his wimple'. As the nun says for the second time, 'But behold the hand of him that betrayeth me is with me on the table', the honky tonk piano strikes up: it is cut off in mid-stream by the slam of the door as the speaker exits repeating 'But woe unto that man by whom he is betrayed.' In *Vesalii Icones*, it is the final dance in which the dancer is not only 'stripped down' by the images of Vesalius, but is physically naked as well. Both pieces challenge the audience's

---

[36]     Davies, Peter Maxwell, *Le Jongleur de Notre Dame* (London: Chester, 1978), p. iii.

ability to see clearly, and to see the evil among us; and the foxtrot demonstrates on both occasions that we have failed and are servants of the wrong master. The foxtrot in *Eight Songs* does something different: it reveals a man close to death. The revelation in *Blind Man's Buff* also leads to death, but in fact Davies takes the notion of death one stage further, for the ghost of The Boy King returns – 'resurrected' to use Davies's word – to sing the moral of the tale. And that moral also has much in common with *Revelation and Fall,* as well as *Vesalii Icones,* in that it is not about 'blindness' but about the inability to see clearly, and to distinguish good from bad.

What Davies's use of older dramatic forms and his reliance on ritual suggest is that despite the outrageous events that take place in them and their expressionist style, his works of music theatre, if not conservative, at least fit into an overall picture of dramatic traditions. This is not to say that their interpretation is therefore obvious, or easy, or even definitive. As Davies himself has said:

> In all my music-theatre pieces there are various interpretations, and it is up
> to you to make your own.[37]

What such use of ritual and identified forms does do is to make possible a meaningful interpretation. Davies though has given at least one direction. Paul Griffiths in conversation with the composer suggests 'There's never any redemption in your music: one's left really not knowing what to take seriously.' He responded: 'Absolutely. No comment!'[38] The view has been expressed that Davies's music theatre works after *Vesalii* 'broke no new ground, and lacked much of the theatrical force of their predecessors'.[39] This can only be said to be true if *Eight Songs* and *Vesalii Icones* represent what might be termed the furthest extreme to which Davies was prepared to go.

---

[37] Milnes, *op.cit.*, p. 1071.
[38] Griffiths, *Peter Maxwell Davies*, p. 112.
[39] Clements, 'Peter Maxwell Davies', *New Grove Dictionary of Opera*, ed. Sadie (London: Macmillan, 1992), vol. I, p. 1091.

# 4

# Structure and effect in
# *Ave Maris Stella*

## *Joel Lester*

Polemic litters the history of new music – the 'new music' of any age, whether its innovators proclaimed their creations 'le nuove musiche', 'the music of the future', the 'avant-garde' (or even, in a recent instance, the 'derriere garde'!). From the early seventeenth-century, battles between Artusi and Monteverdi over the legitimacy of Monteverdi's counterpoint (prefigured in several earlier squabbles in sixteenth-century Italy and followed for several decades by similar battles as that 'new music' spread to other cultural centres), through the vicious sarcasm hurled by supporters of Brahms and Wagner in feuds that extended long after the deaths of the principals, to the disputes over the very definition of music in the twentieth-century – in these and other wars, heated words were the weapons. Even when one party has tried to be conciliatory, or has tried to stay above the fray, new music that has challenged an existing repertoire has inspired cultural wars. That Rameau had the highest respect for Lully's operas mattered not a whit to his opponents in the campaigns between the Lullistes and Ramistes of the 1730s, one of a vast number of cultural wars fought over music in pre-Revolutionary France.

Twentieth-century battles over new music have most often been disputes over compositional process and issues of musical expression and meaning. If the popular image of the nineteenth-century composer was of a distressed soul pouring out his passion in heartfelt expression, the comparable conception of the twentieth-century composer who created such distressing modern music has often been of a coldly calculating mind working according to some sort of compositional system. To be sure, composers have not been helped by the proclamations of their colleagues about their latest discoveries in the realm of compositional process. It was one thing for Schoenberg to draw upon political sloganeering to declare the emancipation of the dissonance: who would speak up for the enslavement of dissonance? Although Schenker basically did that in his famous analysis of a portion of Stravinsky's *Concerto for Piano and Wind*

*Instruments*,[1] it was quite different for Schoenberg to announce the twelve-tone system, which to many seemed the very antithesis of artistic creativity. Even as musically sensitive a cultural figure as Thomas Mann, whose novels and shorter works exhibit considerable evidence of careful 'abstract' structural planning, caricatured the twelve-tone system in *Doktor Faustus*.[2] The music of Webern, proclaimed as path-breaking by the postwar inventors of totally serialized music, remains for many concert-goers the incarnation of such mechanically created music, and all the information about the extra-musical inspirations of many of Webern's pieces detailed in Hans and Rosaleen Moldenhauer's 1979 biography has done little to change that impression.[3] Likewise, because Berg used a twelve-tone set that outlines four triads in his Violin Concerto, he is viewed as the 'romantic' within the Second Viennese School, even though analysts have repeatedly demonstrated the intricate serial structuring of his music.

What all too often seems to get drowned out by the raucous polemic about new music is the beauty of the musical experience itself. This was a continual experience for me during the twenty-two seasons from 1970–91 in which I was violinist (and occasionally violist) of the Da Capo Chamber Players, a chamber ensemble whose repertoire focused on recent music. I never failed to savour the experience when we performed music by a composer whose music was reputed to be all 'brain', yet the composer's comments at a rehearsal would focus entirely on applying unnotated rubatos to help sculpt the phrases. And likewise, I never failed to relish the comments on staying faithful to minute notated details, because of their structural importance, in rehearsal remarks by a composer whose music was known for its luscious sonorities. Such experiences repeatedly reinforced my deep belief that music is an art that can draw simultaneously upon seemingly conflicting human capacities, communicating the ineffable through intricate structures that reflect the highest levels of human intellect.

Hardly any of the hundreds of recent compositions I performed in those years intrigued me more because of this combination than Peter Maxwell Davies's *Ave Maris Stella* (1975), a work I first encountered when Da Capo prepared it to occupy the second half of the programme at its tenth anniversary concert in the Alice Tully Hall (Lincoln Centre, New York) in 1980. I knew some other Davies works, and had been struck by their eclecticism, in which medieval influences abutted sonorities that had been unknown before the twentieth century. Even

---

[1]    Schenker, in 'Fortsetzung der Urlinie-Betrachtungen', *Das Meisterwerk in der Musik 2* (Munich: Drei Masken Verlag 1926), pp. 37–8. Facsimile edition (Hildesheim: Georg Olms, 1974). English translation by Orin Grossman (1973), in 'Thirteen Essays from the Three Yearbooks, *Das Meisterwerk in der Musik* by Heinrich Schenker: An Annotated Translation', (Ph.D., Northwestern University, 1973).

[2]    Mann, *Doktor Faustus* (Stockholm: Bermann-Fischer, 1947). English translation by Helen Tracy Lowe-Porter (New York: Knopf, 1948).

[3]    Moldenhauer and Moldenhauer, *Anton von Webern: A Chronicle of his Life and Work* (New York: Knopf, 1979).

within that company, however, *Ave Maris Stella* stood out. Its calm but rapturous opening cello solo effectively introduced a piece that included the broadest range of musical gestures and manners of expression.

The title's medieval invocation (citing its eponymous, often-set hymn) seemed nowhere present before the concluding alto flute phrase (notated in medieval neumes), yet that phrase seemed to emerge quite effectively from the music (not unlike the manner in which the citation from Beethoven's 'An die ferne Geliebte' emerges through a long series of thematic transformations to conclude the first movement of Schumann's *Fantasy*, op. 17, and then retrospectively colours the listener's perception of so much of the preceding music). Music of the greatest rhythmic precision occurred simultaneously with freely-written improvisatory rhythms in many passages. Yet all certainly belonged together. The more I relished learning the music, and the more I became involved in the piece, the more my theorist's curiosity was piqued as to how it came to be.

The recurring intervals in the various phrases of the cello solo that occupies the opening section soon revealed the underlying nine-pc row shown in the first nine notes of Ex. 4.1. The remaining phrases in the cello solo arise from rotations of this row from right to left (that is, the last pitch becomes the first pitch of the next rotation), as shown in the remainder of Ex. 4.1.

Ex. 4.1: *Ave Maris Stella* – the row rotations in the cello solo

The interval structure of the pitch row generates the lush, romantic aura projected by the cello solo. Specifically, all intervals but one in the row are triadic intervals: major and minor thirds, perfect fifths, and their inversions. The last six pitches form two triads that belong to a single key: E major and D major triads that both belong to A major. This intervallic and triadic profile is possible because the row is a statement of pc set [0,1,2,3,5,6,7,9,10] (Forte set 9–11), as shown in Ex. 4.2. Like its complement, the major triad, this pc set is heavily weighted with minor thirds, major thirds, and perfect fourths. In addition, because the pc set contains no gaps in its scalar structure, each pitch in the set is step-connected both above and below to its adjacent pitches.

0   1   2   3   5   6   7   9   10

Ex. 4.2: *Ave Maris Stella* – pc set [0,1,2,3,5,6,7,9,10] (Forte set 9–11) as the source of the opening cello phrase

The contour of the opening cello phrases (shown in Ex. 4.3) projects these 'tonal' features of the underlying material. Within the first phrase (bars 1–5), with only one exception (the G#-A motion in bars 3–4), all intervals are stated in their closest position (that is, as thirds rather than as sixths or tenths, and as fourths rather than as fifths or elevenths). The melody, for instance, opens with two ascending major thirds (notated C#-E# and B#-E), each followed by a descending perfect fourth (E#-B# and E-B). And many non-adjacent notes are step-related: one can easily hear a descending chromatic scale-segment from the opening C# (C#-B#-B) and from the high E# in bar 1 (E#-E). The entire melodic phrase spans only a minor ninth: and the phrase ends almost precisely where it began registrally following a registral peak shortly after the mid-phrase.

These features impart a nineteenth-century tonal aura to the opening melody. This effect is heightened by the accompanying instruments. The cello begins entirely alone for two bars, with the marimba joining in shortly afterwards solely to resonate at the unison two crucial pitches: E and G# in bars 2 and 3. The alto flute enters in bar 3, imitating the cello melody a perfect fourth lower or perfect fifth higher at a slower, unmeasured pace.

The immediately succeeding phrases grow more complex in various ways. The register spreads: the second phrase (bars 6–10) spans an octave and a tritone; the third phrase (bars 11–15) spans just a semitone less; and the fourth and fifth phrases (bars 16–20 and 21–25) each open up to two octaves plus a whole tone. Yet connections with the more traditional first phrase abound.

The first interval of the second phrase is A-G♯, presented as the same minor ninth just traversed in the opposite direction three bars earlier. The last five pitches of the second phrase (B-F♯-D♯-E-C♯) are a literal transposition of the comparable pitches in the first phrase (E-B-G♯-A-F♯). Since the second phrase presents the row rotated at T7 (that is, a perfect fifth higher), the transposition of this segment up a fifth also recalls part of the immediately preceding alto flute melody.

The serialized rhythmic structure of the cello solo complements the overall effect of a slowly unfolding melody. The numbers in parentheses below the score in Ex. 4.3 are the durations of the notes measured in quavers while the rests at the end of each phrase are counted as part of the duration from the last note in the phrase to the first note in the next phrase. The durations are fully serialized. Like the pitch series that governs the cello's pitches, the row of durations also rotates in each of the nine phrases, but this rotation is from left to right, the opposite of the rotation in the pitch series: that is, the first duration of one row becomes the last duration in the next rotated row.

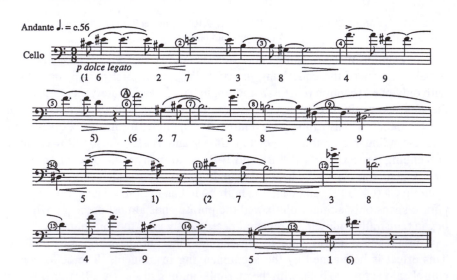

Ex. 4.3: *Ave Maris Stella* – bars 1–15, cello part

The serial structure of pitch and rhythm here is central to creating the effect of the passage. Using the same pitch row for each cello phrase retains a commonality of intervals and overall harmonic colour for all the phrases. At the same time, the row rotations and transpositions allow evolution in the pitch field and in the local ordering of pitches. Likewise, using the same durational row for each phrase ensures that each phrase is exactly the same length and uses the same durations, while rotating the row provides variety within this field of commonality.

All these factors are appropriate for the opening of an expository section. In *Ave Maris Stella* there are nine sections (just as there are nine notes and nine durations in the pitch and duration rows of the cello's phrases), each leading *attacca* into the next section. The first section overall (the cello solo) functions as the exposition of the basic materials in the manner discussed above, and also gradually prepares for the higher level of activity of the second section. The first section does this in several ways, most obviously by the introduction of new instruments and the corresponding introduction of additional rhythms and registers. The viola joins during the fourth cello phrase, performing the entire nine-phrase pitch-and-duration complex of the cello part, but in retrograde and at a faster tempo. The basic counting unit for the duration row is now one-fifth of a dotted crotchet, faster than the quaver counting unit of the cello part. The piano finally enters during the seventh phrase, structured like the viola (that is, featuring a faster retrograde of the cello solo), but with the demisemiquaver as the basic counting unit.

These serial procedures produce growth of textural activity, an increase in rhythmic activity, and the accumulation of timbres over the entire section. The aspects of the music that are not controlled serially support this growth of activity. Register, for instance, expands throughout the section. In the cello solo, as already noted, phrases grow from thirteen semitones (barely more than a single octave) in the first phrase to, eventually, forty-one and thirty-nine semitones (over three octaves) in the eighth and ninth phrases. The viola and piano parts, even though they are each based on the same pitch and duration rows as the cello part, cover a wider range than the cello in many parallel phrases. And, of course, as new instruments enter, the total register of the ensemble expands. Ex. 4.4 graphically illustrates the registral, rhythmic and timbral shape of this first section of the composition.

The increase of activity leads to the dramatic entry of the clarinet – the sole instrument absent from the opening section – to begin the second section of the piece. This second section is about as long as the first in time, but since its tempo gradually speeds up and the overall rhythmic profile is more active, many more notes are needed to fill in the time. The serial techniques are arranged so as to provide these additional notes. The rhythmic series of the clarinet solo in section two is the same as that of the cello solo (and, therefore, as the viola and piano parts) in section one. But, each successive duration in the series occurs an

| Section 1, Phrases: | 1 | 2 | 3 | 4 | 5 | 6 | 7 | 8 | 9 |
|---|---|---|---|---|---|---|---|---|---|
| Rhythmic values | ♪.♩. | ♪.♩. | ♪.♩. | ♪.♩. | ♪.♩. | ♪.♩. | ♪.♩. | ♪.♩. | ♪.♩. |

Instruments:
alto flute
marimba
piano
viola
cello

Ranges:
● = cello
○ = ensemble

Ex. 4.4: *Ave Maris Stella* – various musical elements as they expand during the nine phrases of the opening section

increasing number of times: the first duration occurs once, the second duration occurs twice, the third duration occurs three times, and so forth, as shown in Ex. 4.5. The second half of the clarinet solo repeats the duration series, but with the number of repetitions in reverse order: nine times for the first duration, eight times for the second, and so forth. Throughout the section, some of the longer durations are broken up by short flourishes or re-articulations of the pitch, further animating the rhythm.

$$(1 = ♪)$$

1   6   6   2   2   2   7     7     7     7   etc.

Ex. 4.5: *Ave Maris Stella* – the durations of the clarinet solo at the opening of section two

The resulting repetition of durations gives rise to easily perceived changes in the meter. This is in contrast to the more leisurely 9/8 bars maintained in section one (the cello solo). Increased dynamic levels (*fortes* and, in general, more rapid changes between dynamic levels), greater densities of texture and rhythmic activity, taken along with the gradual *accelerando*, contribute to the accumulating drive of the section.

The pitches in the clarinet solo are also based on the pitch row of the cello's solo in section one, but consecutive pitches in the clarinet solo derive from more than one row rotation. Ex. 4.6 illustrates the complex manner in which the repeated durations complement the pitch structure. The first duration of the row (a quaver) presents the first pc of the first phrase of the cello solo. The second duration (a dotted minim), stated twice (because it is the second duration in the row, as explained above), draws upon the first pitch from the second cello phrase and the second pitch from the first cello phrase. The third duration (a crotchet), stated thrice, draws upon the first pitch of the cello phrase three, the second pitch of cello phrase two, and the third pitch of cello phrase one. The same process continues throughout section two. If a repeated pc would arise from this procedure, the repetition is omitted.

This process may sound mechanical, but some aspects of its structure are quite easily audible. As Ex. 4.6 shows, the pitches from the first cello phrase (the C♯, F and C in the first three bars) are the last pitches of the repetitions of each duration in the row. They are also invariably the loudest pitches in each short phrase division: and they are the only pitches that are followed by rests. A careful listener who remembers the opening cello solo and who is aware of the dynamics and rests in the clarinet solo will hear the clarinet solo as a rhapsodic expansion of the opening cello phrase. At the same time, the adjacent pitches in the clarinet solo still produce the intervals of the basic row: minor and major thirds and perfect fourths.

Reinforcing these connections to the sounds of section one are fragments of the opening cello-solo phrases in the instruments that accompany the clarinet solo. As the clarinet begins in bar 46, for instance (as shown in Ex. 4.6), the piano right hand plays rapidly the pitches of the cello's second phrase, a phrase that begins on the same A that is in the clarinet solo at that point. The left hand of the piano part plays in retrograde the pitches of the third cello phrase, but transposed so as to begin on that same A. The alto flute shortly joins the piano in deriving

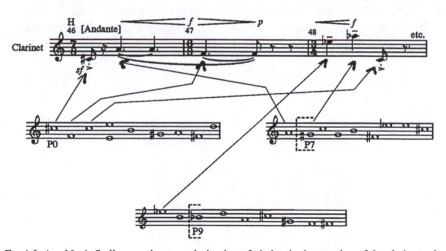

Ex. 4.6: *Ave Maris Stella* – section two, derivation of pitches in the opening of the clarinet solo

similar counterpoints to the clarinet melody. Just as the marimba merely resonated at the unison on a few pitches of each phrase throughout the cello solo in section one, giving a slow harmonic resonance to this expository passage, here the clarinet pitches are the source for transposed versions of the cello phrases of section one, versions that grow out of unisons but expand the harmonic field in this more active section.

Similarly imaginative processes create each of the later sections of *Ave Maris Stella*. The serial processes are always arranged and complemented by the other parts so as to produce the musical effects appropriate to that section of the overall composition.

In sum, *Ave Maris Stella* emerges from this analysis as a highly structured, one might even say highly mechanically structured, piece, yet, it is clear that all its precompositional features did not arise from some speculative musings about what might arise sonically if this or that precompositional element were explored. Rather, each structure observed above clearly arises as a way of shaping a musical gesture: even-length phrases in the cello solo join irregular rhythms that gently cover the leisurely meter to complement the pitch rotations and impart an improvisatory sense to the expository opening. The rather different precompositional structures of the clarinet solo allow the second section to be an extravagant diminution of the cello solo as clearer meters emerge. Innumerable other features both here and throughout the piece eventually lead to the alto flute's statement of fragments of the Gregorian hymn that close the piece.

Just as the polemics of the past fade into obscurity while the quality music of the age remains alive – just as, for instance, we can enjoy both Brahms and Wagner, or both Palestrina's *stile antico* and Monteverdi's *prima prattica*, or both tonal and atonal masterworks, all with no regard for the raucous disputes that have tried to build walls between these supposedly antithetical repertoires – in the same way we can savour its musical qualities while we relish the carefully planned serial elements that produce the structure and effect in *Ave Maris Stella*.

# 5

# Peter Maxwell Davies's recent music, and its debt to his earlier scores

*John Warnaby*

No contemporary composer has demonstrated a deeper understanding of music history than Peter Maxwell Davies, and it is a preoccupation he has pursued throughout his career. Likewise, politics have invariably elicited strong reactions, particularly when unduly influenced by ideological considerations. Though Davies's recent style has evinced a greater degree of detachment than hitherto, these factors should not be discounted any more than in his earlier scores.

1987 was a decisive year in Davies's career. He disbanded The Fires of London ensemble, which had dominated his composing activities for the previous twenty years, having relinquished the directorship of the St Magnus Festival in 1986. He also began to cultivate links with various orchestras, so that his orchestral output during the subsequent decade has been particularly fruitful. The ten Strathclyde Concertos, on which he embarked in 1986, have been completed, together with additional concerti for trumpet, piccolo and piano. He has also written three of his six symphonies, a full-length ballet, a choreographic poem and several shorter works including the first two parts of a projected cycle of fourteen works covering different genres, entitled *Orkney Saga*. These have been inspired by the texts George Mackay Brown provided for an exhibition in St Magnus Cathedral, Kirkwall, commemorating the role of Orkneymen in the Crusades. There have also been several pieces of a popular character, and a sequence of music theatre works for young children dates from this period. More recently, he has composed his second full-scale opera, *The Doctor of Myddfai*, together with three substantial creations for soloists, chorus and orchestra, including the oratorio *Job*.

All this is in sharp contrast to the relatively fallow period Davies was experiencing when he first visited Orkney in 1970. The intensely expressionist works of the later 1960s had left him with some 'unfinished business', but apart from *Blind Man's Buff*, and *Miss Donnithorne's Maggot*, this was largely set aside once he had become immersed in the writings of George Mackay Brown.

Though his compositional technique continued to evolve, the stylistic changes almost amounted to a re-invention of his musical personality, and it was not until the final version of his opera *Resurrection*, completed in 1987, that he attempted to recapture the ferocity of the *Taverner*-related works.

The libretto of *Resurrection* was originally conceived in response to Davies's experience of American commercialism during the early 1960s, and though it was subsequently modified, it retained the degree of anger necessary to generate the sort of parody on which his compositions had thrived twenty years earlier. However, although the dogmatic application of right-wing policies by the British Conservative Government of the 1980s provided the impetus to complete the opera, the music did not achieve comparable results, owing to the fact that, living in the relatively stable Orkney community, Davies remained detached from the worst excesses of the period. Nevertheless, *Resurrection* amounted to a powerful indictment of the values of the political establishment, and it appears to have been the catalyst which prompted the composer to re-evaluate the themes, symbolism and compositional procedures of his output during the 1960s from the perspective of the 1990s. Accordingly, a network of cross-references with earlier works has evolved, in conjunction with the 'classical' and 'romantic' aspects of his creative imagination, ultimately stemming from an attempt to reconcile the humanist, and medieval-Renaissance traditions embodied in the characters of Zeitblom and Leverkuehn in Thomas Mann's *Doktor Faustus*. In general terms, the symphonies and concerti belong to what might loosely be called the Zeitblom end of the spectrum, where Davies functions as an 'establishment' composer, not least, by providing music for the Orkney community. In contrast, works associated with texts tend to incline towards Leverkuehn's standpoint, exemplifying a critical attitude to authoritarian or ideological interpretations of 'reality'. In both cases, Davies has adopted a broadly modernist approach. There are occasional suggestions of the expressive intensity which dominated his earlier output, but he rarely resorts to the more complex or subversive elements of the modernist aesthetic. There are invariably allusions to traditional forms, with a few indications of post-modern influences, yet the function of the tonal material in the more obviously popular pieces has undergone a considerable transformation. In such works as *Missa Super L'Homme Armé* or *St Thomas Wake*, it performed a defamiliarizing role, usually appearing in unfamiliar contexts, and often satirizing what the composer regarded as bad taste. Glimpses of this practice can be discerned in some recent works, but more frequently it is employed to comic effect, rather than as an expression of genuine indignation.

Hence, *Resurrection* can be described as Davies's last Faustian or thoroughly experimental work, and several parallels can be cited with scores attributed to the fictional Adrian Leverkuehn in Mann's novel,[1] notably, *Apocalypsis cum*

---

[1]    Mann, *Doktor Faustus*, trans. Lowe-Porter, (New York: Knopf, 1948).

*Figuris*, and the *Faust Cantata*. These relate both to Mann's account of compositional processes and also to wider philosophical and theological issues which critics have already discussed in connection with *Taverner*.[2] Particularly important was Mann's thesis that the disintegration of the Austro-German cultural tradition was temporarily suspended by recourse to National Socialism. Accordingly, he interpreted the Faust legend as an allegory for the advent of the Third Reich, the resulting exposure of humanity's capacity for ultimate evil, and the final destruction of Nazism. It was therefore appropriate that the original Darmstadt production, however flawed, should have been in German, insofar as several commentators have detected a conspiracy of silence among the purveyors of postwar culture. They argue that the growing tendency to make reality, itself, taboo, in order to avoid questioning the validity of affirmative bourgeois values, has prevented society recognizing the evils in its midst. Bourgeois culture's capacity to absorb the most extreme forms of expression have made it increasingly difficult to register any kind of protest, but Adorno stated that it was the duty of contemporary composers to espouse the cause of the free individual, repressed by the managed societies of east and west alike:

> Serious music must nowadays be difficult and disagreeable, for charm and pleasure have become means to make men into docile consumers. Not only popular music, but the use made of serious music by the culture industry, encouraged regression to an infantile conditioning.[3]

In responding to Adorno's critique, Davies attempted to avoid the charge of elitism which is invariably levelled at composers of 'difficult' music. Part of his strategy involved turning the weapons of the culture industry against itself, hence the significance of the rock numbers, which carry the main burden of the opera's message, and which are associated with the most important harmonic thinking in the work.

However, the idea of basing *Resurrection* on a sequence of advertising captions may also have been stimulated by the chief protagonist in James Joyce's *Ulysses*. Through the disjunction between the various layers of narrative, Joyce also portrayed the fragmentation of society, stemming from the increasing difficulty of distinguishing reality and appearance, truth or falsity. Mr Bloom's links with advertizing symbolized this issue, and at the culmination of *Resurrection*, Davies underlined the despiritualizing, dehumanizing effects of consumerism through the emergence of an ambiguous Christ figure, who announces 'I am only an advert'. *Ulysses* also encouraged the surreal aspect of

---

[2]    Kerman, 'Popish Ditties', *Tempo* 102, (1972) pp. 20–4. See also Josipovici, 'Taverner: Thoughts on the Libretto', in Pruslin, (ed.), *Peter Maxwell Davies: Studies from Two Decades*, Tempo Booklet 2, (London: Boosey and Hawkes, 1979), pp. 39–46. Also, *Tempo* 101 (1972), pp. 12–19.
[3]    Sadie (ed.), *The New Grove Dictionary of Music* (London 1980), i, p. 112.

the opera. Davies extended the ravings of the hot gospeller to include certain strident politicians of the 1980s, and incorporated autobiographical elements, such as his earlier association with wind-up gramophones. On one level, the work unfolds as a series of cartoons, and this emphasizes the debt to the medieval morality tradition, as the diabolical allusions in Dürer's *Apocalypse*, and the nihilistic elements of the Book of Revelation are reinterpreted in contemporary terms. Another layer includes stylistic features from different phases of Davies's career, such as foxtrots, mock hymn-tunes and self-parodies. Above all, the opera embodies 'the paradox whereby dissonance stands for the expression of everything solemn, lofty, pious, everything of the spirit, while consonance and firm tonality is reserved for the world of hell, in this context, a world of banality and commonplace'.[4] The three distinctive ensembles contribute to one of the composer's most complex scores, not least in the range of symbolism it encapsulates, and this explains the importance he attaches to the work, even though it has so far not gained widespread recognition as one of his central achievements.

The indirect influence of George Mackay Brown on Davies's libretto should also not be discounted. *Resurrection* was the culmination of an extended phase of vocal scores, based substantially on Mackay Brown texts. Particularly important was Mackay Brown's ability to invest realistic detail with symbolic significance. This was unusually pertinent to the opera, where all the characters, together with the events of the narrative, had symbolic value, and it underpinned the satirical dimension. In trying to establish an ideology which dispenses with the notion of evil, bourgeois society has threatened to deprive the imagination of the element of symbolism. By reflecting the extent to which the main developments in twentieth-century culture have contributed to the distortion of reality, the use of parody helps to restore the symbolic to its former status as a means of expressing fundamental truths.

Another feature of Mackay Brown's writing which assumed considerable significance in *Resurrection*, especially as regards the characterization of the family in the prologue, was the emphasis on colloquial speech. Apart from the fact that colloquial speech is inevitably imbued with symbolic value, it is an example of the need to emancipate the text from the constraints of modernist literature, comparable with what Davies sees as the need to liberate music from 12-tone technique. As with the incorporation of popular styles into the music, the use of colloquialisms exposes the extent to which everyday speech has also been reduced to meaningless clichés.

Consequently, in keeping with Davies's Mackay Brown settings, there is a close correspondence between music and text. Concerning the elements of ritual, as well as the diversity of styles in *Resurrection*, which, in his essay on

---

4    Mann, *op. cit.*, p. 375.

Stravinsky, Adorno describes as 'the uncovering of pre-civilized layers of the psyche leading ... to the dissolution of the psyche',[5] it can be claimed that *Resurrection* avoids the charge of the 'regressive sacrifice of the individual to the collectivizing tendencies of society'[6] in that it outlines the ideological interpretation of the chief protagonist's failure to conform to the conventions of society in terms of medical and psychological problems. As with the appropriation of elements of popular culture, this involved a further attempt to turn the tables on bourgeois society by exposing its inclination to regard any kind of non-conformity as a species of illness, using pseudo-scientific jargon to describe its symptoms. Hence, one of the opera's main themes extends both Davies's and Mackay Brown's preoccupation with preserving identity, whether as an individual, or a small community, in an increasingly hostile world.

*Resurrection* also addresses the other problem cited by Gabriel Josipovici in his essay on *Taverner* 'why should anyone sing what can perfectly well be spoken?'[7] Again, the influence of Mackay Brown can be discerned in the way that the difficulty of this question has been reduced through the composer's handling of the relationship between text and music. In contrast to *Taverner*, where the preoccupation with events from English Tudor history conflicts with the presentation of the internal crisis unfolding inside John Taverner's head, the action of *Resurrection* is more clearly centred in the chief protagonist's mind. Suggestions of a linear plot are also considerably diminished, the narrative being restricted to the transformation of the cat into a dragon, plus the gradual reconstruction of the patient, culminating in his resurrection. Both are symbolic, rather than realistic, and this is enhanced by the stylized character of the musical transformations. In comparison with *Taverner*, there is less sense of continuity as the brief scenes alternate with the twenty-four commercials which constitute the main thread of the opera. The fact that these are jingles means they are obviously sung, while the political and religious slogans exhibit similar characteristics. In both instances, Davies parodies the assumption, developed by bourgeois culture in conjunction with the media, that people will accept more readily the veracity of what they are told about a product, or concept, if it is presented in an unreal, fantasy form. It involves a similar suspension of disbelief as when being told a folk tale, or ghost story, and since Mackay Brown often had recourse to the techniques of such tales, it is not surprising that Davies's libretto alludes to such features.

The impression of timelessness tentatively achieved in *Taverner* is also more fully developed in *Resurrection*, through the use of flashbacks and recurring, or

---

[5]   The Open University, Course A 308: *The Rise of Modernism in Music*, Unit 30, p. 59.
[6]   *Ibid.*
[7]   Josipovici, *op. cit.*

closely related, patterns of symbolism, another Mackay Brown trait, resulting in
the replacement of a through-composed drama with a stylized 'number' opera.

Many of the composer's Mackay Brown inspired works might be cited as
models. The most obvious is *The Two Fiddlers*, whose advertising captions,
symbolizing the extent to which late capitalism is sustained by mindless
consumption, proved the prototype of the adverts in *Resurrection*.

The opera was unusual in the context of Davies's Orcadian works in that it
alludes neither to the local community, nor to land or seascapes. It was followed
by a period of eight years during which Davies wrote very few vocal works, apart
from his educational pieces. However, during the later 1980s, Davies worked on
another music theatre project, based on the life of St Francis of Assisi, and the
way his legacy had been distorted by commercial exploitation. Perhaps the
project's failure to materialize can be partly explained by the extent to which the
commercial aspect was satirized in *Resurrection*, but Davies reworked some of
the material in his Trumpet Concerto, based on the plainchant, *Franciscus
Pauper et Humilis*. It has been suggested that the nominal three movements of
the Concerto follow the outline of the opera, in which the chief protagonist was
associated with the trumpet.[8] More significantly, the Trumpet Concerto enabled
Davies to re-affirm his identification with Orkney. Thus, the article
accompanying the recording emphasizes the Concerto's northern, rather than
Umbrian location, thereby underlining the importance of a sense of place, which
Arnold Whittall discerns in Davies's Orkney works.[9]

In keeping with the other concerti, the duration of the Trumpet Concerto is
approximately half an hour, but the extensive orchestral accompaniment and the
tendency towards broad gestures are 'symphonic' in character. The work is cast
as a single movement, based on continuous transformation processes, but
elements of ambiguity are present from the outset. The slow introduction grows
from a sequence of major and minor seconds in the lowest register, which
immediately establish the sombre mood of the orchestral writing. There follows
a leap to a new tonal area, but instead of developing this contrast in terms of a
'tonic\dominant' relationship, Davies introduces a more expansive theme on
strings, whose first note is a tritone distant from the work's initial pitch.

The soloist only enters after the transition to the *allegro*. The style is
declamatory, beginning with the tritone formed from the first pitch of each
introductory 'theme', but in reverse order. The *allegro*, and two subsequent
sections, allude not only to the main divisions of a sonata movement, but also to
the standard movements of a traditional concerto: but in addition, there is a key
passage where some of the work's basic material is revealed on solo horn. There

---

[8]   Notes to Recording of Trumpet Concerto and Fourth Symphony, Collins Classics,
11812.
[9]   Whittall, 'Britten, Maxwell Davies and a Sense of Place', *Tempo* 204 (April 1998),
pp. 5–11.

is also a definite impression that the three sections explore similar material from different perspectives. In this respect, the work can be said to uphold at least one of the principles of serial technique, which the composer practised in his early works, including the Trumpet Sonata, op. 1. In an illuminating article, Richard McGregor has demonstrated Davies's inclination towards certain precompositional procedures, and maintains that these have been influential in the evolution of his style. Besides revealing correspondences between the sketches for works written during different phases of the composer's development, McGregor indicates that Davies may have favoured a particular method of 'reading' set charts since the outset of his career.[10] Accordingly, the Trumpet Concerto is not only the culmination of his preoccupation with the instrument – developed in some of the most demanding passages of his orchestral scores – but also forms part of an overall scheme in which Davies's entire output is unified by his expanding repertoire of transformation processes.

Moreover, the kinship between works is often established at a symbolic level. Davies's recording of the Trumpet Concerto, with John Wallace as soloist, is coupled with the Fourth Symphony, completed the following year. As with the Trumpet Concerto, it marked a return to an Orcadian perspective after the architectural rigours of its predecessor. Yet the Fourth Symphony has equally important links with other works. Quite apart from its position within the symphonic cycle, the Fourth Symphony was conceived as an extension of the three Sinfonias – *Sinfonia Concertante*, *Into The Labyrinth* and *Sinfonietta Accademica* – which established Davies's association with the Scottish Chamber Orchestra in the mid-1980s. As such, it stands in a similar relation to them as that of the First Symphony to the three preceding orchestral scores described in Stephen Pruslin's article, 'Returns and Departures',[11] thereby constituting the finale of a second 'hyper symphony'. Hence, it was designed as 'a point of confluence between his chamber orchestral works and his music for full symphony orchestra'.[12] The image of an eagle taking flight was a further inspiration, and it should always be remembered that the choice of plainsong as source material invariably has symbolic connotations.

The Fourth Symphony is cast as a single entity containing the four movements of a traditional symphony. Consequently, it is descended from both Schoenberg's First Chamber Symphony, and Sibelius's Seventh Symphony. However, the opening notes of the introduction outline a harmonic language which is unique not only to Davies, but even to his symphonic cycle. Hence, the work extends Davies's use of formulations revolving around the tritone, B–F, emphasizing intervals which have a minor third, diminished seventh

---

[10]     McGregor, 'The Maxwell Davies Sketch Material in the British Library', *Tempo* 196 (April 1996), pp. 9–19.

[11]     Pruslin, 'Returns and Departures', in Pruslin (ed.) *op. cit.*, pp. 77–83.

[12]     Notes to Recording of Trumpet Concerto and Fourth Symphony, *op. cit.*

relationship. At the same time, the composer follows a procedure he had previously adopted in *Worldes Blis*, in that the music is impelled forward by being refracted 'through a series of one-sided parentheses',[13] thereby enhancing the tension inherent in the use of the tritone as 'tonic' and 'dominant'. Further contrast is achieved by juxtaposing the abrasive brass against lyrical woodwind, in which three flutes are featured; and by the use of rhythmic modulation, resulting in the rapid alternation of different tempi.

The Fourth Symphony can thus be regarded as inaugurating a phase in which Davies has extended his preoccupation with music history to his own output. It can also be considered a further attempt to reconcile compositional procedures derived from medieval-Renaissance music with the more familiar conventions of the 'symphonic' tradition. In the process, Davies has developed a highly individual brand of symphonic thought, but the Fourth Symphony, particularly, became the subject of adverse criticism, provoking a good deal of discussion about the precise nature of contemporary symphonism.

The debate stemmed from Anthony Bye's contention that Davies's attempt to formulate his own conventions regarding the relationship between 'tonic' and 'dominant' could not be justified in strictly aural terms.

> I don't hear Davies's tonics and dominants. I hear certain pitches given prominence, but no musically meaningful relationship between them. Accordingly, it is a harsh fact that his most successful pieces involve the juxtaposition and balancing of shorter structural units, rather than any pitch controlled dynamic process, which is the distinguishing attribute of symphonic thought.[14]

Bye, and others, have also suggested that the recent works have not achieved the memorability or forcefulness of his earlier scores.

In response, Arnold Whittall pointed to Davies's use of 'pivots and polarities' as points of focus in works as distant and different as the Trumpet Sonata and the Fourth Strathclyde Concerto.[15] He added 'it is in the nature of Davies's modernism that what has seemed in recent years to be a searching for greater clarity and simplicity is, at the same time, a reworking of fundamental aesthetic and technical parities which can neither be completely suppressed, nor conclusively synthesized'.[16] This ties in with McGregor's interpretation of the sketches, while the significance Whittall has subsequently attached to a sense of place clearly relates to the psychological factors which have influenced Davies's œuvre.

---

[13]   *Ibid.*
[14]   Bye, 'Maxwell Davies: Trumpet Concerto; Symphony No. 4', Record Review, *Tempo* 177 (1991), p. 57.
[15]   Whittall, 'The Bottom Line', *Musical Times* 130/1819 (September 1994), pp. 544–50.
[16]   *Ibid.*

The Fourth Symphony was crucial in that it addressed the same structural issues as *Worldes Blis*, but without depending on either the large orchestra, or the intense expressionism of the earlier work. Stylistic reintegration had been achieved, and the fractured manner of the 1960s had been exorcized in *Resurrection*. Yet creative tensions remained, and the greater variety of form and content in the three latest symphonies, as compared with their predecessors testifies to the difficulty Davies has experienced in finding alternative meanings for the 'polarities' on which he has always relied.

The problem is inherent in the fact that Davies's compositional method is ultimately based on isorhythmic cycles – alternating blocks of material which frequently create contrast, but which are often derived from the same source, usually plainsong. Hence, although Davies has consistently generated extended structures by means of transformation processes, the elements of contrast they embody have more in common with variation, or double variation form, than with conventional developmental procedures. Thus, while Hans Keller's criticisms of Davies's First Symphony[17] reflected a traditional outlook, perhaps they already pointed to the absence of what Michael Hall calls 'a way between the goal-orientated structures of classical composers, ... and the fragmentary, almost completely static style'[18] of the Darmstadt composers. As Davies retreated from the fragmentation of expressionism, which he had adopted at least partially as a means of protesting against the tyranny of total serialism, he attempted to compensate for the introduction of elements of goal orientation, and even suggestions of conventional harmonic procedures, by incorporating new features into symphonic discourse.

Davies did not return to the symphony for another five years, but in the two suites he drew from the ballet *Caroline Mathilde* he reflected the approaches to structure adopted in *St Thomas Wake*, and *Worldes Blis*, while also following the narrative outline of the ballet. Accordingly, the suite derived from Act I establishes the main elements of the drama and is based on musical themes which are harmonically unrelated to signify the incompatibility of the principal protagonists, but which are stylistically akin to the popular music of Caroline's lifetime. Variants of this material support the choreographic characterization of the main participants. They are generally presented in alternation and are progressively transformed as the plot unfolds. As in *St Thomas Wake*, there is a sequence where successive versions of the original are subjected to increasing distortion while remaining recognizable. The suite is thus modelled on variation form, whereas the suite associated with Act II is far more 'symphonic' in outline. It includes a substantial *passacaglia* and concludes with a large-scale movement in accordance with the extended climax of the ballet.

---

[17]    Keller, 'The State of the Symphony, not only Maxwell Davies's', *Tempo* 125 (June 1978), pp. 6–11.

[18]    Hall, *Harrison Birtwistle* (London: Robson, 1984), p. 8.

More decisive was the composition of *Chat Moss*, which provided the basic material for the Fifth Symphony. On one level, it formed a pendant to the much larger score, *The Turn of the Tide*, in that it was written for either school, or professional orchestra: at the same time, it inaugurated a series of short orchestral pieces inspired by childhood recollections. This has encouraged speculation that the Fifth Symphony seems, through the vulnerable agency of the child, to begin to make tentative links between the existential furnace of the notorious works of the late 1960s and the polar retreat that many commentators have heard in many of the Orkney pieces. An unlikely union between the first and third person narratives that 'set Mahler and Sibelius ... at odds with each other'.[19] Such a 'reading' might explain 'the new plainness of utterance' that Julian Beecroft detects in the Symphony,[20] and it may account for the fact that Sibelius's influence is particularly evident. There is a greater use of triadic material, with suggestions of modality, rather than tonality, while its single movement, lasting 25 minutes, establishes an obvious connection with Sibelius's Seventh Symphony. In this connection, Beecroft cites several structural and textual correspondences.[21] Yet the thirty-four sections of varying length indicate that Sibelius's influence is stylistic, rather than technical. They relate to Davies's long-standing method of generating isorhythmic cycles based on different types of material, and appear to confirm Bye's previously cited contention that Davies's 'most successful pieces ... involve the juxtaposition and balancing of shorter structural units, rather than any pitch controlled dynamic process, which is the distinguishing attribute of symphonic thought'.[22] The alternation of slow and rapid episodes is more convincingly handled than in the Fourth Symphony, giving rise to a compact structure. Disparate sections based on woodwind, brass and strings, respectively, are superseded, in the second half, by more sustained passages, culminating in the main climax for full orchestra, followed by an extended final section almost entirely for strings and derived from an expansive cello theme. The result is a binary form, not unlike Davies's larger stageworks.

An alternative approach involves interpreting the Fifth Symphony in terms of Sibelius's *En Saga*, with which it was programmed at its premiere. This would explain the prominence given to flutes, especially at the outset, as well as the general woodwind sonorities, which are frequently redolent of Sibelius. It may also account for the work's programmatic content, which is never stated, but clearly implied by the allusion to bird calls in the quieter episodes.

The Fifth Symphony's links with Davies's output of the 1960s are not made explicit, but the constant interaction between three distinct layers of activity can be traced back to *St Thomas Wake* or *Vesalii Icones*. The major difference is that

---

[19]   Beecroft, 'Maxwell Davies's Fifth Symphony', *Tempo* 191 (December 1994), pp. 2-6.
[20]   *Ibid.*
[21]   *Ibid.*
[22]   *Ibid.*

the symphonic drama stems from the transformation of the initial material through the complex network of magic squares, rather than through the influence of parody and distortion, associated with extra-musical factors.

To some degree, the Sixth Symphony can be regarded as an enlargement of its predecessor, again involving an interplay between three distinct layers of material. Like the Fifth Symphony, the Sixth Symphony is based on a pre-existing work, and the fact that *Time and the Raven* is much larger than *Chat Moss* may have contributed to the size of the Symphony itself. The compositional technique is comparable to that of constructing a parody mass on a pre-existing motet. In Davies's oeuvre, it dates back to the two *Fantasia on an In Nomine of John Taverner*, and hence, it is not coincidental that the Sixth Symphony shares with the Second Fantasia a three-movement structure with extended slow finale

One of the most perceptive comments in Beecroft's discussion of the Fifth Symphony concerns the 'tension between the real and the phantom that is one of the basic fascinations in Davies's music',[23] and this applies even more to the Sixth Symphony in that the forms of the individual movements are ambiguous. Thus, although the work returns to the architectural scope of the first four symphonies, it does so in order to question the 'symphonic' nature of the different components. The 'plainness of utterance' is taken further and, as in the Fifth Symphony, contrast is achieved through the juxtaposition of slow and fast tempi. A good deal of the instrumental writing is also economical, particularly in the outer movements and, consequently, the orchestra is often deployed as a collection of smaller ensembles, in a manner reminiscent of Mahler.

The three movements are arranged symmetrically, with the outer movements balancing one another around the shorter central section. The sense of goal orientation is thus tempered by a hint of cyclic form, reinforced by the fact that the melody from *Time and the Raven*, which opens the Symphony, returns in transformed guise, at the conclusion of the finale.

In his introduction, Davies describes the first two movements as, respectively, 'a *scherzo* masquerading as a sonata *allegro* and ... a sonata *allegro* masquerading as a *scherzo*'.[24] On the surface, they may suggest the idea of thesis and antithesis, but besides the fact that their formal outlines are similar, the surface detail is determined by continuous transformation processes operating in the background. These not only involve the pitch, intervallic and rhythmic transformation of the *Time and the Raven* material, but are extended to the metamorphosis of one magic square into another, analogous to the evolution of primitive life forms. Ultimately, the transformations rise to the surface, so the third movement can be interpreted as a synthesis of its predecessors. According

---

23   *Ibid.*
24   Programme Book for 1996 St Magnus Festival, Orkney Islands.

to this 'reading', the three movements correspond to the exposition, development and recapitulation of 'classical' sonata-form, but, as Johannes Meph maintained in his review of the first performance,[25] the Sixth Symphony is unique to Orkney, and would have been very different if Davies were living and working elsewhere. The ability to observe natural phenomena in the Orcadian environment has provided a constant source of inspiration, while the comparative stability of the community means that the conventions of the symphony retain their relevance.

At the same time, the symphony's link with *Time and the Raven* strengthens its international credentials. Unlike the overture, it does not achieve universality through the incorporation of 'mock' national anthems or other quotations. Instead, it follows Mackay Brown's example by re-examining the entire tradition from a local perspective.

The Strathclyde Concerto project meant that Davies's exploration of the symphonic tradition was extended to cover the conventions of the 'classical' concerto. This was largely determined by the fact that the repertoire of the Scottish Chamber Orchestra concentrated mainly on the late eighteenth-century, thereby encouraging the classical aspect of the composer's personality. Nevertheless, while each of the concertos was conceived in terms of a small orchestra and emphasized the element of dialogue, rather than confrontation, the individual items presented a particular interpretation of the concerto principle. This was largely determined by the character of the solo instrument, or instruments, for whom Davies designed a specific orchestral accompaniment. There were six solo concertos, two double concertos, a concerto grosso, involving a concertante group of six players, and a concerto for orchestra. Each has a duration of approximately half an hour, and in almost all of them a continuous sequence of transformations is projected over a traditional three-movement design.

To some extent, each of the concertos reflects other works which Davies was writing concurrently, and in one instance the subject-matter responsible for the work's inspiration and character can be traced back to the late 1960s. Thus, *Strathclyde Concerto No. 3*, for horn and trumpet, shares an affinity with the Trumpet Concerto and Fourth Symphony, while No. 5, for violin and viola, has three distinct layers, like *St Thomas Wake,* one stemming from the overture to Haydn's opera *L'Isola Disabitata*, and another from Jan Albert Ban's *Vanitas*, with a text akin to the monody of *Worldes Blis*. Brief extracts from both pieces are presented at the outset, and the transformation of this material provides the substance of the first movement. There are distant references to both pieces towards the end of the movement, but by this stage the composer is preoccupied with extending the development section of the 'classical' concerto.

---

[25]    Meph, 'Past or Future? Peter Maxwell Davies: Symphony No. 6', *Musical Times* 137/ 1842 (August 1996), p. 33.

Although, on one level, the second and third movements observe the conventions of traditional concerto-form, further allusions to Haydn and Ban confirm that the work was conceived in terms of continuous transformation processes. The monochrome sonorities are in keeping with Ban's *Vanitas*, and possibly an engraving in which the song appears. The resulting mood, if not the orchestral texture, is similar to the gradual unfolding of the monody in *Worldes Blis*, but in terms of its precompositional workings, *Strathclyde Concerto No. 5* shares certain links with the Trumpet Concerto.[26] Equally interesting is the uniformity of the string textures which establish a connection with the English pastoral tradition that Davies would not have countenanced in the late 1960s. It assumes even greater significance in view of the fact that he has accepted a commission to write an Antarctic symphony, commemorating Vaughan Williams's *Sinfonia Antarctica*.

*Strathclyde Concerto No. 9*, for six woodwinds and strings, has close ties with the Fifth Symphony, in that they share some of the same precompositional material. Likewise, the concerto has an episodic structure, in which fast and slow music alternate, making it the least conventional of the Strathclyde series as regards both form and instrumentation. Essentially, it is a single-movement concerto grosso, with a concertante ensemble comprising piccolo, alto flute, cor anglais, E flat and bass clarinets and contra-bassoon. As such, it looks back to the *Sinfonia Concertante*, for wind quintet, strings and timpani, which formed part of the triptych inaugurating Davies's association with the Scottish Chamber Orchestra. By contrast, *Strathclyde Concerto No. 10*, for orchestra, is possibly the most conventional of the set, with a traditional three-movement design. To some extent, it sums up the complete cycle, but without referring directly to any of the preceding concertos. Finally, its virtuosity is more sustained than any work Davies has written for the Scottish Chamber Orchestra since the Fourth Symphony. Nevertheless, its style is resolutely concertante, rather than symphonic, thereby preserving the distinctive features of the two cycles, irrespective of the stylistic characteristics they share. The tritone conclusion is typical: indicating the possibility of further concertos, which has already been realized in the comparatively small-scale Piccolo Concerto, and the much larger Piano Concerto.

Paul Conway has described the latter as 'a piano-concerto-about-piano concertos',[27] referring to the many pianistic styles which have been incorporated into its 35-minute span. Yet the work also evinces 'symphonic' tendencies, insofar as it is concerned with integrating elements of 'classicism' and 'romanticism' into a contemporary, possibly 'modernist', sensibility. The structure is similar to the Sixth Symphony, with two substantial outer movements

---

[26]    McGregor, *op. cit.*

[27]    Conway, 'Recent Maxwell Davies Premieres', *Tempo* 204 (April 1998), pp. 36–7.

framing a briefer middle section, the latter providing a lyrical interlude in a predominantly dramatic score. The combination of florid passagework with a mainly percussive approach to the keyboard contains echoes of the piano style Davies frequently employed when writing for The Fires of London, but the gestures have been amplified, so that for the first time, the soloist is capable of matching the power of the orchestra. This is particularly evident in the finale, but the suspicion remains that while Davies has stamped his personality on the salient features of the piano concerto's history, he has failed to add significantly to our understanding of the genre. Perhaps the piano concerto has become such a potent symbol of bourgeois values that it would take an exceptionally radical approach to give it new meaning, and this may explain Davies's reluctance to tackle the form until a comparatively late stage in his career.

During, and subsequent to, the period of the Fifth and Sixth Symphonies, as well as the later Strathclyde Concertos, Davies renewed his interest in the literature of George Mackay Brown, though this did not necessarily entail conventional settings of the author's texts. A projected third ballet ultimately became the choreographic poem, *The Beltane Fire*, and this represented a new departure, not only because it welded elements of his 'popular' and 'symphonic' styles into a cohesive form, but because it adhered to the narrative outlines of a typical Mackay Brown short story. Mackay Brown did not write a story entitled *The Beltane Fire*, but the subject-matter underpinning Davies's symphonic drama alludes to many of Mackay Brown's perennial themes: the impact of the Reformation on the rituals and ceremonies of medieval Orkney society; the need to preserve the community from the influence of external forces; the borderline between history and legend, etc. Davies creates musical equivalents for the different aspects of the narrative, and the ensuing transformations of the thematic material graphically illustrate the plot. In the process, different facets of his creative personality are fused, thereby forging links between Orcadian and Scottish folk music, the solemn church music of the Reformation, and contemporary composition. On one level, *The Beltane Fire* is concerned with a sense of place, but at the same time it raises wider issues, such as the composer's relationship to modernism and post-modernism, considered by Arnold Whittall elsewhere in this volume.

The later orchestral score, *A Reel of Seven Fishermen*, directly influenced by a Mackay Brown poem, explores similar territory, but in the meantime, another sequence of Mackay Brown texts inspired *The Three Kings*, the first of three substantial works for soloists, chorus and orchestra, written on either side of his opera *The Doctor of Myddfai*, which also contains a significant choral element. These were Davies's first choral and orchestral works since *Veni Sancte Spiritus*, dating from 1963, but in keeping with the earlier work, as well as with choral scores involving small instrumental forces, the influence of Stravinsky is more discernible than in other genres.

*The Three Kings* is a cantata, to texts Davies had previously set in *The House of Winter*, written for the King's Singers in 1986. It was initially conceived as early as 1984, but did not appear until 1995 and it established the pattern of Davies's subsequent choral writing. But while these works are among his most traditional scores, they also have a communal importance, enabling non-professional musicians to participate in major events. They are in addition vehicles for the expression of the composer's religious impulse, which has always existed, notwithstanding his innate hostility to many aspects of organized religion. In keeping with the ritual element in Mackay Brown's narrative, plainsong is used extensively in *The Three Kings*, both as source material and as a means of unifying the structure. Elsewhere, it plays a less prominent role, most notably in *The Doctor of Myddfai*, where allusions to traditional Welsh hymn-singing enhance the atmosphere of the story.

With hindsight, *The Doctor of Myddfai*, rather than *Resurrection*, can be regarded as the true sequel of *Taverner*, partly because of the libretto's obvious political overtones, but equally because of the opera's two-act form, its many characters, plus chorus and full orchestra. At the same time, David Pountney's libretto has an Orcadian resonance in that it elaborates a familiar legend associated with a specific location in Wales, and depicts a small community trying to retain its identity in a world increasingly dominated by vast bureaucracies.

*The Doctor of Myddfai* is set in the near future, and its preoccupation with a mysterious disease further enhances its topicality. As with Davies's other operas, the plot revolves around a conflict between good and evil, with the chief protagonist paying a heavy price for the unique position he occupies in society. Like *Taverner*, he is driven by an inner compulsion, as he tries to grapple with the power of the state, embodied in the figure of the Ruler, and to reconcile conflicting forces, characterized by different musical styles. Typically, the roles of the main protagonists are transformed as the drama unfolds, and these influence the transformation processes applied to the basic musical material. Accordingly, specific motifs, frequently associated with certain instruments, are used to define the characteristics of a particular individual, or a particular scene, thereby ensuring a close parallel between music and text. Hence, the Doctor is often accompanied by alto flute, while the chorus, symbolizing the people, generate the main climax of the opera. Their contributions allude to traditional Welsh hymn-singing, and their appearances in Act I already create a memorable impact, particularly in relation to the detached style of much of the instrumental writing, which satirizes officialdom with music of an ironic cast. However, the chorus's full power is reserved for Act II, as they alternate with other episodes, helping to create a more sustained discourse than in the kaleidoscopic scenes of Act I, and propelling the drama to its conclusion. In contrast to what he regards as the sentimentality of most popular religious music, Davies approaches the

Welsh hymn-singing tradition in the manner of genuine folk music. In this connection, a comparison with the evangelical tune in the main act of *Resurrection* is revealing, especially as it also plays a crucial role in the latter stages of the work.

The power of the chorus in *The Doctor of Myddfai* appears to have convinced Davies that oratorio could serve his dramatic requirements as effectively as opera, with its extensive theatrical apparatus. *Job* fits naturally into the sequence of Davies's dramatic scores, and following *The Three Kings*, it was appropriate he should turn to a biblical narrative which had fascinated him throughout his career. At the same time, there was the influence of William Blake's engravings, as well as Vaughan Williams's *Masque for Dancing*, and the story offered a striking contrast to the bureaucratic jargon used to symbolize the oppressive power of the state in *The Doctor of Myddfai*.

The oratorio is scored for four soloists, chorus and orchestra, and its central protagonist represents a thread of continuity in Davies's oeuvre in that, like John Taverner and St Magnus, he is involved in a metaphysical 'dialogue' with the forces of good and evil, and beset by temptation. However, in response to the poetic text, Davies avoids the expressionism of the former, and builds on the measured detachment associated with Mackay Brown's characterization of the latter. The result is a work whose essential conservatism has definite affinities with the English choral tradition, notwithstanding the composer's graphic depiction of the events of the drama. Accordingly, the orchestra functions as 'commentator', not only underpinning the chorus in the 'portrayal' of the participants, but also underlining the changes of mood embodied in the narrative.

The overall form of *Job* is cyclic, with plainsong-like material providing a 'frame' for the main body of the work. The six movements of *The Jacobite Rising*, again featuring four soloists, chorus and orchestra, are also cyclic, but the character of the work is very different. Various texts have been selected, most of which are either directly, or indirectly, related to the rising, but an extract from the poetry of Wilfred Owen contains a general comment on war, while a phrase from a sonnet by Edwin Muir functions as a refrain, unifying the structure. The centrepiece of the work, and its most dramatic section, is a setting, in a somewhat Ivesian manner, of 'Hey, Johnnie Cope', but although this introduces a new element into Davies's choral writing, any suggestion of novelty is offset by the work's tranquil conclusion, in response to Sorley McLean's poem *Hallaig*.

Despite the prospect of further works for chorus and orchestra in the near future, Davies remains primarily concerned with orchestral music. His commitment to the symphonic tradition implies a relatively conventional approach to orchestral writing, but this has not precluded the development of several series of orchestral scores, apart from the Strathclyde Concertos, each with its own distinctive purpose. The substantial three-movement *A Reel of Seven Fishermen* continues the 'story-telling' approach established in *The*

*Beltane Fire*, this time evoking the mood of a Mackay Brown poem about the perils of the sea. Its turbulent middle section has autobiographical significance, stemming from a personal encounter with the sea. Likewise, an expanding sequence of shorter pieces has been inspired by recollections of childhood in Manchester, and these fulfil a similar function to the concert overtures, *Time and the Raven*, or *Maxwell's Reel, with Northern Lights*.

Davies has also continued to cultivate an overtly popular style, but the most significant recent development, not confined to purely orchestral music, may well prove to be the *Orkney Saga* project: inspired by tapestries displayed in St Magnus Cathedral, Kirkwall, and containing brief captions by Mackay Brown. These will provide the starting point for each piece in the cycle, of which the first two have already been completed. They reflect what the composer has called 'a great spiritual journey', and their individual durations of approximately twenty minutes correspond to the playing times of some of the composer's most completely successful creations.

*Orkney Saga I* indicates an entirely fresh approach to the orchestra, with a tautness of construction and originality of form that looks back to Davies's earliest output. Its successor is built on a conventional *passacaglia*, but employed with haunting effect, especially in the final bars when a boy treble sings the twelfth-century *Hymn to St Magnus* in conjunction with a related fourteenth-century plainsong which the composer previously used in *Hymn to St Magnus*, and may prove to be the basis of the overall scheme.

Finally, this survey would not be complete without referring to Davies's continuing involvement with music education. Besides the project for Longmans, involving several music theatre pieces for younger children of different age groups and musical abilities, he wrote *The Turn of the Tide* for professional players in such a way as to allow for the interpolation of contributions by young performers. Its preoccupation with environmental issues also relates it to several of the composer's other works.

As with other outstanding creative figures, Davies's achievement is not easily categorized, especially as every aspect of his creative personality thrives on ambiguity. Claims have been made for him as a modernist, a post-modernist, an essentially British composer, or a European composer whose sensibility has been nourished by both the Austro-German and Nordic traditions. Then there is Davies the symphonist, as opposed to the exponent of music theatre, the music educator and populist, extending his activities as provider of functional music for the local community. These have become increasingly important as the Orcadian composer, for whom a sense of place is crucial, has replaced the much-travelled pre-Orcadian, constantly searching for a role in society.

Above all, there is the metaphysical composer, grappling with theological or philosophical issues, or creating abstract arithmetical patterns which reflect the proportions of primitive life-forms. This is closely related to 'the search for a historical, as well as a personal continuity' which, as Beecroft has pointed out, 'has been one of Davies's abiding concerns, and offers a clear thematic link between his Orkney and pre-Orkney compositions'.[28] Many regret the detachment of his recent works as vigorously as others once criticized the expressive intensity of his output during the later 1960s. There is a suspicion that, as Douglas Dunn observed in the poetry of Mackay Brown, Davies's music has lost much of its harshness and indignation,[29] yet this appears to reflect a current tendency in the cultural climate. It has been noted that Davies's most radical phase coincided with William Glock's equally radical policies at the BBC, but even at that time Davies had conceived *Worldes Blis* as a means of reintegrating the 'scattered fragments' of his creative personality.[30] The process of integration is still continuing, and, as Arnold Whittall has suggested, 'expressionistic rhetoric' is no longer required, given the possibility of renewal informing Mackay Brown's texts.[31] As Davies contemplates his earlier output from the perspective of the 1990s, it is clear that the many nuances of style to be found in his recent scores have the potential for further synthesis, including a greater degree of harmonic stability. How this will be interpreted by commentators on new music remains to be seen, but the 'spiritual journey' of the *Orkney Saga* project, the forthcoming symphonies, springing from a close identification with environmental issues, and the prospect of a cycle of string quartets give rise to optimism that some of Davies's most profound music has still [1999] to be written.

---

[28]   Beecroft, *op. cit.*

[29]   Dunn, 'Finished Fragrance: The Poems of George Mackay Brown', *Poetry Nation* 2 (1974), pp. 80–92.

[30]   Composer's programme note for *Worldes Blis,* in Griffiths, *Peter Maxwell Davies* (London: Robson, 1982), pp. 149–52

[31]   Whittall, 'The Bottom Line', *op. cit.*

# 6

# Compositional processes in some works of the 1980s

*Richard McGregor*

Davies's choice of source material is usually related to plainsong from the *Liber Usualis* as is well known, though this is of course not the only material which he uses as the stepping-off point for his precompositional procedures. As Peter Owens has discussed in his article for this volume, works which are chronologically close to each other may use the same material, although Davies suggested in a discussion with the author that it will usually only be 'two or three works' which are related. In practice this manifests itself in two ways. On the one, hand there are pieces which are clearly 'satellites' of a larger work, but there are also occasions where two or perhaps three substantial works are related to each other at this first level of composition. It is worth noting that there are also cases where source material reappears in a later work – usually in a summative context.

The plainchants and other sources which underpin the works of the 1980s are presented below. This list is necessarily incomplete because Davies will make cross-references between works which are not always straightforward to detect.

| Work | Source |
| --- | --- |
| Piano Sonata | [as Symphony no. 2?, *Nativitas Tua* LU p. 1627 and *Panem di Caelo* LU p. 1035] |
| Brass Quintet | [charts available – no sources noted] |
| *Image, Reflection, Shadow* | *Lux Aeterna* [LU p. 1815] |
| *Sinfonia Concertante* | [no precompositional material available] |
| Organ Sonata | [From 'The Lamentations of Jeremiah' not considered here – LU pp. 626, 669, 715ff. may apply] |
| *Into the Labyrinth* | *Dies Irae* [LU p. 1810] *Victimae Paschali Laudes* [LU p. 780] |
| *Sinfonietta Accademica* | *Dies Irae* [LU p. 1810] *Victimae Paschali Laudes* [LU p. 780] |
| Symphony no. 3 | *Sancte Michael Archangele* [LU p. 1655] |
| Violin Concerto | [no precompositional material available] |
| *Strathclyde No. 1* | *Dum Compleréntur* [LU p. 884] |

| | |
|---|---|
| *Resurrection* | *Laetentur Coeli* [LU p. 387] |
| | *Puer Natus* [LU p. 408] |
| | *Herodes Iratus Occidit* [LU p. 427] |
| | *Victimae Paschali Laudes* [LU p. 780] |
| *Strathclyde No. 2* | *Franciscus Pauper et Humilis* [LU p. 1644] |
| | *Dum Compleréntur* [LU p. 884] |
| | *Ego Sum Pauper* [LU p. 1647] |
| Trumpet Concerto | *Franciscus Pauper et Humilis* [LU p. 1644] |
| | *Ego Sum Pauper* [LU p. 1647] |
| | [bundled with these sketches but not obviously from this work, *Laetentur Coeli* [LU p. 387]; *Puer Natus* [LU p. 408]; *Herodes Iratus Occidit*; *Cor Meum* [p. 1474]? – possibly *Resurrection* material incorrectly bundled] |
| *Strathclyde No. 3* | [charts available – no sources noted] |
| | *Dum Compleréntur?* [LU p. 884] |
| *Symphony No. 4* | *Adorna Thalalmum* [LU p. 1359] |
| | *Dum Compleréntur* [LU p. 884] |
| *Strathclyde No. 4* | *Cumha crobh nan teud* |

Ex. 6.1: Partial summary chart of source material for Davies's principal works of the 1980s

There are no precompositional charts or sketch materials available for *Sinfonia Concertante*, whereas those for the Brass Quintet are quite detailed, although one has to sift out the sketches from those of *Image, Reflection, Shadow* with which they have been bundled. The two works were written back to back as was the composer's general custom until quite recently. The charts for the Brass Quintet are interesting because they use set square/magic square complexes derived from 4, 6 and 9 notes, multi-set forms more common to the later symphonies and which led to the Fifth Symphony's set generators as explained in my companion article in this volume.

The processes which operate for *Image, Reflection, Shadow* will be explored hereafter in some detail. The plainchant *Lux Aeterna* appears to have been used for only this work whereas *Sinfonia Accademica* and *Into the Labyrinth* share *Dies Irae* and *Victimae Paschali Laudes* – the latter turning up (resurrected?) in *Resurrection* some years later (and see also Peter Owens's discussion in this volume of works using these two plainchants).

Davies's programme note for *Strathclyde Concerto No. 1* states that this concerto 'has a lot in common with [the Violin Concerto] sharing some details of melody ... the oboe's opening figure, emerging from the string sound towards the first unaccompanied solo, comes from the earlier concerto'.[1] The melodic connection to the earlier work is not entirely obvious but may refer to either the first movement of the Violin Concerto at letter H, or the descending line which

---

[1]     Programme note by the composer for *Strathclyde Concerto No. 1*.

leads to the second movement. A programme note by John Warnaby draws attention to the fact the 'the violin's concluding figure reveals some of the basic material of the work'.[2]

Interestingly the first three pitches of the Oboe Concerto G♯,E♯,Fx – enharmonically A♭,F,G – are pitches which haunt the opening of derived sets in Davies's work: see for example the set for the Trumpet Concerto beginning F,G,A♭, etc. (quoted in my article for *Tempo*);[3] the set chart given in Ex. 6.2 beginning G,A♭,F, etc.; the extended set G,A♭,F [C♭,D♭,E♭|A♭,B♭,G|C♭,D♭,D, A♭,B♭] and its relation, the α labelled set, in *Strathclyde Concerto No. 3* (see Ex. 6.11). It may be that it is accidental that these pitches also open *Ave Maria – Hail Blessed Flower* the 1961 carol setting Davies wrote for Cirencester, though perhaps, more significantly, they are a transposition of the opening D,F,E pitches from Taverner's *In Nomine* which had such a pervasive influence on the works of the 1960s.

There are no sketches for the Violin Concerto currently available and those for *Strathclyde Concerto No. 1* are rather sparse but do contain a partial set transformation chart which converts the violin 1 line of 6 after C in the second movement to the oboe line at D (Ex. 6.2). This series of pitches was later used by the composer to provide one of the source sets for the Fourth Symphony. The set chart which results, as I have outlined in my companion article in this volume, suggests a closer relationship with the plainchant *Adorno thalalmum tuum* used in that symphony than is in fact the case. This connection will be discussed later.

From notes relating to *Resurrection* in the sketches it is likely that references to *Hymn to St Magnus*, *Worldes Blis* and *The Lighthouse* will be found within the musical text. However, at the moment it is not possible to say if there is some deeper compositional connection between these works and *Resurrection* or whether Davies simply quotes from the earlier works.

| 1 | G | A♭ | F | E | B♭ | B | A | D | E♭ | C | A | G |
|---|----|----|----|----|----|----|----|----|----|----|----|----|
| 2 | A | A♭ | G♭ | G♭ | B♭ | C | B♭ | D♭ | E♭ | D♭ | B♭ | A♭ |
| 3 | B | A♭ | G | G | B | D♭ | C | C | E | D | B | A |
| 4 | D♭ | A♭ | A♭ | A♭ | C | C | D♭ | C♭ | F♭ | E♭ | C | B♭ |
| 5 | E♭ | A♭ | A | A | D♭ | E♭ | D | B♭ | F | E | C♯ | B |
| 6 | F | A♭ | B | B | D | E | E | A | F♯ | F | D | C |
| 7 | G | A♭ | C | C | D | F | F | A♭ | G♭ | G♭ | D | D♭ |

Ex. 6.2: partial transformation set from the sketches for *Strathclyde Concerto No. 1*

2    Programme note by John Warnaby quoted in <http://www.maxopus.com>.
3    McGregor, 'The Maxwell Davies Sketch Material in the British Library', *Tempo* 196 (April 1996), pp. 9–19.

The sketch materials for the Trumpet Concerto appear quite substantial but the actual compositional processes involved are quite obscure and Davies has acknowledged,[4] that there may be some difficulties in analysing this piece. The composer did not specify exactly what these difficulties would be but almost certainly the fact that the Trumpet Concerto was intended as 'part of a preliminary working-out of some of the musical possibilities arising from [the plainchant], in preparation for the composition of a chamber opera on St. Francis'[5] suggests that there might be some material missing. The non-appearance of such an opera to this date relates to the fact that Messaien's opera on the same subject appeared in the late 1980s and according to Davies 'no one was interested in producing it'. The plainchant material which is bundled with the Trumpet Concerto probably does not belong to this piece but is related to *Resurrection* which has no charts in the British Library collection.

I have already discussed some of Davies's compositional treatments of the set charts but the remainder of this article will concentrate in some depth on aspects of several of the works detailed in Ex. 6.1 above, in order to demonstrate how the material is developed from the charts into the first draft score. This will clarify some of the developments which took place in the composer's style during the decade.

In terms of sketch material the first movement of *Image, Reflection, Shadow* is very rewarding – the score annotations are quite consistent on the sketch and translate onto the set charts with relative ease. As is quite common in Davies's music there are two related set charts. They are derived straightforwardly from the plainchant *Lux Aeterna* and marked clearly in the sketches.

The following prime forms are obtained: A,G,F,B,C,E|B,C,E,F,A,G (the second hexachord is simply a reordered version of the first – although in fact it was from the second hexachord that Davies obtained the E for the last note of the first hexachord). The second hexachord is then transposed up one semitone as is clearly shown in the sketches. This procedure is very similar to that found in the Second Symphony.

A   G F              B C  [+E *ed.*]                    B C        E F     A G

*Lux Ae--- terna luceat e-is Domine|Cum sanctis tuis in aeternum qui-a pi-us es*

Ex. 6.3: *Image, Reflection, Shadow* – derivation of the set squares from plainchant *Lux Aeterna*

---

4     Conversation with the composer 15 November 1996 in Manchester.
5     Composer's programme note for the Trumpet Concerto.

From these two hexachords a number of different set charts are formed. In the first place, Davies simply constructs the normal set transposition squares based on successive notes of the hexachord (that is, there are prime forms only, no inversions). In Ex. 6.9 these set charts have not been numbered consecutively but according to the point at which they first occur in the piece. Davies refers to his initial squares as simply α and β (Ex. 6.4), although α itself, as the original set chart, is not heard as such in this movement.

The set chart which provides the next layer of pitch working is a transformation set which takes the first line of α and changes it to βR (the retrograde of β at transposition level (T)8) as in Ex. 6.5 below – in the summary chart Ex. 6.9 it is labelled [2].

Davies refers to this as NT which probably means New Transposition. The version of α→βR which leads to OT (probably Original Transposition) is not actually heard until the end of the movement, and even this is not entirely certain – see Ex. 6.9 at score letter L in piano labelled [8]. The essential difference is that whereas the OT retains the starting note 'A' for every line NT employs the successive notes of the set to end on the 'dominant' 'E'. A further hexachordal transformation converts βR (NT) to β (OT) at (T)1 (Ex. 6.6).

The next set chart is, as usual, derived from the application of the 6 x 6 magic square (the square of the Sun) to the pitches of α (3 in Ex. 6.9). Davies's label for this square (Ex. 6.7) is α [ ⪴ ⌐ ∋ ⍓ ] which means α *sol* (i.e. sun) *square*. The set labelled [4] in Ex 6.9 is a derived version of the β hexachord subject to the application of the same 6 x 6 magic square. Davies has no hieroglyph for this and simply calls it □β (Ex. 6.8).

| A | G | F | C | B | E |
|---|---|---|---|---|---|
| G | F | Eb | Bb | A | D |
| F | Eb | Db | Ab | G | C |
| C | Bb | Ab | Eb | D | G |
| B | A | G | D | C# | F# |
| E | D | C | G | F# | B |

| C | Db | F | Gb | Bb | Ab |
|---|---|---|---|---|---|
| C# | D | Gb | G | B | A |
| F | Gb | Bb | Cb | Eb | Db |
| F# | G | B | C | E | D |
| A# | B | D# | E | G# | F# |
| G# | A | C# | D | F# | E |

Ex. 6.4: *Image, Reflection, Shadow* α and β hexachords – source transposition sets [1] (not used in movement one) and [5] in Ex. 6.9

| A | G | F | C | B | E |
|---|---|---|---|---|---|
| G | F | Eb | A | A | Eb |
| F | E | D | F# | G# | D# |
| C | C | A | C | Eb | C |
| B | C | A | Bb | Eb | Db |
| E | F# | D | C# | A | G# |

Ex. 6.5: *Image, Reflection, Shadow* – transformation set α →βR NT – see Ex. 6.9 reference number [2]

| E | F# | D | C# | A | G# |
|---|----|---|----|---|-----|
| F | G# | Eb | D | A | G# |
| G | A | E | E | Bb | G# |
| A | B | E | F | Bb | A |
| B | C | F | F# | B | A |
| C# | D | F# | G | B | A |
| Has rhythm square overlaid | | | | | |

Ex. 6.6: *Image, Reflection, Shadow* – transformation chart βR to β (T)1 – see Ex. 6.9 reference number [6]

| E | D | F | G | F# | A |
|---|---|---|---|----|---|
| G | A | G | D | F | F# |
| C | Eb | Ab | Db | D | G |
| C | Bb | Eb | Ab | G | F |
| B | C# | A# | D# | A | D |
| B | B | C | C | G | E |

Ex. 6.7: *Image, Reflection, Shadow* – α magic square labelled [3] in Ex. 6.9

| Ab | A | F | D | F# | C |
|----|---|---|---|----|---|
| C# | B | D# | E | D | F# |
| F# | F# | Cb | Bb | E | D |
| Db | G | C | Cb | Eb | F |
| A# | G# | G | F# | B | A |
| E | Bb | Db | Gb | Db | Ab |

Ex. 6.8: *Image, Reflection, Shadow* – ?β magic square labelled [4] in Ex. 6.9

Finally, coming much later on in the movement, is a transformation set which converts α to β (T)1. In Ex. 6.9 this is designated [7].

This series of set charts is quite typical of all the sketch working as a whole – that is to say there are often α and β sets, sets labelled OT and NT, charts which are derived from transformation processes and charts which have been derived using an appropriate magic square.

Here then is the outline plan of the movement showing the deployment of this thematic content (*sol squ*, that is, ⅁ Γ Ⅎ ᴎ = sketch label).

| | | |
|---|---|---|
| flute (alto): | [synoptic]?[6] | |
| clarinet: | α line, β line with [Bb] to α/β one transformation? | |

**Score A**

| | | |
|---|---|---|
| clarinet: | βR to α, [R] [NT set backwards] | [2R] |
| violin: | α to β R NT | [2] |
| cello: | α [*sol squ*] [magic square version]{reading left | [3] |
| | { to right down | |
| | diagonals* | |
| alto flute: | α [*sol squ*] 1R, 2R +? | [3] |
| piano [rh]: | [*sol squ*] | [3] |
| | | lines 1–3 |
| piano [lh]: | □β [magic square version] | [4] |

**Score C**

| | | |
|---|---|---|
| flute (alto)/cello: | | |
| | α [*sol squ*] [1–3]prime | [3] |
| | [6–4] retrograde | |

**Score D**

| | | |
|---|---|---|
| flute (alto): | α [*sol squ*] 1R, 6R or [↰] | [3] |
| violin: | □β | [4] |
| cello: | α [*sol squ*] retrograde | [3R] |
| cimbalom: | ?? | [?] |
| piano [rh]: | β set notes reordered | [5] |
| piano [lh]: | α to βR NT | [2] |

**Score F**

| | | |
|---|---|---|
| flute (alto): | late entry: α circular [*sol squ*] [◉] | [3] |
| clarinet: | α to β R NT | [2] |
| cello: | α [*sol squ*] diagonals left to right | |
| | reading up | [3] |
| cimbalom: | [2nd draft score is labelled β] | |
| piano: | β 1 [+ α 1] +3+4 [R lines] | [5] |

**Score I**

| | | |
|---|---|---|
| flute (alto): | α [*sol squ*] circular continues | [3] |
| clar./cello: | β R to β | [6] |
| violin: | β first line - repeated?? | |
| | [Davies label (∋①)] | [?] |

**Score J**

| | | |
|---|---|---|
| flute (alto): | □β read along/up ↗ | [4] |
| clar./cello: | β R to β, concluded | [6] |
| clarinet: | [thereafter] β to α | [7R] |
| violin: | α [*sol squ* ] | [3] |

---

6   Roberts's term for music which is based on a set but freely written. Roberts, 'Techniques of Composition in the Music of Peter Maxwell Davies' (Ph.D., University of Birmingham, 1985) p. 73.

| cello: | □β diagonals reading right to left down | [4] |
| cimbalom: | 2nd draft score has 'top voice α' 'lower voice β' | |
| | | [variant of F] |
| piano [rh]: | | [?] |
| piano [lh]: | □β alternating P/R, to α [*sol squ* ] | |
| | alternating P/R to ?synoptic | [4][3][?] |

Score L

| flute(alto)/clar: | □β shared set | [4] |
| vln/cello: | α [*sol squ*] shared set | [3] |
| cimbalom: | α to βR NT P and R versions shared/interleaved | [2] |
| piano: | α to βR OT ?? 1,2→$OT_6$ at T11 | [8] |
| [M] | α to βR NT paired sets | [2] |

Score N [coda]

pitch content not yet defined[7] [cimbalom c.f. with F]

*Note the use of the diagonals reading the thematic line, a typical
opening ploy of many of Davies's set-based works

Ex. 6.9: *Image, Reflection, Shadow* – first movement summary

Pruslin writes[7] that 'the title relates in part to the compositional process whereby a given contour (image) often appears simultaneously in inversion (reflection), while a composite of both contours (shadow) acts as a third layer' although the piece also has a poetic 'programme' with reference to the poem by Charles Senior printed at the back of the score. This description of the relationship of the pitch content to the title may not be entirely accurate for the first movement as I shall show presently. Pruslin also refers to the duos created by the wind, strings and piano/cimbalom although in fact as Ex. 6.9 shows the disposition of duos or pairings is somewhat more complex than that.

At letter A violin has the transformation set of α to βR NT, paired with clarinet in retrograde, while cello and alto flute state variously the α magic square. The piano right hand although chordal is related to this in an accompanimental role based on the first three lines of the magic square. The left-hand part which appears imitative at first is more of a support to the transformation sets in clarinet and violin. The section from C to D features a continuation and development of the alto flute/cello pairing (note that although not labelled as such in the sketch this would be the equivalent of Davies's 'middle eight' section such as is found throughout the various sketches). This is a 'reflection' in the sense that it is like a long statement of the α magic square

---

[7]    Pruslin, 1996 writing for the webpage says: 'at the end of the lyrical first movement [Davies] refers to the climax of the earlier work, in which a long, deeply "inhaled" *ostinato* passage finally explodes with shattering intensity'. In connection with this discussion of *Image, Reflection, Shadow*, I am grateful to Rodney Lister for his observations.

line by line from 1–6 but with the cello's 4–6 bent backwards like a hairpin so that the last note of 6 starts at the same time as the first note of 1.

The varied 'reprise' of the first section which occurs from letter D to letter F closes this internal ternary shape by presenting the opening material in altered instrumentation. Thus the alto flute and cello continue their pairing, while the violin takes the β pitch square from the piano which in its turn has chordal articulation of the β set in the right-hand, and a chordal version of the original clarinet part (albeit reflected in the opposite direction) in the left-hand. The cimbalom part was added later as will be discussed subsequently. At D its pitch content is difficult to assign, although it may relate in part to the clarinet's line in the *Adagio* introduction.

At letter F the cello and later alto flute present two more readings of the α magic square using diagonal and circular movement round the square. The clarinet has a reprise of its statement from letter A, but in reverse, no doubt related to the title. The *Moderato* at letter I signals not only a change in tempo but a change in set choice. From this point until letter L the β set is more predominant. The alto flute and cello at letter J have two readings of the magic square – the cello's diagonal reading clearly a reflection of its α square reading at letter F. The cimbalom also has a varied version of its statement at letter F so that this section from letter J to letter L becomes an elaborate double/variation on the earlier section – in other words the earlier section is embodied as a 'shadow' within the later one.

Finally, at letter L, the instruments make their 'proper' pairings according to type and the set statements are shared between the paired instruments.

So much for the interplay of pitch material in this first movement but as indicated earlier, the background to this work is of some interest. Examination of the sketches reveals that the cimbalom part, or at least the detail of it, is largely missing from the first draft. According to Davies's agent Judy Arnold[8] the work was written movement by movement and the first performance was of the first movement only. This arose because Davies wished to spend some time familiarizing himself with the cimbalom which was being specially built for Greg Knowles and there was a delay in delivery of the instrument. Consequently the piece had to be learnt in stages and so delayed the performance of the complete work until 22 August 1982 at Lucerne. This makes the lack of a cimbalom part on the first draft all the more interesting. There are no indications on the score as to what the instrument should do so it may be that the notes for this are in the composer's diary which he kept from 1972.[9]

---

[8]   Conversation with the author – December 1998.
[9]   See Nicholas Jones's transcribed conversation with the composer at <http://www.maxopus.com>.

Some of the squares defined in Examples 6.4 to 6.8 have rhythmic values attached to them which have not been reproduced here, and in addition some annotations to the charts have been omitted – in particular the circular path traced through α [3] beginning in the middle and working outwards in anticlockwise direction. Square [3] also shows a cross-hatched grid indicating the diagonal readings of the square inward from the four corners – in the manner described by Roberts in his original article for *Contact*,[10] and later developed in his thesis.[11]

There are several other charts used in the rest of the work which are variants on those given above, usually transposed and sometimes swung around on an axis. There are, however, three larger set transformations. Identified in the sketches as for the second movement there is a 12-note collection containing two hexachords – namely the first line of α [α1] and the last line of β [β 6] – transforming by six steps to a middle line, and this middle line turned retrograde, with some changes in order leading by six steps back to the retrograde of the first line of [α 1] [β 6] with some reorderings.

Another α-related 20-note set transforms by seven steps to an 18-note statement which is in fact the first three lines of α [*sol squ*] [3]. (A similar 20-note process is to be found in the charts for Symphony No. 4). In like manner, an 18-note β-related statement transforms into the last three lines of α [*sol squ*] [3], a 16-note statement. This version of the α set is given below in Ex. 6.10. The origin of the initial line is not obvious and may even be from another work.

| C | D | F# | Ab | Bb | E | F# | F# | Ab | F | Eb | Gb | F | Cb | Db | Eb | G | C# | A | B |
|---|---|----|----|----|---|----|----|----|---|----|----|---|----|----|----|---|----|---|---|
| A | Bb | E | Gb | Ab | D | E | Eb | Gb | E | Db | E | Eb | Bb | B | Db | F | Bb | Ab | A |
| F# | Gb | D | E | F# | C | Eb | D | F | Db | B | Eb | D | A | A | B | E | Ab | G | F# |
| D# | D | C | C# | D | Bb | Db | C | Eb | B | A | Db | Db | Ab | G | Ab | D | Gb | F | E |
| Bb | A | Ab | B | B | Ab | C | Bb | Db | A | A | B | | G# | F | Gb | C | E | E | C# |
| G | Gb | G | A | | G | Bb | Ab | B | Ab | E | Ab | | G | Eb | E | Bb | D | Eb | Bb |
| E | D | F | G | | F# | A | G | A | G | D | F | | F# | C | Eb | Ab | C# | D | G |

Ex. 6.10: *Image, Reflection, Shadow* – α chart transformation to α magic square lines 1–3

| G | Ab | F | Cb | Db | Eb | Ab | Bb | G | Cb | Db | D | Ab | Bb |
|---|----|---|----|----|----|----|----|---|----|----|---|----|----|
| G# | A | F# | C | D | E | A | B | G# | C | D | Eb | A | B |
| F | F# | Eb | A | B | C# | F# | G# | F | A | B | C | F# | G# |
| B | C | A | Eb | F | G | C | D | B | Eb | F | F# | C | D |
| C# | D | B | F | G | A | D | E | C# | F | G | G# | D | E |
| D# | E | C# | G | A | B | E | F# | D# | G | A | Bb | E | F# |
| A# | B | G# | D | E | F# | B | C# | Bb | D | E | F | B | C# |
| D | Eb | C | F# | G# | A# | Eb | F | D | F# | G# | A | D# | F |

Ex. 6.11: *Strathclyde Concerto No. 3* – extended Mercury α magic square (the original 8-note version is in bold)

10    Roberts in *Contact* 19 (Summer 1978), pp. 26–9.
11    Roberts, 'Techniques of Composition', *op. cit.*

The first line of the chart is noteworthy for the predominance of whole tone intervals which carry the resonance of the *Taverner* 'Death chord' [D,F♯,E,G♯]. It is possible that the chart at Ex. 6.10 is the progenitor one of those which generates material for *Strathclyde Concerto No. 3* (Ex. 6.11) though clearly not in respect of actual pitch content. The two charts are here presented side by side which permits some points of similarity to be noted.

By way of further comparison, it will be useful to examine some of the principles which appear to underlie the generation of set charts for the Third Strathclyde at this point, as they demonstrate some interesting features. Ex. 6.11 is one of the two 'extended' squares for the work, the other, not presented here is a 9-note x 19 based on the square of the Moon, and labelled β.

There is a Mercury (8-note) magic square based on G,A♭,F,C♭,D♭E♭,B♭,D (but see also the discussion on *Strathclyde Concerto No. 1* following), using the magic square orientation by top line 8,58,59,5,4,62,63,1 and giving the first line pitch sequence D,E♭,C,D♭,B,B♭,F,G. An interesting by-product of the transformation process is that the opening notes (D,E♭,C ...) of the magic square are a perfect fifth transposition of the original set (G,A♭,F ...). In addition the final line of the magic square A,G♯,F,G♯,F♯,D♯,A♯,D has quite a strong correspondence with the original set.

A 9-note set (G,C♯,D,D♯G♯,F,F♯,E,A) generates the square of the Moon (using Davies's usual number orientation – top line 37,78,29,70,21,62,13,54,5). This results in square lines which are simply palindromic round the fifth note (for example, first line G,F♯,G♯,D,G♯,D,G♯,F♯,G – see Ex. 6.16). The following (Ex. 6.12) transformation square (α→β, but not so labelled by Davies) is also found. Two adjustments will be noted from the extended version of α found in Ex. 6.11. The reason for these minor adjustments is not clear.

| G | Ab | F | C | Db | D | Ab | Bb | G | B | Db | Eb | D | Ab | Bb |
|---|----|---|---|----|---|----|----|---|---|----|----|---|----|----|
| G | Gb | E | A | B | C | Gb | Ab | F | A | B | B | Bb | Ab | C |
| G | E | Eb | G | Bb | A | F | G | Eb | G | A | Ab | G | Ab | D |
| Gb | D | D | E | A | Gb | E | Gb | D | F | G | F | E | Ab | E |
| Gb | C | Db | D | G | E | D | F | C | Eb | F | D | Db | Ab | Gb |

Ex. 6.12: *Strathclyde Concerto No. 3* – transformation set α→β

Only one other set chart is found in the sketches and this is simply the transposition set of the Moon square β laid out such that each subsequent line begins underneath the next note diagonally instead of vertically. This results in a rhomboid-shaped square from which Davies abstracts the verticals which he uses as chords most notably at score number 14, as well as the opening which is discussed hereafter.

It is obvious then that the precompositional chart material for *Strathclyde Concerto No. 3* is much more straightforward than for *Image, Reflection, Shadow* and in general this is true for works composed after 1989. Stephen Pruslin writing in 1996 lays out the initial thrust of the piece:

> in the present concerto, Sir Peter has afforded us a rare aural glimpse of the musical material actually assembling itself, first, in the orchestra from the ninefold Square of the Moon and then, in the trumpet, from the eightfold Square of Mercury.[12]

Davies speaks quite specifically in his introduction to the work in the soundbyte recorded on the webpage for this work. He draws attention to the opening where:

> it was the first time in any piece of music I've written that I let the listener into the way a magic square is constructed out of the basic material ... at the beginning of the concerto ... the magic square, its mechanics and its derivation are, for the first time, exposed very clearly on the surface of the music.[13]

As will be seen from Ex. 6.13 below, which is the opening of the work, the imitative entries follow each other at a crotchet's distance. As a consequence the rhombus shape of β referred to above, is laid out. The entries follow the diagonal line downwards although some initial notes are missing where they already occur in the texture somewhere else. In Ex. 6.13 some of these missing notes have been indicated by annotation.

This passage is immediately followed by a decorated but nonetheless clear statement on the trumpet of the opening line of the Mercury magic square [α] which leads into pitch statements of each line in turn, initially with decoration, and then, from score number 2 (marked 'calmo' in the sketches but not on the final score), with no decoration or repetition at all. The rhythmic values are determined by the numerical sequence of the magic square, *modulo* 8. The horn's first, highly decorated, entry at score figure 1 + 7 can be simplified to reveal the first line of the original α transposition square (G,A♭,F,C♭, etc.). In Ex. 6.14 the main notes are ringed to clarify the set material. The decorative writing here is a logical extension of the thematic elaboration which is found in, for example, the first movement of the Second Symphony at full score figures D, F and so on, translated into the concerto framework.

Decoration returns to the set statements when the horn takes over the fifth pitch statement of α at score letter 3. It is then joined in quasi-canonic echo by

---

[12]    Pruslin, 1996, writing about *Strathclyde Concerto No. 3* for the website <http://www.maxopus.com>.

[13]    Davies's spoken introduction to *Strathclyde Concerto No. 3* for the website <http://www.maxopus.com>.

Ex. 6.13: Opening section of *Strathclyde Concerto No. 3*

Ex. 6.14: *Strathclyde Concerto No. 3* – trumpet and horn first entries

Ex. 6.15: Trumpet Concerto – opening solo trumpet line two bars before C *et seq.*

the trumpet which has the final retrograde of the extended form of the α set (as in Ex. 6.11). The main notes of decorated sets can usually be determined by applying the numerical rhythmic sequence derived from the magic square to calculate the duration of each note/group.

This contrasts with the opening solo line of the Trumpet Concerto (Ex. 6.15) where, though the semiquaver patterning is not dissimilar to that of the horn above, the set derivation is less clearly defined. For the listener the linear focus is more evident in *Strathclyde No. 3* and this is true for the later symphonies as I have shown in the accompanying article.

Davies's use of 'tonalities' as reference points (for example, F minor for the Second Symphony) finds expression in tonal areas defined by harmonic content. Thus the diminished 7th which is found throughout his long-term harmonic structuring gives a certain focus to the 'tonality'. Intervals taken in isolation out of the diminished 7th then give more direct connections with traditional tonal centres. For example F and Ab in the Second Symphony give F minor by implication. A similar tonal centring is felt at the beginning of the third movement of *Image, Reflection, Shadow*, for example, where E and G tend towards 'E minor' with the D acting as a flattened leading note. In the works of the 1980s and 1990s these tonal inflections are increasingly allowed into the decorative arabesque passages for solo instruments, replacing the earlier practice of repeating notes already used from the set/square. The trumpet's first entry in Ex. 6.14 has a strong A minor association in the scalic rise. Similar tonally inflected arabesques are apparent in *Strathclyde Concerto No. 4* for clarinet.

Consideration of the third and fourth Strathclydes shows some interesting points of comparison. Like the Trumpet Concerto these are both one movement works with the elements of individual movements discernible within them. The sketches show that in both there are usually no more than two distinct thematic lines at any one time. In the earlier piece the ideas are often derived from the two distinct sets while in the latter the opposing thematic material derives from the transposition square on the one hand and the magic square on the other (as expressed in Davies's notation on the draft score). Both have a section where one finds cross-reading of the magic square, alternatively to the right and then to the left (Davies labels this βουστροφηδον (boustrophedon) literally, 'turning like oxen in ploughing' and used figuratively of writing which has this characteristic).[14] Normally in the sketches Davies draws the directional movement across the square as a graphic (e.g. ⧕ or ⧕). In other works such as Symphony No. 2 where there is significant use of German words in the sketches,

---

[14]    Sometimes written βουστροφ or βουστροφος boustroph/boustrophos) in the sketches. The use of this term is relatively localized within these particular works – about the same time Davies was commenting in pre-concert talks of the difficulty of explaining the magic square processes in words. (Source of the definition: Liddell and Scott, *A Greek-English Lexicon*, Clarendon Press, Oxford, reprinted 1978).

Davies uses 'grundgevidret' and 'querschnitt' to describe diagonal readings of the square. However, no German words are used in these concertos.[15]

In both cases the βουστροφηδον lines are given to the solo instrument. In *Strathclyde Concerto No. 3* it is the trumpet at score number 47. In the sketch this is labelled ⨅⨅.Ɛ ♐ βουστροφος, that is, 'nine (magic) square reading up and down alternately'– this distinguishes it from the horn solo from eight bars before figure 46 in the score which has a different label showing its origins – Ɛ ♐ HLƆ βουστροφηδον, that is, '(magic) square Mercury reading left to right and right to left alternately'. The 9-note square is given in Ex. 6.16 and the trumpet part derived from reading from bottom right upwards is seen in Ex. 6.17 (it should be noted that some omissions and reordering are evident but no repetition or decoration is found).

| G  | F#  | G# | D  | G# | D  | G# | F#  | G  |
|----|-----|----|----|----|----|----|-----|----|
| E  | C#  | G# | A  | C  | A  | G# | C#  | E  |
| Bb | F   | D  | F  | Bb | F  | D  | F   | Bb |
| B  | B   | D# | D# | A# | D# | D# | B   | B  |
| C  | A   | C  | Ab | Ab | Ab | C  | A   | C  |
| Bb | Db  | D  | F  | Gb | F  | D  | Db  | Bb |
| B  | D#  | F# | C  | D  | C  | F# | D#  | B  |
| E  | E   | C# | D# | F# | D# | C# | E   | E  |
| A  | D   | C# | G  | E  | G  | C# | D   | A  |

Ex. 6.16: *Strathclyde Concerto No. 3* – the 9-note magic square

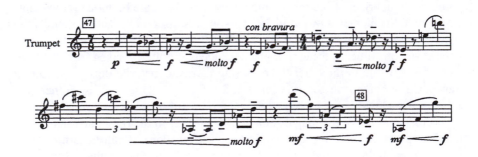

Ex. 6.17: *Strathclyde Concerto No. 3* – trumpet part at score number 47

---

15     McGregor 1996, *op. cit.*

A similar section (labelled $\ni \delta\!/$ *Boustroph*) is found in *Strathclyde Concerto No. 4* at score number 15 reading the square from bottom left (that is, row 10 of the [10 x 10 Uranus] magic square) alternatively left to right and right to left .

The accompanying parts in all the Strathclyde Concertos are straightforward rhythmically and often chordally based. In the sketches thematic derivations are usually annotated but the chordal passages are not.

Such a straightforward approach makes a strong contrast with the opening movement of *Image, Reflection, Shadow* as detailed in Ex. 6.9 above. This is of course partly explained by the fact that the earlier work was written for The Fires, disbanded in 1987 before the third and fourth Strathclydes were written and that the soloist focus of concerti demands a different approach. The disappearance of The Fires from the scene therefore served to contribute to the evolution taking place in the composer's style at this time. Davies knew that the level of complexity created for six specialist players would no longer be possible in the concerti.

It is therefore not unreasonable to assume that *Strathclyde Concerto No. 1* stands at the crossroads of this change – perhaps even more so than the Violin Concerto written just before. The movements of *Strathclyde No. 1* are clearly dated – the first two completed at Bunertoon on 11 and 16 August (1986) respectively and the third movement slightly later, on 4 October at London. Davies does not always date his pieces exactly so the chronology here is helpful. The piece was not actually performed until eighteen months later, after *Resurrection,* although as suggested earlier, the opera appears to have connections with other works but not *Strathclyde No. 1*. Although there is a difficulty in relating the Oboe Concerto in detail to the Violin Concerto, Davies is quite explicit in his programme note:

> This concerto has a lot in common with the *Violin Concerto* I had recently written for Isaac Stern, tackling some of the same formal problems and sharing some details of melody: for instance, the timpani are used in both works entirely to give rhythmic impetus in development or transformation sections, and the oboe's opening figure, emerging from the string sound towards the first unaccompanied solo, comes from the earlier concerto. There were musical problems unsolved, material still capable of extension, still worrying me from the older work.[16]

The linking of formal problems is not surprising considering the genre. However, the melodic linking will need greater exploration if the exact relationship between the works is to be elucidated. The lack of sketches for the earlier work and the lack of substantive precompositional material for the Oboe Concerto inhibits any immediate comparisons. However, the connections which exist at

---

[16]    Davies, programme note for *Strathclyde Concerto No. 1* as quoted on webpage <http://www.maxopus.com>.

the precompositional level between the first and second Strathclydes and the Fourth Symphony suggest that the source plainsong may have a greater currency than may be immediately obvious. In writing about this plainsong in the programme note Davies says:

> The plainsong itself is heard clearly at the opening of the work, in the violas, and is subject to transformations of various kinds – intervallic, permutation, magic square – throughout.[17]

The interconnectivity operating in this work may prove difficult to unravel completely. The 7-note set (goal line of Ex. 6.2) which generates the magic square of Venus as detailed in my companion article in this volume at Ex. 7.1 is derived from the plainchant *Dum Compleréntur* by a simple process (and verified, up to a point, by one of the few pieces of precompositional working in the sketches):

| | Dum | com-pler- | én- | tur | dies | Pen- | te- | co- | tes | |
|---|---|---|---|---|---|---|---|---|---|---|
| | E | G | AC | C | C | CD | C | A | B | A | G |
| (T3) | G | B♭ | CE♭ | E♭ | E♭ | E♭F | E♭ | C | D | C | B♭ |
| opening | C | E♭ | F A♭ | A♭ | A♭ | A♭B♭ | A♭ | F | G | F | E♭ |
| Inv. | F | D | CC | A♭ | G | [sic] | | | | | |
| Retro | G | A♭ | CC | D | F | | | | | | |

[above labels *sic*]

Ex. 6.18: *Strathclyde Concerto No. 1* – partial set derivation

However this is clearly not the whole story and a later sheet suggests a second pitch profile (and Davies calls this *Dum Compleréntur* in the sketch):

E, F, DC, G, GAG B, C, B, BAG, ABG, GFFF, FE, DFGAB, GAFD, DFGAGGCEFD

Ex. 6.19: *Strathclyde Concerto No. 1* – alternative set profile plainchant (unidentified)

This appears to lead to the second set in the following manner:

E, F, D, C, G, G, F, B  (C),A,F, E (suggested derivation)
G, A♭,F, E, B♭,B, A, D, E♭,C, A, G (pitch set at T3)

This plainchant is not taken from that which produces the original *Dum Compleréntur* set (see p. 884 of the *Liber Usualis*). However, there are two clues in the first draft score which suggest a partial solution. Firstly, the third movement is prefaced with the Latin 'Veni Creator Spiritus' which is the *Liber Usualis* chant on p. 885 following *Dum Compleréntur*. More significant,

---

[17]    *Ibid.*

however, is a reference to 'Veni Sancte Spiritus' in Davies's personal script at what became score letter I. This reference suggested that a connection between the present work and Davies's 1963 choral work might be feasible. In addition the plainchant *Veni Sancte Spiritus* is used in *A Mirror of Whitening Light* (and Symphony No.1) and as Roberts points out, the source in that case is an isolated antiphon 'Ad invocandum Spiritum Sanctum' which generates a Mercury square based on G,**E,F,D**,F♯,A,G♯,C (the emboldening is mine).[18] Cross-referencing between compositions is a undoubtedly a feature of many works and in the companion article to this I demonstrate a clear example from Symphony No. 6.

In Davies's early *Veni Sancte Spiritus* the opening section is actually based on the words of *Dum Compleréntur* although a connection with the *Liber Usualis* is not immediately apparent. However, there does appear to be a connection of pitch content between the second movement of the Oboe Concerto and the trumpet part at figure H in the earlier work (note four sketch bars are missed out in the final version).

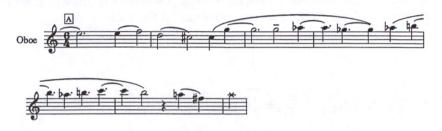

Ex. 6.20: *Strathclyde Concerto No. 1* – second movement at figure A

Ex. 6.21: *Veni Sancte Spiritus* – trumpet one part at figure H

---

[18]    Davies, programme note for *A Mirror of Whitening Light* as quoted in Griffiths, *Peter Maxwell Davies* (London: Robson, 1982), pp. 163–5; see also Roberts in *Contact* 23 (Winter 1981), pp. 26–9.

The pitch sequence in the Oboe Concerto viz. E,F,D,C♯,G,A♭,(G♭),B,C,A (F♯,E)
corresponds to the trumpet's F,G♭,E♭,(G),D,A♭,A,C,D,B♭ (repetition omitted)
except for the penultimate note and the relative change of position of the
bracketed note. Without question the source has been the same and interestingly
the oboe part from figure A follows the original, as written out in the sketch (see
Ex. 6.19), virtually note for note including repetition but with chromatic
alteration towards figure B.

That even this might not be the whole story is suggested if we return to the
material associated with the 7-note set charts for Symphony No. 4. There is no
indication that these are the missing charts for the Oboe Concerto, but, also
bundled with the charts are some rough drafts of a version for voice and oboe of
an *Alma Redemptoris Mater* utilizing the two rotations of the magic square
identified as [2] and [3] in 'Max the symphonist' (Ex. 7.1). The first six bars of
the oboe part which uses set chart [3] – at first with little repetition and
decoration but increasingly elaborated – is given at Ex. 6.22. This can be
compared with the first four bars of score letter A and the first three of letter B
of *Strathclyde Concerto No. 1* second movement at Ex. 6.23.

Ex. 6.22: *Fourth Symphony* sketches – bundled pages α, 1 and 2 *(Alma Redemptoris Mater)* –
oboe part from 'page 1' (with voice part)

Ex. 6.23: *Strathclyde Concerto No. 1* – oboe solo at A (four bars) and at B (three bars)

There is no suggestion at this stage of any direct connection with Davies's 1957 sextet *Alma Redemptoris Mater*. However, the oboe line in the third movement of that work from bar 38 to 69 is a diatonic descent C,B,A,G, (A,G,),E which when compared with the opening pitches of the *Dum Compleréntur* plainchant E,G,A,C might demonstrate a chance correspondence, but with a composer like Davies one can never be certain that this is not a deliberate cross-reference.

This potentially complex series of cross-references actually underpins a movement which is relatively straightforward formally and texturally. In terms of structure and content the second movement of the Oboe Concerto makes a strong contrast with the first of *Image, Reflection, Shadow* analysed earlier. As can be seen in Ex. 6.24, the movement is structurally clearly ternary with a smaller ternary unit making up the first A section – a form within a form, or rather, an internal structure that summarizes or prefigures the whole, typical of the composer's approach to formal considerations (and in that sense not dissimilar to the first movement of *Image, Reflection, Shadow*). A certain amount of numerical correspondence between sections is apparent, including the use of 28, one of Davies's preferred numbers (as shown in the 'eagle wings' Ex. 7.3 in the article 'Max the symphonist') but not necessarily providing clear evidence of the stricter sectional control found in earlier works.

In the same way, the pitch material (notwithstanding the earlier discussion) is not readily reducible to chart-based originals except within the B section (as indicated, where a transformation process allows the main thematic idea to evolve into the *Dum Compleréntur* set). On the other hand, the trichord enclosed by a minor third is particularly prominent throughout as the starting point of both harmonic and melodic material. It is not very likely that the pitch content here is quite as free as it might appear, but at present the actual process of pitch generation remains obscure.

Within the space of this article it has been possible to highlight only some of the compositional processes Davies used in the 1980s. These can be directly compared with the procedures of the 1960s and 1970s which are much better known. However, it has been possible to explore in some depth areas of interconnectivity which exist between works in relation to the deployment and disposition of source material across a wide time-span. This logic of compositional processes and the relationship between works is explored further by John Warnaby in his article for this volume.

It would appear that, having loosed somewhat the pitch control factors in the first two Strathclydes, Davies decided to revisit his constructional processes thereafter, making the pitch processes more overt – hence the opening discourse of *Strathclyde No. 3*. That such overt processes are indeed operating within the later symphonies is one particular focus of the next article.

| Score | Adagio | A | B | | | C |
|---|---|---|---|---|---|---|
| Duration | 44 | 60 | 36 + | 36 + | 48 | 74.5 |
| Section | Introduction | Opening section based on 'alternative plainchant' | Varied repeat T11 | Middle Eight | Varied Reprise | 7 statement transformation Figure x . Statements 1 to 6 alternating vln 1/vln2 |
| | | FIRST SECTION | | | | SECOND SECTION |
| Trichord base | A,Bb,C/C#,D,E/ E,F,G | D,E,F | C#,D#,E | C,C#,Eb (D,F,G) | D,E,F | G,A,Bb (B,C#,D) F,G,Ab |

| Score | D | E | B | F | | C | G |
|---|---|---|---|---|---|---|---|
| Duration | 60 | 28 | | 16 + | 28 | | 44 |
| Section | Oboe - statement 7 / - varied rpt + 4th / -statement 7 reprise | | | 4 bars incl 2 bars 'cadenza small slow' [PMD] | | Varied Introduction repeat | Varied reprise 4/4 for 6/4 |
| | | | Climax | | | | Codetta / Harmonic summary |
| | | | | | | REPRISE | |
| Trichord base | G,Ab,C/C,Db,F/G,Ab,Cb | G,Ab,Gb (D,Eb,Db) | F,G,Ab | | | F,G,Ab | D,E,F C pedal / F,Gb,Ab |

Ex. 6.24: *Strathclyde Concerto No. 1* – second movement structural summary

# 7

# Max the symphonist

*Richard McGregor*

Some thoughts on *scherzos* and slow movements in the light of the composer's words about his compositional processes.

This article is designed to be read in conjunction with my other contribution to this volume. The thrust of this article builds on the discussion in *Tempo* 196 (April 1996)[1] in that it continues my investigations into the formal structures of the symphonic *scherzos* and slow movements which I initiated there by looking at Davies's Second Symphony.

The sheer scale of Davies's symphonic output militates against a thorough analysis in an article such as this, and therefore it seemed useful to concentrate on making comparisons between the symphonies even though this necessitates a non-consecutive approach to the study. Nevertheless it is quite obvious that there are a number of constants as well as some developments which can be discerned in Davies's approach to aspects of symphonic form over the twenty years or so between the First and Sixth Symphonies. Some of the developments reflect a conscious change over time in the composer's approach to his basic material.

Although slow movements and *scherzos* are traditionally middle movements, Davies is by no means constrained to present them in these positions. Ever conscious of his symphonic antecedents, and in particular Mahler and Sibelius, he often uses formal structures which can be related to past practice, as he perceives it, but which at the same time tend to undermine expectations. In the First and Fourth Symphonies, for example, he speaks of ghosts of established forms, and so '[in the First Symphony] there is *scherzo* of a kind … reduced to a "ghost" in the form's far hinterground'[2] and '[the] *Fourth Symphony* harbours a "ghost sonata"'.[3] Recent symphonies have shown a desire to blur the strict divisions and articulations between movements. So, for example, '[in the Fourth

---

[1]   McGregor, 'The Maxwell Davies Sketch Material in the British Library', *Tempo* 196 (April 1996), pp. 9–19 and *Tempo* 197 (July 1996), pp. 20–2.

[2]   Composer's programme note for his First Symphony.

[3]   Davies interviewed by Stephen Pruslin – the phrase is Pruslin's apparently quoting the composer: see Pruslin 'Peter Maxwell Davies's Symphony no. 4' in *Musical Times* cxxx/1759 (September 1989), pp. 520–3; also found on webpage <http://www.maxopus.com>.

Symphony] I have become interested in disguising restatements or recapitulations as transitions',[4] and, in the Sixth Symphony there is a '*scherzo masquerading as a sonata-allegro*', while overall there is '"play" at surface level with "classical" musical form, background layers of slow, independent transformations, sometimes suddenly exposed'.[5] This evolution in his formal thinking clearly owes much to the tangible influence of Sibelius.

Davies has always been preoccupied with formal structures as the carriers of musical argument. As early as 1963 in an interview with R. Murray Schafer he remarked that 'I have to define the architecture of the piece before I start ... each time we write a piece we must think about the form in advance, if it is not going to be shapeless'.[6] Seventeen years later in an interview with Paul Griffiths he comments that 'I can't work without having a feeling for a work's proportions and the basic material before I put a note on paper'.[7]

Despite these statements, it is clear that the late 1980s mark a shift in Davies's attitude towards both the musical detail which articulates these forms and his desire, or lack of it, to talk about the processes. In his pre-Prom talk for the Fourth Symphony he began by declaring that 'as I get older I feel very strongly that I want less and less to talk about ... the music that I write', later asserting that 'one is composing against a background of material which you've learnt for that specific piece, and you are working freely with that and when necessary ... harmonically adapting it slightly'.[8]

The latter statement suggests that there is a conscious move away from the stricter writing of the 1970s works, and this is confirmed by his comments regarding the composition of the Fourth Symphony in which he says that 'one has to have a rigorous harmonic and rhythmic structure on a large and small scale. But within that there has to be freedom to choose and make every moment work for you' and that within the work there are 'systematic transformations of interval and contour – [which] took a few weeks to work through, absorb and become assimilated enough to carry around in my head as a background matrix' to the extent that 'the raw material and its associations became an almost personal mythological base'.[9]

This move away from more rigorous and all-embracing serial set working seems to have coincided with a greater explicitness on the composer's part in relation to the creation of 'serious modal expression [for] the twenty-first century'.[10] Whereas Davies believes this to be an important step in respect of any

---

4    *Ibid.*
5    Composer's programme note for his Sixth Symphony.
6    Schafer, *British Composers in Interview* (London, 1963), pp. 173ff.
7    Griffiths, *Peter Maxwell Davies* (London, 1982).
8    Composer's pre-Prom talk on the Fourth Symphony, 10 September 1989.
9    Composer's programme note for his Fourth Symphony.
10   Interview with Stephen Pruslin as n. 3 above.

'legacy' which he might leave to subsequent generations, his critics have been quick to use this fact, *inter alia*, to demonstrate his lack of relevance for the rising generation.[11] It may be that Davies's use of the terms 'tonic' and 'dominant' is too redolent of 'classical' archetypes for its own good (as likewise his 'key' references – such as to F minor in the second movement of the Second Symphony). Whatever some commentators believe the composer should have done or how he should or should not express himself is, however, irrelevant. Davies has never been afraid to allow the quality of his work to transcend analytical rhetoric.

This is not the place to discuss at length the compositional processes through which the composer generates his primary pitch material for the symphonies, although this will certainly be the basis of a more extended study subsequently. While it will be necessary to give some specific references to precompositional material for the Fourth and Sixth Symphonies particularly since the sketches are not generally available at this time, the organizational principles are generally consistent for all the symphonies and have been illustrated for the Third Symphony by Nicholas Jones.[12]

Before beginning to deal with some analytical detail it is necessary to clarify one particular piece of the composer's terminology. To assist those who wish to pursue the sketch material further I follow the composer's terminology in referring to the ordinary transposition chart as the 'set square' (Davies – $\ni.\mathbb{O}$ = set) and the derived form as the 'magic square' (Davies – $\ni \delta\!|$ = square).

Following on from my analysis of processes operating in second and third movements of the Second Symphony it is useful to compare the *scherzo* of the Second Symphony with the *scherzo* of the Fourth Symphony. This reveals that the rhythmic movement is comparable – in the later symphony the rhythms are, as Davies says, 'all physical' – there are strong *ostinato*-related bass figurations which promote harmonic stasis although the rhythmic figurations themselves are not constant. The pitch-chart material from the sketches consists of the following:

1. 7-note set square and derived Venus magic square – this looks like a chromatically inflected set derived from the 'manuscript' version of *Adorna thalamum tuum* but in fact it is a derived form of *Dum compleréntur dies Pentecóstes (Strathclyde Concerto No. 1 –* movement two, score letter D) [initial note G]

2. A version of the Venus square at T9

3. The original Venus square flipped round its diagonal [i.e. what were inversion statements now appear as primes] [initial note D]

[11]   Some criticism of Davies's work is referred to in Whittall's 'Cross-currents and Convergences: Britten, Maxwell Davies and the Sense of Place', *Tempo* 204 (April 1998), p. 7.
[12]   Jones '"Preliminary workings": the Precompositional Process in Maxwell Davies's Third Symphony', *Tempo* 204 (April 1998), pp. 14–22.

4.    A 9-note set square (and a few lines only of a complementary inversion
      square) – this set is clearly derived from a first only sieve[13] of a
      chromatically altered version of the chant *Adorna thalamum tuum* from
      *Liber Usualis* [LU] p. 1359 [initial note G]

5.    A 9-note Moon square [Davies's usual configuration – see for example
      *Ave Maris Stella*]

6.    The same Moon square flipped about its diagonal as in 3. above [initial
      note D]

7.    Two versions of a transformation set converting the 9-note to the 7-note
      [initial note D]

8.    Transformation set [twenty notes], twenty statements [initial note F line
      1 to initial note Eb line 20] – the derivation of the initial statement is
      unclear but appears to have links with the 7-note set at 1. and 2. above.
      The relationship of the destination line [20] with the other sets is not
      clear. Davies labels the two pages of this transformation set as α and β

9.    An interim working of a 12-note set which is first-only sieved within
      itself to indicate a 7-note set contained inside the 12. This set appears to
      derive in part from 1. above [initial note D]

10.   A 10-note set and associated Uranus [composer's labelling in the Sixth
      Symphony] magic square. This set is derived from 9. with some of the
      repeated pitches reinstated and one reordered. The last three notes of the
      set are the same as the opening of 4. above [i.e. G,A,C] [initial note D]

Ex. 7.1: Fourth Symphony – significant precompositional workings

In addition there is a rough working on one page which shows the derivation of
a 10-note set which was apparently extrapolated by means of a geometric shape
drawn onto [2.] above.

There is no full set chart for the 10-note set and it seems therefore to be a
localized working. This is not all the precompositional working for this
symphony but the rest is not significant to the summary which follows.

As far as the deployment of the 7-, 9- and 10-note sets is concerned, Davies
hinted at the relationship with the formal macrostructure in his Pre-Prom talk,
although in the context of the work as a whole. Having just mentioned the
blurring process by which one movement moves into another, he continued:

> you can have operating through the whole piece, a very slow transformation
> process, where the material is in a state of bending and preparing for the
> next thing the whole time, so that, there's actually very little literal repeat,
> although I think, because the harmony recurs, and outlines recur although

---

[13]    'Sieving' – a term first used by David Roberts to describe Davies's extraction of a
prime set from the original plainchant.

the actual notes are probably going to be different, you will have a sense of reprise, although I'm playing with your sense of reprise and of points of arrival and departure which are smudged all the time.[14]

This statement can usefully be illustrated with reference to the *scherzo* of the Fourth Symphony in Ex. 7.2.

The Introduction establishes C as the harmonic focus, soon becoming the *ostinato*-like figuration referred to earlier on the notes D,F,Ab,C – the D,F,Ab a diminished triad characteristic of Davies's harmonic vocabulary (compare, for example, with its harmonic function in the Second Symphony).

The set statement noted on set line 1 (Ex. 7.2) is incomplete, reflecting more extended use of the Venus square in the first movement. The reference to the 20-note transformation set (8. above) is brief but represents its first appearance in the symphony (cellos and basses *pizzicato* 8 bars before score number 18). The connections with the Venus square [2.] are made more explicit by the alto flute at score figure 18 stating an abstracted dual statement of the Venus square as shown.

A further variant reading on the Venus square [2.] precedes partial references to the transformation set 9→7 [7.] at score number 20 as the upper part of a dual set statement with the Venus set [1.]. This section illustrates Davies's statement that 'increasingly I have used forms incompletely leaving their completion implicit, or perhaps taken up and reworked or completed in another movement or in some cases, in the next work'[15] since this combination of sets was first heard in the first movement at score number 9, with the difference that the lines were reversed in the earlier movement.

The comparatively straightforward combination of sets from score number 20 to score 21 is followed by an obscure passage from 21 whose origins are very difficult to clarify. In the sketches, unlike the immediately preceding section, there are no set labels of any kind. In Davies's later sketches one encounters this all the time – there are sections where the labelling is precise and unequivocal, and there are sections with no labels at all. Since the sections which are labelled are generally clearly relatable to the set charts and the sections which are unlabelled do not generally fit easily into the chart structures this suggests that these are areas where Davies is exercising his 'freedom to choose and make every moment work for you',[16] or it may be that this is the sort of section he means when he refers to 'a preparation for a transformation' or 'material got in[to] a state of readiness to be transformed'.[17]

---

[14]  Composer's pre-Prom talk on the Fourth Symphony, 10 September 1989.

[15]  Interview with Stephen Pruslin as n. 3 above.

[16]  *Ibid.*

[17]  Composer's pre-Prom talk on the Fourth Symphony, 10 September 1989 (although in fact these sections are directly comparable to what Roberts refers to as 'synoptic paraphrase' ['Techniques of Composition in the Music of Peter Maxwell Davies' (Ph.D., University of Birmingham, 1985), p. 73] – see also Peter Owens's article in this volume).

| Summary of set square choice - Symphony 4 movement 2 (Scherzo) | | |
|---|---|---|
| SCORE | | |
| Comment | INTRO | Ref. to 20-note transf. |
| Instruments | [2.] vc/cb | [8.] vc/cb |
| Set line1 | [2.] 1.2.6 | [8.] 7? |
| Set line 2 | | |
| Accomp. | D,F,Ab,C bass [timp] | [cont.] |
| SCORE | Fig18 | Fig19 |
| Comment | | [2 bars] 10 set anticipated? |
| Instruments | [2.] alto fl | |
| Set line1 | [2.] 1/2 abstracted, 3/4, 5/6 | 7/1Rep. | |
| Accomp. | | [timp] bass reprise |
| SCORE | [continues] | [continues] |
| Comment | [2 bars] | |
| Instruments | [full orchestra] | [str./wind] |
| Set line1 | | [3.] 1-4 related pairs = [7.] NT 1 - 4 |
| Set line 2 | [2.?] 1 - 7 derived | |
| SCORE | Fig20 | Fig 21    //Fig22 |
| Comment | Clearer [7.] transformation set | |
| Instruments | Flute [7.] Alto Fl [1.] | [3.] brass; [7.] str. // [ ] horns |
| Set line1 | [7.] 1 - 4, 4R?, 3 [O.T.] | [3. Varied]    //[1.M.S.]traced lines |
| Set line 2 | [1.] 1 - 7 / Reprise [1.] 1,2,1R | [7.] 2OT, 3NT ?  // [ ] |
| Accomp. | D;B;G#;F;D [vc] | [[timp C,D.F.Ab,G] |
| SCORE | Fig23 | Fig24 |
| Comment | [9.] prep. set for 10-note set | [9.] becomes 'cantus' |
| Instruments | [1.] str.: [8.] hn/wind: [9.] alt. fl.+ | [8. same]; [2.] trpts; [9.] bass cl. |
| Set line1 | [9.] 2 | [9.] 1 - 7 |
| Set line 2 | [8.] 1/2 (part) | (2 cont) - 12 [latterly in canon] |
| Set line 3 | [1.] 3 - 6 re-ordered/dyads | [2.] 1 - 5 |
| SCORE | Fig28 | Fig29 |
| Comment | Climax | [9.] set mainly retrograde |
| Instruments | [cont.] | line 2 cl/b.cl.: line 3 lower str. |
| Set line1 | [9.] 5 Reprise | [8a./8b.] 10R/20R |
| Set line 2 | 13 - 20 [6 lines climax] | [9.] 1,2R,3,4R,6R,7R |
| Set line 3 | [5],6.7 | [9.] 7 - 1 |
| SCORE | | Fig31    Meno mosso |
| Comment | [8.] overlaps end of [9.] | Coda; [4.] 9-note set leading to Adagio |
| Instruments | upper str then lower str | line 2 fls; line 3 hns/trpts; [4.] cor. ang. + |
| Set line1 | [8.] 15R    [8.] 11R | [7.] (1),2,3    // [4.] 1 |
| Set line 2 | [8 ] 5R    [8 ] 1R | [7 ] 1/ |
| Accomp. | | Db.BbGb.D (bsn/cb)>> CDFA (timp) |

Ex. 7.2: Fourth Symphony – second movement, summary thematic statement chart

At score number 23 the set structure again becomes clear – here the 20-note set transformation is stated complete following the instrumentation but not necessarily the rhythm or octave placing of the set chart [8.]. This set is used through to score number 29 but as shown in Ex. 7.2 the entry sequence is compressed to give density of texture and subsidiary climax. Simultaneously, a new set appears [9.] and this clearly has the function of leading to the 10-set [10.] of the final movement.

The movement is concluded from score number 29 with a complete restatement of the 10-note preparation set [9.] backwards from line 7→1 as a 'tenor' above which the opposite 1→7 is heard, although using mainly retrograde sets as shown on the chart. The strings approach score number 30 with partial references to set statements from [8.] and these continue from five bars after 30. The fourth and fifth bars after 30 are unlabelled and isolated in the sketches (i.e. they look as though they are part of the violins set statements but are not). Score letter 31 has an incomplete reference to the chart set [7.] over a harmonic bass which has become Db,Bb,Gb,G. The *meno mosso* is simply a reference back to the 9-set [4.]. The structural model for this movement is therefore clearly one of evolution with throw-backs and throw-forwards all controlled by the 20-note transformation set.

I have spent some time discussing the set statements for this movement because, when taken in conjunction with Davies's comments about the compositional processes, as he perceives them, this movement clearly demonstrates the logic of some of the compositional choices he makes. It also provides a useful comparison with the Fifth Symphony where the sets are designed in such a way as to be able to generate new ones, hence the transformation process which is suggested in this movement of the Fourth Symphony becomes even more 'organic' within the later work. The idea of 'developing' sets may be what lies partly behind Davies's recent statements about bringing the 'workings' to the surface.[18]

Despite their similarities in rhythmic configurations, the structure of the Fourth Symphony *scherzo* is quite different from that of the Second Symphony where subsections of the formal structure repeat seven times, albeit with internal development.[19] The number 28 may be symbolic for the composer – in the sketches for the Fourth Symphony one finds stuck on the verso of folio 14 a diagrammatic formulation which represents the eagle's wings which Davies identifies as a source of inspiration for the piece. This numerical structure is the basis of the slow movement in the symphony. I have reproduced the diagram below – it will be seen that the central number is 28 and Davies annotates this number as 'the dimensions of the temple'.[20]

---

[18]   *Ibid.*
[19]   McGregor, April 1996, *op. cit.*
[20]   Sketches for the Fourth Symphony on page 14v.

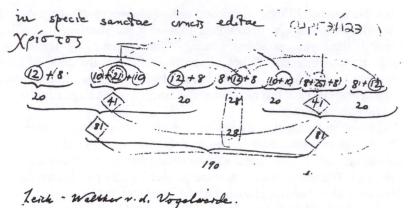

[John MacQueen, *Numerology*, Edinburgh University Press 1985 pp. 66-7]

Ex. 7.3: Numerical structure diagram for Fourth Symphony third movement

*Source*: John MacQueen, *Numerology* (Edinburgh University Press, 1985) pp. 66–7

A different approach to *scherzo* is found in the Sixth Symphony. As a three-movement work the most obvious omission would be the *scherzo* – however the composer's programme note clearly indicates otherwise since 'the first movement proper is a *scherzo* masquerading as a *sonata-allegro*'.[21] Davies here is deliberately playing around with the listener's conception of sonata form. The dual function of the first movement is interesting since it gives indication that the origins of the formal shape lie in an area of cross-fertilization between the influences of Sibelius and Mahler. The first draft score for this movement is also noteworthy from an analytical perspective since it is one of the most clearly annotated first scores in the whole collection of sketches. This may again be a result of bringing the working to the surface.

To understand this piece and the significance of the first movement in the whole structure it is important to know more about the source material than the composer has disclosed in his programme note.

The aboriginal song that underpins the occasional piece *Time and the Raven* provides one of the source sets for the work. Davies refers to the original as 'Améwara Inatáija Verses'. The second source set is derived from a melody 'Die Gesang der gelben Blume' by Hans Henne Jahnn from *Perrudja*, a book owned by the composer (see p. 4 in Ex. 7.4 below). These two sources are complementary in the sense that they both describe descending scales. From the discussion that follows the table it will be obvious that the choice and manipulation of these sets contributes to the modality of the work in an important way.

---

<sup></sup>21     Composer's programme note for his Sixth Symphony.

The third source set for the work is, as usual, plainsong – in this case *Immolabit hedum multitudo* from *Liber Usualis*, page 926. There is, unusually, a fourth set – this is derived from an early piano work *Parade* written in 1949 and is therefore a clear autobiographical reference on the composer's part. Davies rediscovered this early work in the 1980s (probably while the sketch material was being collected together). In conversation he remarked that the piece shows many of the things he now does 'already there', and he incorporated a reference to it in Symphony No. 3.

Davies has, to this date, neither written nor spoken about this source material for the Sixth Symphony. However, as suggested earlier it is a particular useful work to consider in detail, not just because of the lack of comment by the composer on the work's origins (other than the obvious link with *Time and the Raven*), but because the set charts are very full and worked out (although everything is relative – the charts for *Taverner*, for example, are extensive). In addition, the labelling of the musical argument is remarkably consistent and regular throughout the whole of first draft. Having a precise labelling by the composer allows for consideration of the actual reasoning behind set choices rather than the more speculative approach that one has to adopt for many works of the 1980s and 1990s.

The complete set of precompositional workings is as follows:

| Page | (label) | Content |
|---|---|---|
| 1 | α1 | Phrases 1,2,3 of **Améwara** with derived note row (significant note repetition [e.g. over a bar] is retained) |
| 2 | β2 | Phrases 4,5,6 as above |
| 3 | γ3 | Phrases 7,8,9 as above |
| 4 | α4 | Original and subsequent derivations of 10-note row for **Die Gesang** |
| 5 | β5 | Plainsong – **Immolabit hedum multitudo** L.U. p 926, 9-note set [with derivation shown] |
| 6 | | Pages 1–3 derived **Améwara** sets only shown rewritten |
| 7 | | As page 6 but all statements one semitone lower |
| 8 | (i)I | Sieved set transposition chart – 6-note [last note an octave below first – based on page 6 **Améwara**] |
| | II | 8-note transposition chart based on page 6 **Améwara** [no. 2] |
| 9 | (i)III | Transposition chart – 9-note – origin obscure [possibly inflected from page 6 **Améwara** row 5] |
| 10 | | **Améwara** → **Gesang** set transformation OT 1-5 and NT 1-5 [i.e. original **Améwara** set at T3 → **Gesang** T0] |
| 10 | | [verso] possible set abstraction for *Job* [ex Venus square] |
| 11 | | **Gesang** 10-note set [URANUS] transposition set square and derived magic square |
| 12 | | **Gesang** → **Immolabit** OT/NT transformation sets |
| 13 | | **Immolabit** 9-note set [LUNA – the Moon] and magic square |
| 13bis | | First five notes of each line of p. 13 magic square reading downwards and converted into chords |

| 13ter | | First five notes of each line of p. 14 magic square reading downwards and converted into chords |
| 14 | | **Immolabit** inversion set [LUNA] and magic square |
| 15 | | **Immolabit** → **Parade** transformation sets OT/NT [9-note→12-note] |
| 15 | α | [also labelled xy] [page contains one bar 'line 27' of first draft score] **Gesang** [dual lines] → **Immolabit** NT transformation set |
| 15 | α | [verso] **Immolabit** magic square expressed as dyads |
| 16 | | **Parade** set [MERCURY – 8-note] and magic square |
| 17 | | **Parade** → **Gesang** [labelled 'wieder' by PMD] OT/NT 8-note →7-note [the **Gesang** set is the alternative 7-note ascending form – cf. page 18] |
| 18 | | **Gesang** 7-note set ['wieder'] [VENUS] version – from original 10-note form on page α4 [inverted] |
| 18 | [verso] | pivots' from **Parade** set [page 16] and detail from **Améwara** set [i.e. scales] |
| [19] | [not numbered by PMD] | |
| | | Set from page 11 reading diagonal lines starting in top left corner [this appears to have a connection with *Strathclyde Concerto 10*] |
| [20] | [not numbered by PMD] | |
| | | Set from page 11 reading diagonal lines starting in top right corner |

[Note: discussion with composer suggests that some of the charts for the Fifth Symphony were used again in the Sixth and in *The Doctor of Myddfai* – although the exact nature of the relationship is as yet unexplored.]

Ex. 7.4: Precompositional chart material for the Sixth Symphony (complete)

It seemed useful to present the above summary, not least of all because the precompositional charts do not always survive the transfer to the British Library collection (for example the Violin Concerto) and at the time of writing these have yet to be deposited, but also, it appears that this does represent a full collection of precompositional workings for the symphony (and can be compared with the list for Fourth Symphony above). In the discussion which follows set charts will not necessarily be given complete as that would take up a disproportionate amount of space, but sufficient will be given to allow reconstruction of the original. This is obviously much more difficult with transformation sets and therefore, when quoted, these are given complete.

The label '*scherzo* masquerading as *sonata-allegro*' derives in part from the first movement placing, but the lack of rhythmic *ostinato* features which usually characterize many of Davies's symphonic *scherzo*s promotes the initial perception of 'normal' *sonata-allegro* by the listener. Davies takes great delight in playing with our preconceptions of classical forms – so, in the second

| | | Precompositional chart page number |
|---|---|---|
| Score letter | Introduction to figure A | 1 |
| Main line [hauptstimme] | Amewara sets rr[1i], 2[ii] | 6,7 |
| Subsidiary line [nebenstimme] | Gesang Uranus set at T4??? | 11 |
| Score letter | Fig A - Fig E | |
| Main line [hauptstimme] | Amewara sets rr3(i), 4(ii), 5(i), 6(ii) etc to9(i) | 6,7 |
| Subsidiary line [nebenstimme] | Transformation Amewara to Gesang set lines rr1+2, 2+3, 3+4,4+5 | 10 |
| Score letter | Fig E - Fig I | |
| Main line [hauptstimme] | Gesang square Uranus [10] rr 1 - 5, 6 reordered, 7 chords [Fig G], 8-10 | 11 |
| Subsidiary line [nebenstimme] | Gesang set rr 1R, 2R, 3, 1 Rpr, 2P+R, 4, 5R, 5 Rpr, 7 chds, 7 Rpr, 8, 9, 10 chds | 11 |
| Score letter | Fig I - Fig K | |
| Main line [hauptstimme] | Amewara set rr 8R, 7, 6[P/R?], Repr 8, 7R, 5, 2R | 8 |
| Subsidiary line [nebenstimme] | Amewara II(i) r7 / II(i) r10 | 10 |
| Score letter | [continues] | |
| Main line [hauptstimme] | Gesang square rr10, 1, 8 (?=10), 7, 2, 7, 6, 5 | 11 |
| Subsidiary line [nebenstimme] | Gesang set rr1R + 1 / 2R / | 11 |
| Score letter | Fig K - Fig L | |
| Main line [hauptstimme] | Amewara set III(ii) rr1 - 9 | 9 |
| Subsidiary line [nebenstimme] | Gesang set r3 | 11 |
| Additional line | Amewara set III(ii) r3R | 9 |
| Score letter | Fig L - N | |
| Main line [hauptstimme] | Amewara to Gesang Transformation rr4R / 5 Reprise (+R) / [synoptic?] | 10 |
| Subsidiary line [nebenstimme] | Amewara to Gesang Transformation OT rr1 -5 / 5R / [synoptic?] | 10 |
| Score letter | Fig N - Fig O | |
| Main line [hauptstimme] | Gesang to Immolabit Transf. NT rr1-3, 4 in basso | 15 α |
| Subsidiary line [nebenstimme] | Amewara set II(i) rr4+5R, 3, 1/1R | 8 |
| Additional line | Immolabit set r 8 / Reprise | 13 |
| Score letter | Fig O - Fig P | |
| Main line [hauptstimme] | [Ges - Immol] 4 - 9 // [Ges - Immol] 1+2, 3+4 | 15α |
| Subsidiary line [nebenstimme] | Amewara II(i) set 1R / square r1 | 8 |
| Additional line | Immolabit set r1R | 13 |
| Score letter | Fig P - Fig R | |
| Main line [hauptstimme] | Gesang to Immolabit rr5+6, 7+8, 9+1 / [nebens.] Immol. square rr1-5 | 15α |
| Subsidiary line [nebenstimme] | [quasi canon] Immolabit [Luna] set [haupst.] rr1-3, 4R, 5, 6R, 7, 8R, 9 | 13 |
| Additional line | Gesang [Uranus] set rr1 - 5 | 11 |
| | [new additional line]　　　　　Gesang square r10 | 11 |
| Score letter | [poco adagio] | |
| Main line [hauptstimme] | Immolabit set inversion rr1, 2?R | 14 |
| Additional line | Reprise Gesang R / [square ] r1 | 11 |
| Additional line 2 | [continues] | |
| Score letter | Fig R - Fig S | |
| Main line [hauptstimme] | Gesang to Immolabit transformation set rr 1-9 NT | 15α |
| Subsidiary line [nebenstimme] | Immolabit square [R] / synoptic? | 13 |
| Additional line | Gesang set r1/square r4 | 11 |
| Score letter | [continues] | |
| Main line [hauptstimme] | Immolabit set r1/square r5 - set r2 | 15α |
| Subsidiary line [nebenstimme] | Gesang to Immolabit dyadic transf. [not labelled] / Immol set r1/square r5 | 13 |
| Additional line | Synoptic accompaniment? | 12/13 |
| Additional line 2 | Immolabit Inv 1 / square 5 | 14 |

Ex. 7.5: *Sixth Symphony* – first movement summary – set deployment chart

movement 'a *sonata-allegro* disguised as a *scherzo*'[22] one finds the harmonic/ rhythmic figurations absent from the first movement. The chart shows the main thrust of the musical argument for the whole of the first movement (Ex. 7.5).

The three main ideas (that is, excluding *Parade*) are all present in this movement. It is not so easy to sectionalize the movement effectively (but see Ex. 7.7) because although some thematic material may be more prominent at one point, that same material has in some cases already been foreshadowed in the musical argument and often might be accompanied by its own transformation.

This is undoubtedly the structural idea to which Davies refers when he speaks of 'deeper motions, life-forms, slowly breathing away below and determining the active surface'.[23]

The stable surface level created by the statements of the Améwara theme (Ex. 7.4, pp. 6, 7) is undermined by the immediate process of transformation which takes place underneath as the Améwara set is transformed (Ex. 7.6) into the Gesang set (Ex. 7.4, p. 10). This juxtaposition is deliberately further blurred, but also made 'harmonic', by the deployment of two consecutive set lines simultaneously.

| | | Amewara | | | | | | | | | |
|---|---|---|---|---|---|---|---|---|---|---|---|
| | 1 | C | Bb | G | G | F | Eb | C | C | Bb | G |
| | 2 | C | Bb | Ab | G | F# | E | Db | Db | C | Bb |
| OT | 3 | C | B | Ab | Ab | F# | E | D | Eb | D | Db |
| | 4 | C | Bb | A | Ab | G | F | Eb | D | E | F |
| | 5 | C | B | Bb | Ab | G | F# | E | Eb | F | A |
| | 1 | C | Bb | G | G | F | Eb | C | C | Bb | G |
| | 2 | A | G | F | E | D# | C# | A# | A# | A | G |
| NT | 3 | F# | F | D | D | C | Bb | Ab | A | Ab | G |
| | 4 | Eb | Db | C | B | Bb | Ab | Gb | F | G | Ab |
| | 5 | C | B | Bb | Ab | G | F# | E | Eb | F | A |
| | Gelben Blume | | [set label - sic] | | | | | | | |

Ex. 7.6: Sixth Symphony first movement – set chart for transformation of **Améwara** set to **Gesang** set – as Ex. 7.4, p. 10

---

22   *Ibid.*
23   *Ibid.*

The passage at score letter E is a straightforward exposition (quasi-*sonata-allegro?*). No change of speed or instrumentation is indicated on the score, nor is there any suggestion that the rhythmic material is other than intuitive. It is not clear why the Améwara set is presented as it is (from letter I to letter J), with a mix of primes, retrogrades and reprise, and followed by the Gesang magic square which utilizes variant directional readings of set lines, unless Davies imagines this to be a sort of 'double' on the opening section (the 'double' being his preferred descriptor for processes he views more as variation than development). If this interpretation is correct then the passage from figure K to figure M is a second 'double', containing elements of partial repetition (never exact – Davies prefers to use the term 'reprise' for this feature). This latter passage acts as a bridge to a new feature (quasi-second subject?) at letter N.

At this point, as can be seen from Ex. 7.5, the thematic bass sets are the dyadic transformations of the Gesang → Immolabit sets, overlaid by a transposition (the eighth line) of the set square (Ex. 7.4, p. 13) which emphasises the A♭ (a semitone slip from the original A at the beginning of the movement) start note also found in the accompanying Améwara set. This leads to a 'double' just before letter P which features dual line statements, a parallel to the musical argument at letter A but here using different sets. This parallel with the opening of the movement continues since the set square and magic square linear statements of Immolabit following letter P are comparable to the layout of the Gesang set from letter E.

The final section, marked '*poco adagio*', relates particularly to the Immolabit set but typically the references are made less explicit by virtue of the partial statements which are employed. From letter R onwards the only constant is a third deployment of the Gesang→Immolabit transformation, a reprise of its first statement at letter N.

The *scherzo* elements of this movement are perhaps not as clear as the *sonata-allegro* elements – particularly since later reprised sections do not return to the opening Améwara material. However, if the Gesang set is perceived as principal theme, rather than Améwara, the *scherzo* connections become clearer. If (t) indicates the controlling presence of a transformation set, the structural plan of the movement is as follows, with more 'traditional' structural descriptor below:

$$M + M(t)G; \ G; \ M; \ G; \ M; \ M(t)G; \ G(t)I[1]; \ G(t)I[2]; \ [I]; \ G(t)I \ (3)$$
$$A; B; \ A1; B; A1; \quad A; \quad B/C1; \quad B/C2;[D]; \quad B/C3$$

(M= Améwara, G = Gesang, I = Immolabit)

Ex. 7.7: Sixth Symphony – first movement basic structure

The above consideration of the Sixth Symphony first movement's formal structure leads usefully into consideration of the Fifth Symphony completed in 1994. Unusually, in the sketches for this work there is a detailed formal plan for the symphony (unusual not in the sense that Davies never plans this out on paper, but rather that it is rare to find such a plan in the sketches – this may have something to do with the 'speed at which it was written').[24]

The approach to this symphony is comparable to the sectional method adopted in a variety of works and which I have noted in relation to the *scherzo* of the Second Symphony[25] in that the whole symphony is made up of alternating *adagio* and *scherzo* movements interrelated not only in the long-term exposition of the *scherzo* or *adagio* material but also in the subsection by subsection progression of alternating *scherzo* and *adagio* material (with, in addition, three interruptions, or *lacunae*). Julian Beecroft, writing in *Tempo* 191,[26] identifies the thirty-four subsections for this work, but, Ex. 7.9 based on the composer's formal plan, suggests that there are fewer than this. On one level the symphony is like a series of large interlocking ternary forms. The numbering of the pages in the sketch material does suggest that a least some elements of the first sketches were done consecutively rather than necessarily in chronological sequence. For example in the summary chart below (Ex. 7.9) *adagio* 1 at letter B can be directly related to *adagio* 2 at letter W (that is, pages 1A/1B to 2A/2B).

The chart in Ex. 7.8 illustrates, without going into great detail, the types of set used. The letters 'a' and 'b' (composer's labels) refer to the original Mercury set transposition square and magic square from which the smaller charts are derived.

The basic premise of the set generation is that given a z-note transposition square from which a z-note magic square is derived, then the z-note magic square minus final note = a y-note transposition square from which a y-note magic square is derived and so on. Thus, for example, given an 8-note set transposition square, from which is derived the magic square of 8 notes, the resultant 8-note magic square minus final note = the 7-note set transposition square from which a 7-note magic square is derived, and so on until a 3-note square is achieved. When first received from the composer, the precompositional material for this symphony apparently contained no set chart material at all. However, some of the sets bundled with the Sixth Symphony, but not yet identified as having been used in it, turned out to be those required for the Fifth Symphony – lacking, however, the 7- and 8-note charts. Fortunately these were straightforward to reconstruct and will probably turn up subsequently associated with another work, possibly *The Doctor of Myddfai*.

---

[24]   Composer's pre-concert talk on his Sixth Symphony, 22 June 1996, in the Phoenix Cinema, Kirkwall, Orkney.

[25]   McGregor, April 1996, *op. cit.*

[26]   Beecroft, 'Maxwell Davies's Fifth Symphony', *Tempo* 191 (January 1995), pp. 2–5.

| 'a' | Bb | B | C# | Eb | D | D | C# | A | | 'a' | A | Bb | C | D | Eb | Db | B | Bb |
|---|---|---|---|---|---|---|---|---|---|---|---|---|---|---|---|---|---|---|
| | B/Db | G | D | E | F | C# | B | C | | | Bb | B | C# | Eb | E | D | C | B |
| | E/Db | E/D | E/D | F# | D | Eb | Db | G | | | C | Db | Eb | F | Gb | D/E | D | C# |
| | Eb | E/D | F# | G# | D | G | F | G | | | D | Eb | F | G | G# | F# | E | Eb |
| | E | Eb | F | A | Ab | F# | E | Eb | | | Eb | D/E | F# | Ab | A·· | G·· | E· | E |
| | C | Eb | F | F | F# | E | E | C# | | | Db | D/E | E | F# | G | F | Eb | D |
| | Bb | Db | Eb | Eb | E | E | C | B | | | B/Db | C | D/E | E | F | Eb | Db | C |
| | B | Bb | C | E | Eb | Db | B | Bb | | | Bb | B | C# | Eb | E | D | C# | B |
| 'b' | G | F | E | D | Eb | Eb | E | G# | | 'b' | G# | F# | F | Eb | D | E | F | G |
| | F | Eb | D | C | B | Eb | E | E | | | F# | E | Eb | Db | C | D | Eb | F |
| | E | D | C# | B | D# | D | Eb | C# | | | F | Eb | D | C | B | C# | D | E |
| | D | C | B | A | Eb | Bb | B | Bb | | | Eb | C# | C# | Bb | A | B | C | D |
| | C# | C# | C/C# | Ab | Bb/A | B | C | D | | | D | C | B | A/Bb | Ab | Bb | B | C# |
| | F | C# | C | C | B | C# | D | E | | | E | D | C# | B | Bb | C | C# | Eb |
| | F# | D | Db | Db | C | D | D# | B | | | F | Eb | D | C | B | Db | D | E |
| | F# | F# | F | C# | D | E | E | G | | | G | F | E | D | C# | Eb | E | F# |

The 'a' and 'b' are as in the composer's sketches - apparent variants are shown

Ex. 7.8: Fifth Symphony – Mercury (8-note) set charts (reconstructed)

The detail of the formal structure and the main set layout for the work is summarized in Ex. 7.9.

A greater understanding of Davies's thinking behind this symphony can be gleaned from an analysis of the second *adagio* (dual statement) section of the work which runs from letter W to A2.

In the sketches this section is laid out on seven lines of condensed score (recalling the procedure adopted in the Second Symphony *scherzo*). Each of the lines articulates 28 quavers (this suggests the 28 which was associated with the eagle's wings in the Fourth Symphony as discussed earlier and may perhaps represent a conscious link with the earlier symphony – what Davies sometimes alludes to as 'unfinished business'). The section is labelled 'Venus satz' in the sketch – a parallel with the first *adagio* which had the Mercury set as its basis. The top right-hand corner of the first page has a German motto *'du kannst nur gar tun C2 und wieder war tun'* which seems to have been added after the music had been written since it encloses the two bars of melodic line (letter W + 5/6) which in the sketch is in mid-treble clef register with no instrumentation indicated (in the full score violins, violas and cellos have the line in triple octaves).

The section divides into three sub-units in the sketches as a ternary structure, the first three lines (3 x 28) are numbered consecutively 33 to 35, the middle section (or 'middle eight' in Davies's terminology) numbered 36a, 36b and the returning 'A' section (labelled 'Reprise') numbered 37a, 37b. The 'tenor' voice on the sketch (trombone in the full score but not indicated as such on the sketch) is a rhythmic *cantus* based on the magic square-related number permutation common to all Davies's serial-based working (that is, 1,5,2,6,3,7,4; 5,2,6,3,7,4,1; etc.). The associated pitch set states the 'a' version of the Venus set. Underneath the *cantus* is a bass line that utilizes the 'b' version of the Venus set whose

| Score Figure | PMD page Number | Content summary | Description of material |
|---|---|---|---|
| | 1 | *Domine/Haec Dies* | *Adagio* introduction |
| B | 1A | Mercury [8 square] canon *Haec Dies* | *Adagio* - 1st dual statement |
| | 1B | (b) | |
| | Prelim 2 | | |
| J | [1] | Jupiter b [4]square | 1st *Scherzo*     *Allegro Moderato* |
| | | *Haec Dies* 'a' square [sketch label] | |
| L | 2a/2b | Jupiter sets   p2[...] | Trio [Middle Eight] |
| N | 3a ('AT') | | Reprise |
| P | 4 | | Codetta |
| | [4-5] | 'Einschub' [PMD label] | Interrupted Squares on brass -*Adagio* - 1st 'lacuna' |
| R | 5 | *Adagio* | Dual Transformation |
| | | [no sketch notes here] | *Allegro Moderato* Transition |
| S | 6 | | Reprise of 1st *Scherzo* |
| T | 7 | (begins T2 of letter S) | Quicker - itself a transition to |
| V | 'AT' | | [c.f. *Chat Moss* material] |
| W | 2A/2B | 'Venus [7] movement' a and b squares | *Adagio* 2nd dual statement (in 3 parts ) |
| A2 | bis | Venus square | *Lento molto* 2nd lacuna |
| | V(enus) α | End of Transition — *Scherzo* | *Allegro* - 2nd *Scherzo Rondino* |
| D2 | | (sol set [6] = square Venus [7]) | |
| E2-G2 | β | Mars set to Saturn [5 set/square to 3 set/square] | |
| G2-H2 | γ | Sol set/square [6 set] [NB sun = 'sol'] | |
| I2 | | 'Fibonacci' | *Lentissimo* - 3rd lacuna |
| I2 + 4 | 1 | [*Allegro*] | *Allegro*, shadow of 2nd *Scherzo* |
| J2 | 2 | Sun set b | |
| K2 | 1 | Mercury [8] square a and b | 3rd *scherzo* with horns overriding |
| L2 | 2 | | |
| | 3 | | |
| N2 | Einschub | 'Zwischen' [PMD label] | *Adagio* - 3rd dual statement slow |
| O2 | 1 | Venus square 'a lot only' | *Allegro* 3rd *scherzo* reprise (shadow) |
| P2 + 4 | 2 | | |
| Q2 | | [c.f. I2/N2] | Adagio - 4th dual statement, slow quasi chorale |
| R2 | [1] | [c.f. H2 + 4] | *Allegro* 4th *Scherzo* |
| S2 | [2] | [Mars square [5]to Sol Square [6] c.f. E2] | [ Sets Sol = Square Venus c.f. 2nd *scherzo* A2 - D2 |
| T2 | 1 | | *Adagio*, *Lento*, *Adagio* - 5th dual statement |
| V2-X2 | 2 | [9 square] | - slow dissolution |

Ex. 7.9: Fifth Symphony – structural summary for the whole work

rhythmic articulation is also controlled. These two parts together articulate the 28 durations of each subsection as for example in Ex. 7.10 where they can be seen as the second and fifth lines.

Above this foundation two distinctive instrumental groups oppose each other. The four horns in two parts have a dyadic statement of a derived version of the Venus set (labelled $\flat 2 \propto$ = Ve(nus) $\alpha$ ) as seen in the third and sixth lines of Ex. 7.10. In the first sketch draft the more complex rhythmic elaboration is absent and was evidently added later. The undecorated rhythms are quite repetitive but they do not appear to have been serially determined.

Against this is placed the string texture which can be seen to consist of decorated versions of the retrograde set statements in descending order (7R, 6R, etc.) although the durational length of the set statements varies considerably (in Ex. 7.10 these are the first and fourth lines).

Ex. 7.10: Fifth Symphony – second *adagio*, score letter [W] – [X+4] [sketches transcription]

The middle section from letter Y is scored for wind only (and unusually in the printed score a 'piano' reduction is given of this section). In the first draft score instrumentation is indicated, whereas in the first section it was not, and the controlling durational pattern is in both lower parts in *cancrizans* movement for each statement. The *ostinato* figuration of the full score is simply suggested by unstemmed notes in the 'tenor' area of the draft score (Ex. 7.11).

Ex. 7.11: Fifth Symphony – second *adagio* (full score letter Y, first six bars only) (sketches transcription)

The reprise section appears to cross refer to the string parts of the first section without quoting them directly – specifically there are similar rhythmic gestures and the pitch elements are used but with some re-orderings and elaborations. The lines may be compared in part in Ex. 7.12.

This appears to be an example where the composer chooses to abandon the set charts to make a freer variation on the original, an interpretation supported by the fact that the sketches do not contain any set chart references for the upper part, although remaining for the lower parts.

(a)

(b)

Ex. 7.12: Fifth Symphony – comparison between violin parts letters [W] (Ex. 7.12a) to [Z] (Ex. 7.12b) (sketches transcription)

Ex. 7.12a

Ex. 7.12b

The fairly straightforward structural and thematic working which will have been observed to characterize these later symphonies can be contrasted with an example from Symphony No. 3.

The final movement of the Third Symphony is a large-scale Mahlerian structure – in fact Davies refers specifically to the ninth in his programme note (although it is Mahler by way of Sibelius's Seventh Symphony as a sketch reference to the trills at score letter O makes clear). A detailed analysis of this expansive movement would not be appropriate here. However, in order to understand the relationships which are explored in this movement it is necessary to expand on Nicholas Jones's helpful article in *Tempo* 204. Jones gives the reader a useful insight into the interpretation and structuring of diverse thematic elements. However, it is important to note that the composer's numbering sequence does not always necessarily indicate the order in which the charts should be read. Thus the set chart (Ex. 7.13) on sketch page 15r (d2 sketch 1 – composer's label and page number) must precede the working out of the set matrix on page 14r (d2). In the example below only the first six lines of the transformation chart are given (that is, following the sketches, where page 15r presents the first six lines, and the concluding six are on page 16r).

This chart explains the otherwise apparently arbitrary transformation sequence on the page labelled 14r (d2), that is, successive entries of the

| D | G | A | F | E | C | B | A# | F# | G# | C# | D# |
|----|----|---|----|----|----|----|----|----|----|----|----|
| Eb | G | A | F | E | C | B | A# | F# | G# | C | D# |
| F | G | A | E | E | Db | Bb | Bb | G | Ab | B | Eb |
| Gb | G | A | E | Eb | Db | Bb | Bb | G | Ab | Bb | Eb |
| G | Ab | A | E | Eb | D | A | Bb | Ab | A | Bb | Eb |
| Ab | Ab | A | Eb | Eb | D | A | A | Ab | A | A | Eb |

Ex. 7.13: Third Symphony – set chart from precompositional working page 15r
(d2 sketch 1 –composer's label)

transformation set have been transposed to begin on successive notes of the 12-note pitch series, or rather, of two combinatorial hexachords, each of which is treated as an independent unit. These are labelled α and β not unlike *Image, Reflection, Shadow* discussed in my article 'Compositional processes in some works of the 1980s'.

In a similar way page 18v needs to be understood as having been worked before page 10r, which shows the regular stepwise transformations (for the most part) which lead to the pitch sequence C,D♭,E,A♭,G,B – the prime of a transposition square of the sun (Sol) which gives rise to a 6 x 6 magic square labelled 'Metin square' in the composer's script. Metin is a direct reference to Davies's partner at the time and is one of a number of hidden autobiographical references to be found in the symphonies (cf. *Parade* in the Sixth Symphony) which have recently found an overt expression in the series of occasional pieces based round localities associated with the composer's youth.

It will be clear then that the chart material relationships in this symphony are highly complex and would merit a more extended study in their own right. It would not be inappropriate to speculate that Mahler's tragic autobiographical statement in the last movement of the Ninth Symphony provided the 'model' for Davies's own emotional reactions, *inter alia*, to his father's decline.

The thematic basis of the initial sections of the final movement, following some initial introductory material, arise from the transformation set (prime to inversion) based on the combinatorial hexachords D,G,A,F,E,C/B,A♯,F♯,G♯,C♯,D♯, split, from score letter B, into main thematic line on cellos and accompaniment on upper strings (*vide* sketches pages 15r and 17r). This is repeated in a reworked version for lower brass with more elaborate writing for trumpets and wind above. In this 'double' of the previous section rows 1→6 play simultaneously with rows 12→7 (score letter E).

From letter F a new 7-note (Venus) set square and magic square appears (based on page 19r of the sketches). It can be considered as a partial trope from C,D♭,E,A♭,G,B (now as a 7-note set C,D♭,E,C,A♭,G,B):

$$C,D♭,E,C,A♭,G,B \rightarrow C,E,A♭,B,[F,D♭,E] \rightarrow\ +\ T6 \rightarrow G♭,B♭,D,F, [B,G,B♭]$$

but G♭,B♭,D,F,B,G,B♭ is also a transposed version of the second hexachord of the original chart on page 10r – D♯,G,B,D,E,G at T3 with the addition a new 5th note. These two set forms are superimposed over each other (Ex. 7.14).

At score letter F the main thrust of the thematic material is carried by lower string statements of the set square and upper string statements of the magic square derived from the above. This leads directly into the next section which combines the compositional chart of 17v (6-note Sun set *prime to inversion/inversion to prime* set pairing) in the lower strings and wind with the 'new' 7-note Venus set (sketch page 19r – see Ex. 7.14) in wind (set square) and brass

| 1a | Gb | Bb | D  | F  | B  | G  | Bb |
| 1b | C  | Db | E  | C  | Ab | G  | B  |
| 2a | Bb | D  | Gb | A  | Eb | B  | D  |
| 2b | Db | D  | F  | Db | A  | Ab | C  |
| 3a | D  | Gb | Bb | Db | G  | Eb | Gb |
| 3b | E  | F  | Ab | E  | C  | B  | Eb |
| 4a | F  | A  | Db | E  | Bb | Gb | A  |
| 4b | C  | Db | E  | C  | Ab | G  | B  |
| 5a | B  | Eb | G  | Bb | E  | C  | Eb |
| 5b | Ab | A  | C  | Ab | E  | Eb | G  |
| 6a | G  | B  | Eb | Gb | C  | Ab | B  |
| 6b | G  | Ab | B  | G  | Eb | D  | Gb |
| 7a | Bb | D  | Gb | A  | Eb | B  | D  |
| 7b | B  | C  | Eb | B  | G  | Gb | Bb |

Ex. 7.14: Third Symphony – set charts page 19r – a 7-note set chart pairing [Note: the numbering is editorial]

(magic square reading as verticals). This in its turn leads to the final part of the opening discourse of the movement (score letter L–P) which will be examined in more detail. Ex. 7.15 below shows the thematic lines of this section.

Ex. 7.15: Third Symphony – fourth movement score letters L to M (main thematic lines only)

The viola line presents successive magic square lines with notes omitted, alternately prime and retrograde, a variation, or double, of the first violin line at score letter F, while the tuba presents a linear version of the dual set square (Ex. 7.14) with notes taken from both the [a] and [b] lines in alternate sequence. This culminates at score letters N to P with a 'reprise' in the viola while the tuba completes its set statements, the upper strings forming a harmonic upper layer which Davies relates directly on the sketch score to Sibelius's Seventh Symphony.

Comparison of this extract with those from later symphonies shows that while there is no essential difference in Davies's approach to the primacy of thematic line, nor to his utilization of two parts as effectively Hauptstimme and Nebenstimme carrying the main thematic argument, the derivation of the thematic lines in the symphonies before the Fourth is in fact more obscure and less direct (as, for example, when comparing 'transitions' in the last three symphonies with a comparable passage at figure 16, transition section, in the first movement of the First Symphony, where three set statements are subdivided and interposed within each other). It would require a rather more thoroughgoing analysis than that possible here to demonstrate the implications of this in detail. Clearly, the orchestral treatment of the later symphonies owes much to the opportunities Davies has had to develop his ideas by working closely with the Scottish Chamber Orchestra on the Strathclyde Concertos and, significantly, on the Fourth Symphony itself.

In his First Symphony Davies described 'the transformation from *Lento* to *Scherzo* in the second movement'[27] and noted its affinities with the first movement of Sibelius's Fifth Symphony (just one of a number of places where this symphony lies at the back of Davies's thoughts), and clearly blurring of progression from one area of musical activity to another has been, and continues to be, a vital aspect of his compositional dialectic. But, this process sets up its own tensions, as witness the apparently contradictory statements he has made about the Sixth Symphony: on the one hand in his pre-concert talk he speaks of 'getting rid of even the "ghost" of classical symphonic or sonata form', yet at the same time in his programme note for the CD he still refers to '*scherzo*' and '*sonata-allegro*'. At the Orkney premiere of the Sixth Symphony Davies said of 'classical' formal structures (though specifically of sonata form at that point) that no doubt someone would find them – and perhaps when looking at the first movement I should have avoided attempting to assign structural letter names to material in which transformation processes are in operation.

Nonetheless, the fact that the 'ghosts' of the past continue to haunt Davies's music of the present (whether it be in the formal structures or in the spiritual models from whom he draws inspiration) will not detract from what Stephen

---

27    Composer's programme note for the First Symphony.

Pruslin has referred to as Davies's constant reinvention of the symphony.[28] This is clearly the path he has to tread in order to justify for himself the undertaking of what some would say is a pointless exercise. Much remains to be written about Davies's harmonic vocabulary and its continuing development. Without taking the symphonies as complete entities any wide-ranging discussion of their totality is necessarily incomplete. With his symphonic cycle now nearing completion there comes an ever more pressing need for a large-scale study of these works if they truly represent 'one of the most important symphonic sequences of its time'.[29]

This article has attempted to gain some insights into Davies's compositional process in a very small area of a very large canvas. However the composer's recently expressed view that 'now the relationships are right the detail is less significant except that it articulates the whole'[30] might, I hope, be relevant also to this short study.

---

[28] Pruslin article 1996 for webpage <http://www.maxopus.com>.
[29] Beecroft, *op. cit.*
[30] As n. 24 above.

# 8

# 'A dance of the deadly sins': *The Beltane Fire* and the rites of modernism

*Arnold Whittall*

When Peter Maxwell Davies paid tribute to the 80-year-old Michael Tippett as 'an elemental force, a prime mover', whose then-recent work had 'a transcendent and visionary quality which is a continuing example ... to all who care about the possibility of music today expressing man's highest aspirations',[1] he was implicitly endorsing an understanding of the 'transcendent and visionary' which can be regarded as quintessentially modernist. In those works of Tippett's which Davies might have had in mind – the Third Symphony, *The Ice Break* – there is no possibility of permanently establishing a serenely transcendent state of spiritual enlightenment that floats above the strivings and confusions of things earthly. Rather, there is an acknowledgement that, within the contemporary musical mainstream, spiritual aspirations to the sublime and the serene cannot be separated from the social stresses and tensions of striving itself. Other kinds of musical expression – the ecstatic mysticism of John Tavener's *The Protecting Veil*, the ferociously active exuberance of Brian Ferneyhough's *Études transcendantales* – might manage to escape the aura of the mundane more determinedly and decisively. But Davies, like Tippett, remains too much the humanist sceptic to be able (or willing) to purge his music of tension between the worldly and the visionary. For him, 'expressing man's highest aspirations' always involves the likelihood that such aspirations will be challenged and confronted by forces determined to undermine them.

Peter Maxwell Davies is not given to portentous pronouncements on the nature of modernism, nor any other aesthetic or cultural principle. Nevertheless, his comments on his compositional practice occasionally provide vivid glimpses of how such a commitment to modernism might be technically defined. With reference to both *Saint Thomas Wake* (1969) and the *Strathclyde Concerto No. 5* (1991), Davies has used the image of the strongly contrasted musical styles to

---

[1]    'Foreword' to Lewis (ed.) *Michael Tippett. A Celebration* (Tunbridge Wells: The Baton Press, 1985), p. 7.

which each makes reference forming layers whose 'shifting relationships can be visualized as three superimposed panes of glass through which various musical images are refracted'.[2] The implied concept of modernism as sustained textural multiplicity, with its consequent emphasis on stratification and juxtaposition rather than continuity and synthesis, can also be inferred from Davies's remark about tonality in the Second Symphony as providing not only 'an extremely basic unifying hypothesis', but also something 'of potentially multiple musical significance at any given moment: then it need not reflect a unifying confidence of outlook characteristic of the greatest period of its former exploration, which would be inimical to contemporary experience'.[3]

Distancing the music from 'a unifying confidence of outlook' by way of reference to disparate styles, and to a concept of tonality that is simultaneously unifying and multivalent in the way it functions: these are procedures which are definable as modernist, not least because they can be found in various forms in many of the most significantly progressive twentieth-century composers – and also, if historical and critical models such as those proposed by Adorno are adopted, in certain nineteenth-century composers after and including late Beethoven.[4] To a degree, therefore, Davies's modernist practices continue a well-established twentieth-century tradition: yet they are most remarkable when they align themselves with the procedures of earlier modernist composers, as models, simply to provide a launching pad for Davies's own particularly personal and independent mode of musical discourse. As will be shown with the 'choreographic poem' *The Beltane Fire* (1994), the alternation between material which serves the purposes of the composer's expressionistic symphonism and material evoking either solemn hymnody or exuberant folk-dance suggests that the kind of conjunction, found most seminally in Ives, between a 'supranational' modernist manner and vivid representations of local people and places, is a particularly important model for Davies. At the same time, however, the character of the music itself, and of the way it relates to a particular type of subject-matter in the work's original scenario, requires consideration of other, more mainstream twentieth-century precursors: in particular, Stravinsky.

*The Beltane Fire* was originally conceived as a ballet score, and there are few if any important twentieth-century composers to whom writing for the ballet was as significant as it was for Stravinsky: it therefore comes as no surprise to discover how relevant his example often is to later ballet composers. As Stravinsky showed, there is no reason in principle why ballet music should not be as powerful or as substantial in structure and expression as music for any other

---

    2    Composer's note in the study score, *Strathclyde Concerto No. 5* (London: Boosey & Hawkes, 1994). See also Griffiths, *Peter Maxwell Davies* (London: Robson Books, 1982), p. 152.
    3    Griffiths, *op. cit.*, p. 173.
    4    For the most authoritative account, see Paddison, *Adorno's Aesthetics of Music* (Cambridge: Cambridge University Press, 1993).

genre. Yet it also remains the case that a ballet's dramatic subject-matter, as set out in its scenario, is unlikely to penetrate as deeply into character and situation as the subject-matter formed into texts for vocal compositions and operas. The attraction of ballet, to the composer, may therefore inhere specifically in the particular freedoms – and scope for ambiguity – which the presence of dramatic themes, coupled with the absence of a verbal text, provide. There is also the possibility of aligning the gestural 'language' of ballet music with that of the composer's more abstract compositions. Yet, again, the process of alignment may well create its own ambiguities and complexities, the adumbration of possible affinities between ballets and abstract works which are not so much affirmed as left tantalizingly open to question.

The topic of genre – what precisely is a ballet score, and how exactly does it, or should it, differ from other kinds of composition? – is an issue enabling the composer to call the apparent truths underpinning generally accepted distinctions between genres into question. It offers composers a channel for their scepticism, and, as one of the most resourceful and productive modern musical sceptics, Peter Maxwell Davies has not failed to bring the full power of his compositional technique to bear on music for dance. Although he has not contributed to the genre as frequently, or with such supreme diversity, as Stravinsky, he has shown that ballet is as relevant to his thinking about dramatic composition as opera is, and *The Beltane Fire* is a magnificent demonstration of the rich results of an essentially modernist engagement with fundamental generic issues that can usefully be considered in the light of Stravinsky's own thinking on the subject.

In his *Autobiography* of 1936, ghost-written by Walter Nouvel, but nevertheless ringing true as an authentically personal document, Stravinsky wrote of:

> ... my profound admiration for classical ballet, which in its very essence ... so closely corresponds with my conception of art. For here, in classical dancing, I see the triumph of studied conception over vagueness, of the rule over the arbitrary, of order over the haphazard. I am thus brought face to face with the eternal conflict in art between the Apollonian and Dionysian principles. The latter assumes ecstasy to be the final goal – that is to say, the losing of oneself – whereas art demands above all the full consciousness of the artist. There can therefore be no doubt as to my choice between the two.[5]

Stravinsky's adoption here of the opposed aesthetic categories applied by Nietzsche in relation to his work on the nature of tragedy[6] can easily be interpreted as an attempt to justify his apparent rejection of the explicitly

---

[5]    Stravinsky, *An Autobiography*, tr. anon. (New York: M. & J. Steuer, 1958), pp. 99–100.

[6]    It seems probable that Stravinsky learned of these Nietzschean terms from their use in France by André Gide.

Dionysian, anti-classical, atmosphere of earlier works – in particular, *Petrushka* and *The Rite of Spring* – in favour of the more neoclassical qualities evident in his music after the early 1920s. Yet even if we accept that Stravinsky's neoclassical works are more Apollonian than Dionysian, to the extent that they are predominantly anti-expressionistic, it is difficult to demonstrate analytically that such works – even those with unambiguously serene endings, like the *Symphony of Psalms* – are so divorced in style and technique from the essential precepts of modernism that no trace of the Dionysian remains.

It could of course be argued that the Apollo/Dionysus opposition is nothing more than a red herring, since Stravinsky in his comments seems to make no clear distinction between the possible effects of art and the processes involved in creating it. Must the creator never 'lose himself' as he works to realize his inspiration? Does the 'full consciousness' of the artist necessarily require that the results of his work reject 'ecstasy' as 'the final goal'? Such questions are far from insignificant. Yet what makes the Nietzschean categories valuable, and resonant, in the context of twentieth-century composition in general, is the way they suggest the possibility of a particular field of force between opposite extremes within which music – and pre-eminently modernist music – can move: and some of the most fruitful debates about the nature and function of modernism, in Stravinsky, Davies, and others, have therefore continued to make reference to the terms which Stravinsky himself found it convenient to adopt. So, in plotting certain areas of association between the early Stravinsky ballets and *The Beltane Fire*, we can transform the 'studied conception', 'rule' and 'order' of Apollo into the religious practices of Protestant puritanism, while the ecstasy-seeking realms of Dionysus connect to the pagan fertility rites once prominent in Orkney village life. But with Davies, as with Stravinsky, the specifics of place and time matter mainly because they serve as vivid symbols for wider – and therefore contemporary – topics of concern.

The main reason why *The Rite of Spring*, and, in particular, its explosively powerfully concluding 'Sacrificial Dance', has become such a fundamental icon of modernity in twentieth-century music is that its explicit aggressiveness and violence do not involve the suppression of a sense of the human tragedy that the sacrifice itself brings with it. In these terms, the 'Sacrificial Dance' might be heard as analogous to a dithyramb, a wild hymn expressing the impermanence and desolation of human existence, which Nietzsche saw as the defining attribute of Greek tragedy,[7] and whose wildness and instability are achieved through consistent exploitation of a modernistic stratification of the musical material, reinforced at the very end, as the upper and lower strata of material separate and move in opposite directions.[8]

---

[7]    See Stern, *Nietzsche* (London: Fontana/Collins, 1978), pp. 40–8.

[8]    See *The Rite of Spring*, 'Sacrificial Dance', Fig. 201.

This reading of Stravinsky's music has been deemed 'sentimental' by Richard Taruskin, and he rejects my interpretation of the 'tragic power' of the music's expression of conflict in favour of what he calls the 'terrible dynamism' of an 'absence of conflict'. In Taruskin's view, the final dance 'is presented as anything but horrible – and that's what's horrible. The ballet presents and celebrates an absolute absence of compassion as the necessary correlate of the absence of "psychology", of human subjectivity'.[9] In this view, there is no conflict between the individual victim – the 'chosen one' – and the collective victimizers, rather a common purpose, and Taruskin's own formidably assured initiative leads to the claim that *The Rite*'s modernism lies in a parallelism between the synthesis or fusion represented by its consistently octatonic harmonic elements, and the consistent discontinuities of its form.[10] This emphasis on synthesis and consistency is not in itself sufficient to promote the claim that the music is, after all, more Apollonian than Dionysian in principle. But it gives less prominence to tension and conflict as such than my own preferred interpretation, in which the harmonic idiom, no less than the formal organization, preserves irreducible tension alongside its impulse to integration and convergence – those very qualities, in fact, which ensure that even Stravinsky's most neoclassical compositions do not entirely escape Dionysian, and modernistic, attributes.[11] Whatever the rights and wrongs of Taruskin's ultimate conclusions about *The Rite* as implicated in the evolution of specifically twentieth-century examples of inhumanity (connected, that is, to the fact that Stravinsky did not express overt hostility to the fascist dictators in the 1930s)[12] I therefore see no reason to reject a response to the 'Sacrificial Dance' which involves mixed feelings. Why should one type of reaction – exhilaration at the music's rhythmic energy and brassy tone colours – preclude a simultaneous feeling of sympathy with the Chosen One as victim? After all, we are all capable of mixed feelings, and never more so, I suspect, then when experiencing a modernist work of art whose fractured surface, and avoidance of deep structure along the lines of classical tonal backgrounds, makes it impossible for us to lose ourselves in the kind of underlying regularity of grouping that we respond to instinctively in diatonic music. Stravinsky's music may not directly represent such mixed, conflicting feelings, but it offers an analogy to them, a textural, harmonic and rhythmic representation of persistent conflict which calls into question Taruskin's claim that there is fusion, a lack of conflict, in the music.

---

[9]     Taruskin, *Defining Russia Musically* (Princeton: Princeton University Press, 1997), p. 386. See also Whittall, 'Music Analysis as Human Science? *Le Sacre du Printemps* in Theory and Practice', *Music Analysis* 1 (1982), pp. 33–53.

[10]    Taruskin, *Stravinsky and the Russian Traditions: A Biography of the Works through 'Mavra'* (Berkeley & Los Angeles: University of California Press, 1996), especially pp. 849–966.

[11]    See my review of Taruskin 1996 in *Journal of the American Musicological Society*, 50 (1997), pp. 519–29.

[12]    Taruskin, 1997, *op. cit.*, pp. 362–3.

The issues, and terminology, involved in this discussion of Stravinsky can be equally illuminating when we turn to *The Beltane Fire*, not least because the music for its concluding debasement of those associated with pagan practices seems intended to provoke compassion, however vivid the composer's earlier scepticism about the feelings of both puritans and pagans may have been, and there is certainly a sense in which the concluding music of *The Beltane Fire* 'preserves irreducible tension alongside its impulse to integration and convergence'. Yet this is emphatically not to claim that Davies's work is a conscious reaction to Stravinsky's early ballets: that juxtaposition of folk-like or popular materials with his own style deliberately evokes the precedent of *Petrushka,* or that the use of textural stratification to depict intensifying tension and instability within society directly imitates *The Rite of Spring. The Beltane Fire* may, like *Petrushka,* represent the magical, the primitive, as a threat to more conventional contemporary values. But it does not, like *The Rite,* lead up to a collective ritual of sacrifice, in which dissent is noticeable for its absence, even if it demonstrates many dithyrambic qualities along the way. There are indeed very deep-seated and persistent tensions in the way the music explores the field of force between the extremes of repression and lack of constraint, yet the style and sound have little to do with echoes of Stravinsky. Rather, given that Davies's musical language in the 1990s seems more immediately Schoenbergian than Stravinskian, it might be asked whether Schoenberg's 'Dance round the golden calf' from *Moses und Aron* is not a more salient model than *Petrushka*'s 'Russian Dance' or *The Rite*'s 'Sacrificial Dance' for *The Beltane Fire*'s Dionysian dimension.[13] As will emerge later, however, Davies's attitude to the Dionysian, while not unambiguous, and pulling no punches, can scarcely match Schoenberg's intense love-hate relationship with the pagan barbarism on display in *Moses und Aron.* Nor does his treatment of what we might term the ideology of puritanism have much in common with Schoenberg's sympathetic yet unsparing presentation of Moses in his opera. Above all, what turns the nexus of associations back towards Stravinsky is the ethos of the scenario itself, and the degree to which it encourages the composer to inscribe aspects of place and a particular society into the musical substance.

Ex. 8.1a: *The Beltane Fire* opening (B.Cl.,Vc.,CB only)

---

[13]    For some discussion of the Schoenberg/Stravinsky comparison, see Williams, *New Music and the Claims of Modernity* (Aldershot: Ashgate, 1997), p. 33.

Ex. 8.1b: Fifth Symphony – opening

The opening of *The Beltane Fire* is characteristically dark and questing – a 9-note melodic phrase, the last three notes a six-semitone transposition of the second three (Ex. 8.1a), and underpinned harmonically by a sustained progression from the first note (F) to the fourth (B flat). The initial emphasis on F and B suggests that this work will be another instalment in the Davies symphonic canon, that by now immense span of music, beginning with the First Symphony of 1975–6, and also embracing (among other works) the Strathclyde Concertos, whose 'extremely basic unifying hypothesis' is the strategic recourse to symmetrically divided octaves centring on B, D, F or A flat. The sense of intertextual cross-reference becomes even greater when it is noted that the beginning of *The Beltane Fire* quotes directly from the ending of the Fifth Symphony, composed earlier in the same year, 1994 (Ex. 8.1b). Maybe the image of renewal stemming from the symphony's source chant, the Easter hymn *Haec dies*, is one reason for the connection. But in any case the familiar Davies procedure of deriving different compositions from a common chant or serial source is extended here to show how one work can grow literally out of its immediate predecessor.[14]

In Davies's late-modernist world, such literalism creates a complex context of dependence and resistance, where 'growing out of' provides the stimulus to contradict, distort and reject. *The Beltane Fire* is indeed symphonic, but it is not the Sixth Symphony in disguise, and its generic status as a 'choreographic poem' serves to distance it from its own inherent symphonic attributes as much as to reinforce them. Thus, the special (at least, in Davies's numbered symphonies) single-movement structuring of No. 5, itself reflected in another substantial composition from 1994, the *Strathclyde Concerto No. 9*, is echoed again in the unbroken span of *The Beltane Fire*, even though the musical character of the latter recalls other works more directly – in particular, those many Davies scores of the 1980s and earlier 1990s (for example, *A Spell for Green Corn* and *The*

---

[14]     For more of the technical consequences of compositional intertextuality, see Peter Owens, 'Revelation and Fallacy: Observations on Compositional Technique in the Music of Peter Maxwell Davies', *Music Analysis* 13 (1994), pp. 161–202.

*MacDonald Dances*, both 1993) in which Scottish idioms and materials are explicitly cited or recreated, in strategies generally excluded from the symphonies proper, though not from the Strathclyde Concertos, notably numbers 4 and 5.

In an earlier article, I noted that 'since 1970, and his move to Hoy, Davies has developed a particular enthusiasm for a culture in which tendencies to paganism and piety may be rather more convergent than they are in more urban, mainland settings'.[15] 'Paganism and piety' are indeed the central topics of *The Beltane Fire*, and although it is the clash between them, rather than convergence, which might appear to matter most in the ballet's scenario, I hope to suggest by way of analysis that Davies's reading of confrontation moves beyond 'black and white' opposition into more troubling and ambiguous regions. In this respect, Davies in 1994 was still the composer of *Taverner, The Devils* and *Vesalii Icones*, and the composer's comment with respect to the last of these – 'the point I am trying to make is a moral one – it is a matter of distinguishing the false from the real'[16] – is certainly relevant to *The Beltane Fire*.

Echoing Davies, Paul Griffiths observes of the *Missa Super l'Homme Armé* that 'the questions it raises are those of discerning and communicating religious truth, and in particular of distinguishing what is true from its precise opposite'.[17] In *The Beltane Fire* Davies uses modernist techniques to depict a very unmodernist world and culture, and as a result the music is bound to question the value of attempting to distinguish 'what is true from its precise opposite', simply because it replaces precise oppositions with ambivalent, multivalent interactions, and synthesis with symbiosis. It is therefore the ease with which the Kirk feels it can 'discern and communicate religious truth' which invites the composer's most pointed scepticism, even though, as the music shows, such scepticism cannot eliminate a very real sense of the threat to social justice which the bigotry of established religion often poses.

The most obvious difference between *The Beltane Fire* and such works of the 1960s as the *Missa Super l'Homme Armé* is the presence of a strong sense of regional locality, of the place that was, and is, Orkney. As I wrote in my earlier article:

> ... many of the post-1970s works have an ethnic stratum; song-like, or psalm-tune-like chant offers an emblem of piety and of the determined if futile quest for transcendence, while earthy dance music, usually recalling the hectic Scottish reel, or its slower relative, the Strathspey, represents the human engagement with nature in all its forms.[18]

---

[15]   Cross-Currents and Convergencies: Britten, Maxwell Davies and the Sense of Place', *Tempo* 204 (April 1998), p. 9.

[16]   Griffiths, *op. cit.*, p. 154.

[17]   *Ibid.*, p. 64.

[18]   Whittall, 1998, *op. cit.*, p. 9.

Of all Davies's works from the 1990s, it is the opera *The Doctor of Myddfai* (1995–6) which offers the most elaborate treatment of a cultural conflict between forces promoting sickness and corruption and those dedicated to healing as 'an engagement with nature'. Even there, however, as the scenes between the Doctor and the Ruler make clear, any attempt to regard these characters as unambiguously consistent representatives of 'good' and 'evil' respectively does not work. The music of the opera indicates that, just as the Ruler is by no means an entirely unsympathetic character, so the Doctor, the healer, has more than a few of the attributes of intolerance and intransigence that have been associated with visionaries down the ages. In Davies's mythology, martyrdom – whether of Christian saints or secular protagonists – tends to be invited as much as inflicted, and in this respect the most thought-provoking precedent for *The Beltane Fire*'s scenario is the much earlier opera *The Martyrdom of Saint Magnus* (1976).

In one sense, certainly, that opera provides a kind of negative image of the ballet scenario, offering a more conventional study of warlike, secular forces oppressing and attempting to destroy those committed to pacifism and spirituality. Magnus is to be sacrificed in part because, in his words, 'a curse is fallen on the land … the fissure runs through field and family' and 'there is a black joy abroad, a dance of the deadly sins'. In the opera the message is that 'men who turn from the patterns of God desire always to return to nakedness and savagery' – words that could be heard as the voice of the Kirk in *The Beltane Fire* – and Blind Mary's final line in the opera, 'Saint Magnus keep us from a bedlam of sacrifice' points to the sense in which the disciplines of religion can act as a positive counter to the 'black joy' of unrestricted paganism. It is doubtless because it is not possible for a ballet scenario to develop the subtleties of characterization appropriate to opera that the later work can ultimately be seen as leaving the tensions between two such different social orders unresolved – because, perhaps, they can never *be* resolved. In *The Beltane Fire*, what is perceived by the Kirk as a dance of the deadly sins is, from the opposite perspective, a dance of self-fulfilment and social renewal. Yet even if, according to the ballet scenario, the 'martyrs' are the pagans, the heretics, it is not possible to conclude, from what the music tells us, that they have some kind of absolute truth on their side.

The questioning of the authority of the establishment has always been central to Davies's work, and can be regarded as his most explicit link with the broader aesthetic and cultural practices of twentieth-century modernism. But, as noted above, modernism is not simply iconoclasm, a refusal to conform to some more generally accepted, relatively conservative or traditional set of principles and procedures. In its most basic form, it involves a challenge to classical precepts of integration and synthesis, goal-directedness and hierarchization that depends on continued awareness of those precepts in a truly plural, multivalent social and cultural context.[19] But the modernist claims a closer relation with, and a more direct response to, the fractured nature of the contemporary world, and from this standpoint it is the latter-day classicists who continue to resist such fracturing who are the iconoclasts.

Perhaps the most significant way in which modernism has sought to establish its own seriousness and legitimacy is in devising and presenting particular kinds of ritual or ceremony which are inconceivable from a classical perspective. Here Stravinsky seems to offer the single most crucial archetype, and it is perfectly in keeping with the still-potent disputes about the nature of modernism and classicism that gained in intensity as the end of the twentieth century approached that the particular character of Stravinsky's achievement, in *The Rite of Spring*, in particular, should remain the subject of intense debate and controversy. At this point, therefore, I will resume the discussion of Stravinsky which I began earlier.

For Richard Taruskin, *The Rite of Spring* marked a momentous advance precisely because in it:

> Stravinsky used Russian folk-music as an instrument of self-emancipation from the constricting traditions of Russian art music; and ... by playing, as it were, one tradition against the other – but ultimately fusing them in an unprecedentedly co-ordinated fashion – he found a way out of the cul-de-sac in which Russian music of his day was foundering.

It therefore follows that '*The Rite* was profoundly *traditional* ... neither rupture nor upheaval but a magnificent extension', and its 'signal achievement was a brilliantly original and thorough synthesis of the folkloristic and modernist traditions of Russian art music'.[20]

In his detailed analysis, Taruskin does not entirely exclude the possibility that *The Rite* embraces 'rupture and upheaval' as part of its 'magnificent extension', and, as suggested earlier, it is surely the case that the work's climactic 'Sacrificial Dance' is as much, if not more, an enactment of polarity than of synthesis, since, while it drives towards a centred closure (in terms of a D-based tonality) it simultaneously, and with supreme intensity, subjects that centricity to the threat of disintegration under the sheer weight of the accumulating dissonant superstructure. This music is more stratified than synthesized in any classical sense, and while the characteristics of synthesis are not entirely absent, they are no longer the single most important feature determining the musical action.[21]

Where Taruskin is absolutely correct is in the distinction he draws between the nature of *The Rite*'s musical language, to which alternations between 'folk'

---

[19]    For further discussion of these topics, see Whittall, 'Modernist Aesthetics, Modernist Music: Some Analytical Perspectives' in Baker, Beach and Bernard (eds), *Music Theory in Concept and Practice* (Rochester: University of Rochester Press, 1997), pp. 157–80.

[20]    Taruskin, 1996, *op. cit.*, pp. 905, 847, 937.

[21]    See Whittall, review of Taruskin, p. 523.

and 'art' no longer seem relevant, and that of its immediate predecessor *Petrushka*, in which we can still 'easily separate the "folk-derived" from the "original" elements'.[22] The modernist oppositions of *Petrushka* are therefore a good deal more straightforward, more anecdotal in the sense of deriving from and depending on the specific details of the ballet's scenario, than are those of *The Rite*, which are more structural than stylistic in character. *Petrushka* is also, in this respect, a more relevant precedent for *The Beltane Fire*, a 'rite of modernism' as stylistic disjunction, whereas *The Rite* itself is more a rite of modernism as textural and structural symbiosis.

Stravinsky's avoidance of such stylistic oppositions after *Petrushka* is striking, and persuasive evidence of his search for a 'classical', Apollonian, dimension (unity of style) to balance his continuing pursuit of modernist stratifications and Dionysian intensity in texture and form. He was also by temperament disinclined to choose dramatic subjects which involved explicit confrontations between secular and spiritual domains: indeed, such topics were redundant, given the unambiguous moral perspectives of *Oedipus Rex* and *The Rake's Progress*. By contrast, Peter Maxwell Davies has always relished the opportunity of critically representing the icons and priestly embodiments of Christianity. For him, it is not just the devil, or devils, who merit musical treatment. The saintly – especially when the complexities and conflicts of their motivations can be explored – are even more attractive objects of musical attention and (on occasion) deconstruction.

With this topic the familiar contrast between Davies's earlier expressionism and his later, less vehemently refracted style re-enters the discussion. Of their very nature, the unstable interactions of *St Thomas Wake*, the work whose supercharged confrontations between the three worlds of John Bull, twenties foxtrots and Davies himself provides the most extreme demonstration of the earlier idiom's range and intensity, could hardly be sustained as a stylistic, structural norm. Yet the forcefulness of its inherent ideology – the Davies style representing a contemporary ideal, the Bull a lost, still usable (with transformation) source, the foxtrot a kind of supranational antidote to symphonic expressionism – has remained with the composer as a model from which his later musical thoughts on relations between culture and creativity, and particularly the national and the supranational, can be derived. The Orkney works may be less extreme, less aggressive, even at times verging on a neoclassicism redolent of Hindemith, yet they continue the project of the earlier period in the way they reinscribe contrasts between 'popular' and 'serious', folk and art, local and international, from within the perspective of formal procedures that develop out of the capacious core of the symphonic tradition. The result may seem to the unsympathetic to be a sell-out – a dilution of an earlier expressionistic ideal, and

---

[22]     Taruskin, 1996, *op. cit.*, p. 949.

even a betrayal of modernism itself. My view is that it can best be perceived as a refinement in which the propulsive tensions between evolution and juxtaposition, difference and similarity, are more subtly (and therefore more challengingly) deployed than in works which, for all their dramatic flair and emotional directness, lack a more balanced aesthetic grounding.

Such balance comes by way of the kind of associations inconceivable to Davies in the 1960s: with Sibelius, in particular, and even with Vaughan Williams. Yet while it is true that the particular Nordic vision of nature, in terms of contrasts between starkly monumental and seethingly turbulent states, that links Davies's later symphonic music to Sibelius's later symphonies and *Tapiola* is an unmistakable determining element, that vision has served not to replace but to reinvigorate other, longer-standing associations – the movement between solemnity and sensuality found within the single-movement design of Schoenberg's Chamber Symphony No. 1 (as well as his much later String Trio), and also (still more potently in relation to *The Beltane Fire*) the use of such generic archetypes as dance and chorale – to promote a modernist symphonic structure, as in Stravinsky's *Symphonies of Wind Instruments*.

Davies's youthful scepticism about the traditional, tonal, multi-movement symphonic template might have led him to such flexible yet allusive single-movement fantasia-schemes as found in the *Second Fantasia on John Taverner's In Nomine* (1964) and *Worldes Blis: Motet for Orchestra* (1966–9): it was part of his self-critical sense that, before his own First Symphony, a true mastery of orchestral composition had eluded him, and this promoted the orientation of his 'genuine' symphonic music around the multi-movement models of Beethoven, Tchaikovsky and Mahler. Stephen Pruslin has wisely observed that 'by understanding Beethoven's controlled alternation of stability and flux and adding to it the Sibelian possibilities of self-generating form, Davies tapped into a powerful double inheritance that has sustained him through his ongoing symphonic journey',[23] and it is Sibelius's ultimate advance beyond Beethovenian structuring – the single-movement 'fantasia' of the Seventh Symphony, an advance reinforcing fundamentally 'classical' thematic and harmonic priorities – which is the clearest model for the 'advance' that is Davies's own Fifth Symphony. The sense in which Davies's appropriation of the late-Sibelian model is inextricably bound up with a rethinking of his own earlier fantasia principle is a topic beyond the scope of this study, but it seems clear that the Fifth Symphony's interactive dialogue between contrasting formal prototypes (in Pruslin's formulation, 'a mosaic of 34 distinct sections' at one extreme, and 'one single binary form' at the other) represents a natural distillation of the more elusive debates between what I have described elsewhere

---

[23]    Notes with Collins Classics recording of Symphony No. 5 (14602, 1995).

as fixed and floating modes of discourse in the earlier, multi-movement symphonies and concertos.[24]

In these explicitly symphonic compositions there is an equally explicit 'classical' feature: a tendency for the music to function in terms of a consistent, unified stylistic frame of reference. For this reason, the no less palpable modernism of, for example, the Fifth Symphony emerges in textural and structural juxtapositions that in themselves do not fundamentally fracture the stylistic uniformity. The music does not allude to alien modes of expression, since it has no dramatic topic or scenario by means of which such alienation might be legitimized. Perhaps, then, the most essential quality of all in Davies's development is the acknowledgement that there are two modernisms – that (deriving from Ives, and/or *Petrushka*) which expressionistically explodes a unified style, and that (deriving from *The Rite of Spring*) which ultimately reinforces a unified style. It follows that one reason why Davies has found such long-term musical stimulus in his Orkney environment is that it has shown him a 'relevant' way of continuing or transforming his earlier, more mainstream expressionism while not requiring him to abandon, still less dilute, his no less fruitful concern with a music in which expressionistic conflicts are submerged. No less crucially, of course, the Orkney environment has provided him with a vivid 'ethnic' stratum, a new category of 'found' material quite different in ethos from the foxtrots and other 'foreign' elements of the earlier works.

Looking again at the various compositions of 1994, it might appear that, whereas the short orchestral piece *Chat Moss*, with its steady unfolding of a chant-like melody, to some extent lies behind the Fifth Symphony, the equivalent foundations for *The Beltane Fire* are to be found in *Cross Lane Fair*. Though it evokes the Salford fairground of Davies's youth, *Cross Lane Fair* was commissioned for the St Magnus Festival, and the composer chose to represent his 4/5-year-old self by the combination of Northumbrian bagpipes and bohdran or celtic drum. The latter features in *The Beltane Fire* as well, and the overall form of the *c*.15-minute *Cross Lane Fair* – nine sections played without a break – adumbrates the kind of alternations found in the much longer choreographic poem, whose seven principal sections sub-divide according to the requirements of the detailed dance scenario.

This scenario, devised by Davies himself, implies, as David Nice observes, a 'fundamentally tragic' tone, 'embodying the conflict between the new Reformation clergy and the pagan traditions of the islands'.[25] It should therefore be said again that we cannot simply map Apollonian and Dionysian attributes onto puritan and pagan attitudes respectively, any more than we can regard one as wholly good and the

---

[24]    See Whittall, 'Comparatively Complex: Birtwistle, Maxwell Davies and Modernist Analysis', *Music Analysis* 13 (1994), pp. 139–59, and 'Peter Maxwell Davies and the Problem of Classicizing Modernism' in Danuser (ed.), *Die klassizistische Moderne in der Musik der 20. Jahrhunderts* (Basel, 1997), pp. 143–51.

[25]    This and all subsequent citations are from David Nice's synopsis with the Collins Classics recording (14642, 1996).

other as wholly bad. Indeed, the conflict is tragic precisely because the all-important question of where truth lies is not easily decided, and the moral of the piece seems to involve a bleak view about the prospects for peaceful coexistence, of finding a workable social accommodation between such incompatible cultural traditions. A feeling of the tragic also arises because the music reaches beyond parody or caricature of its component elements, pagan and puritan alike, and it could even be seen as grounds for hope of an eventual *modus vivendi* that the music associated with the Kirk shows itself capable of evolution, of adapting, no less than the pagan dance music, to the composer's own mediating idiom, with its concern to avoid the extremes of 'pure' neoclassicism and hyper-modernistic expressionism. It is therefore in the interaction between aspects of these well-contrasted stylistic and structural tendencies that the confrontation between Apollonian and Dionysian tendencies is most pertinent to *The Beltane Fire*, rather than in the subject-matter and scenario as such, and the score can to this extent be brought into wider considerations of Davies's relationship with so-called 'modern classicism'.[26] For the moment, however, it is time to consider the score itself in a little more detail.

Scene One is set 'In the Barn of the Bu' – the largest farmhouse on the island – and initially depicts an uninhibitedly secular ceremony. As David Nice's synopsis describes it, 'the dancing and drinking of the assembled population are interrupted by the entry of the Greule – the kidnapping ogress of Viking legend', who chases the children and is herself pursued and eventually caught, 'by her vividly costumed sons, the legion of Greuliks, headed by the Skuddlar, who plays the fiddle and leads their dance'. The dancing only gets under way after the short Introduction, already described, which proclaims its preliminary nature by avoiding the kind of stratified textures that emerge in the First General Dance (Ex. 8.2a). Here the lowest melodic line, in Bass clarinet and Contra-Bassoon, continues the Introduction's idea, taken from the Fifth Symphony. At the same time a solo horn, followed by trumpet, has a more literally dance-like tune, and hints of Scotch snaps emerge in the rhythm which will become much more explicit in the work's directly folk-like episodes, such as Interlude Two (Ex. 8.2b). With a melodic counterpoint in the harp as well as chordal harmonic support in the other horns and strings, the initial texture is completed by colourings of the main melodic lines in basses and trombone respectively.

The principal effect of such stratification is to promote the kind of 'floating' harmonic context which is the main means of propulsion in Davies's symphonic music, and comparable contrasts between such music and the points of cadential focus where elements of the 'basic unifying hypothesis' emerge are employed in *The Beltane Fire*, even though the clear-cut thematic repetitions and rhythmic patternings of the First General Dance are an early indication of a degree of regularity that is less apparent in his purely symphonic compositions.

---

[26]    For further discussions see my articles in Danuser (ed.) n. 24 above, and *Tempo* 204 (n. 15 above).

Ex. 8.2a: *The Beltane Fire* – First General Dance; principal melodic line only

Ex. 8.2b: *The Beltane Fire* – Interlude Two (accompaniment omitted)

That regularity is also evident in the brief Second General Dance, which develops the main idea of the first, and is rather more homogeneous in texture, suggesting that the villagers – before the eruption of the sinister, explicitly pagan Greule and Greulik – are more conformist, less extreme in their attitudes.

The Greule's Dance is differentiated from the general dances in various ways, most obviously by excluding strings from the instrumentation and by initial emphasis on a C♯ centre, though this is soon set aside, and the B/F tritone can still be heard. The music of The Greule's Dance may be more grotesque and exuberant in character than what has gone before, with Davies's familiar glissando-whoops in the horns, but the formal outlines are still regular, with thematic repetitions indicating a ternary scheme. With The Greulik's Dance the strings return and the rhythmic and melodic patterning comes closer to folk-like models, though here too the degree of textural stratification (the main dance theme in the violins offset by a smoother theme in the lower registers, and with diverse rhythmic and harmonic punctuations) prevents the establishment of the kind of clear tonal or modal focus that the more explicitly folk-like episodes will reveal. Up to this point, then, only the tendency to focus on more marked, regularly rhythmic patterns (as especially at the start of The Greulik's Dance) distinguishes the music from Davies's symphonic style. But the last two sections of Scene One – The Minister and his Kirk Elders and Sword Dance – are quite different. The hymn-like solemnity of the former is openly mocked, recalling for a moment the unsubtle guying of musical churchiness in Davies's environmentalist polemic *The Yellow Cake Revue* (1980). But there is a tonal instability in *The Beltane Fire* which takes the music beyond parody, and adds to the sense of menace, leaving no doubt of the conflicts to come: there is a world of difference between the unhealthy pomposity (rooted in repression) of the chant-based church material and the uninhibited exuberance of the Sword Dance. Here the bodhran (or small basque drum) makes its first appearance, and the folk-like but pervasively chromatic dance tune (piccolo, then flute) is contrapuntally superimposed onto the Minister's motive to underline their incompatibility.

The Sword Dance itself soon dissolves into the scene's final episode, an *Adagio* touching on the burgeoning romance between the Skuddlar and the Bu-Mester's (farmer's) daughter, and this provides a subtle transition to what follows in reasserting Davies's symphonic style with material that will soon be treated as a 'found', tonal object. The tension between these two musical worlds is explicitly set out with the opposition between the cadence ending Scene One, resolving on the tritone B-F, and the D flat tonality that begins Interlude One. The fact that the cadence which ends Scene One is recalled at the very end of the work (Ex. 8.3 shows both for comparison) is one feature – the importance of recapitulatory elements in Scene Five and the Coda is another – indicating that Davies was by no means concerned to repress analogies between the formal outline of *The Beltane Fire* and a symphonic scheme – expository, fast first movement (Scene One), *scherzo* (Scene Two), developmental slow movement (possibly Scene Three and certainly Scene Four), recapitulatory finale (Scene Five). It follows that the relative heterogeneity of the choreographic poem, as far as form is concerned, makes it possible to 'interrogate' the principles of coherent symphonic structuring rather than simply set them aside.

Ex. 8.3a: *The Beltane Fire* – end of Scene One

Ex. 8.3b: *The Beltane Fire* – Final Scene, ending

As already explained, Interlude One depicts the romantic love between the Skuddlar and the farmer's daughter, a love which, the music suggests, is too sweetly innocent to prosper. Any depiction of a romantic 'voice' by means of a solo violin is difficult to dissociate from the highly perfumed gesturing of Strauss's *Ein Heldenleben*, and whether or not Davies intended to acknowledge (if only to mock) this connection, there is an unmistakable ambivalence in the way the Skuddlar's fiddle, for all its aspirations to folk-like authenticity, seems as much the agent of cultivated delusion as of positive yet pagan ideals. The diatonicism of this love music is therefore soon destabilized, as if to demonstrate the sceptical composer's irritation with such sentimental simplicity, and the music of the Interlude dissolves on a quiet but intensely dissonant chord (Ex. 8.4).

Ex. 8.4: *The Beltane Fire* – end of Interlude One

Scene Two, 'A Field', subdivides into four sections which refocus the conflicts of Scene One. Firstly, two dances, the Ploughing Dance for the men and the Sowing Dance for the women, are well-contrasted fertility rites. The Ploughing Dance has some of the qualities of a *sarabande*, though with an unstable seven-beat metre, and its thematic underpinning – the generative Fifth Symphony tune – suggests a kind of rootedness that has the potential for true, 'modern-classic' stability, even though the tension between its constituent independent strata increases as its cumulative structure unfolds. The Sowing Dance is less stable, and more symphonic in its flowing, clearly stratified lines and steadily cumulative expressiveness, its strongly emphasized mid-point cadence with C♯ in the bass (Ex. 8.5) perhaps recalling the associations between that pitch and the pagan Greule.

Ex. 8.5: *The Beltane Fire* – Sowing Dance: internal cadence point

For this reason, the Sowing Dance is more of a provocation to the Kirk than is the more traditional Ploughing Dance. What immediately follows is not Kirkly disapproval, however, but music for the Skuddlar which is again highly equivocal in its somewhat idealized, tonal romanticism, now in D major, not D flat, and with a rather formal kind of decorative writing in the solo violin. As the music builds to a chromaticized but nevertheless harmonically stable (dominant-rooted) climax, Davies signals potential disaster by introducing his whole-tone 'death' chord on D (Ex. 8.6). .

Ex. 8.6: *The Beltane Fire* – The Skuddlar's Processional, with 'death' chord

The prospect of the climax proceeding to closure is subverted by the chill chorale in which 'The Minister and his Elders break the Spell', but the scene ends with a fully-fledged *pas de deux* for the Skuddlar and the Bu-mester's daughter. Built in cumulative waves like many a Davies symphonic *lento*, and with an increasingly stratified texture, this initially reasserts the D major tonality (though with a new theme) and develops without building a strong climax. As the episode dies away the whole-tone death-chord recurs (three bars before Fig. 40). In the score this love is doomed, and it seems possible from the kind of musical atmosphere created here that the sceptical Davies could be making a distinction between the 'healthy' vigour of collective fertility rituals and the solipsistic sentimentality that typifies individual ideas about love and romance.

Interlude Two, which follows, is cast in the style of 'traditional Orkney-Scottish … dance music', and with its clear-cut modality and regular rhythm (see Ex. 8.2b), the sense of something remembered and quoted, rather than simply composed, Davies creates an ambiguity, a musical 'ideal' which cannot survive for long in the real world of post-expressionist modernism. As with the love music, the dance dies away as its simple purity is corroded under the call of a church bell, and this presages the conflict that comes into full prominence in Scene Three.

Called 'The Kirk', this contains no titled subdivisions in the score, but the synopsis describes a scene 'inside the island church, … The Skuddlar and the Bu-daughter are made to kneel in penance (she is pregnant) … he is made to hand over his fiddle … the congregation mourns'. In a relatively short (just over four minutes) span of music, the irreconcilability of tonal chorale and increasingly chromatic lyric music is explored, and the sense of increasing depth of expression is crucial: now that the lovers have been made to suffer, their music is no longer sentimental, as ripe for parody as that of their puritanical oppressors, and there is even a hint of chorale-style in the Skuddlar's music (solo violin, Ex. 8.7).

Ex. 8.7: *The Beltane Fire* – from Scene Three; 'The Kirk'

Scene Four (The Field) follows immediately, and again there are no titled subdivisions. This is a short (four and a half minutes) but substantial symphonic *lento*, depicting the suffering – drought – that repression inflicts on the community, as a direct result (one infers) of the silencing of the Skuddlar's magic fiddle. The music has the intensity of a symphonic development, and thematic elements from earlier in the work can be heard, as the grand climax of a 'slow, stamping prayer-dance for rain' is generated. The stamping is embodied in inexorable alternations of C and D in the bass from Fig. 59 in the score as an immense *crescendo* prepares a resolution in which B and F once again emerge as basic, *The Beltane Fire*'s prime intertextual link with Davies's symphonic cycle, and its framing representatives, the Fifth and Sixth Symphonies.

Scene Five (The Beltane Fire), has a short introduction with a new folk-like theme (Ex. 8.8), based around the C♯ occasionally identified with pagan forces (the Greule in Scene One), and it is soon clear from the stratified rather than synthesized texture that the attitude here is more positive than parodic.

The Skuddlar and Bu-daughter, freed from captivity, 'lead a wild Bacchanalian dance'. There are three sections, 'A Spell for Water', 'A Rune for Ripeness', and 'A Prayer for Good Ale', and it is perhaps in obedience to the generic constraints of the dance that Davies moves from the relatively symphonic qualities of the first number into a more overtly parodic vein in the waltz-like Rune, even though the clearly defined textural strata ensure that the effect is more subtle, as well as more powerfully Dionysiac, than that of crude pastiche. Either the message is that depth and seriousness are not necessarily and invariably good things, or the essential primitiveness of the distant time in which the ballet is presumed to be set is the key. What is clear is that the spells and prayers are effective. It starts to rain (the B/F outline at score Fig. 75), the general dance resumes, and recollections of material from Scene One become

Ex. 8.8: *The Beltane Fire* – Scene Five; beginning

increasingly prominent. But the Kirk cannot afford to concede the victory to paganism, and the final appearance of chorale material underpins and undermines the continuing dance, shorn for the first and only time of anachronistic tonal simplicity – 'The Skuddlar is arrested, the Bu-daughter arraigned as a witch, and the crowd disperses'.

In the brief Coda 'the Bu-daughter's son, alone before the dying fire, dances a few steps from his sword dance of the first scene, and lies down with outstretched arms in the ashes'. As the composer has stressed, the ending makes explicit that the musical materials associated with the Bu-daughter's son and the Kirk minister share a common source. At the end Kirk and village alike seem to reflect the prevailing sense of disorientation and disillusion, and there is a sense that the extremes of Apollo and Dionysus are equally inadequate as models for lasting social harmony. Technically, the ending is striking for the way it moves from the elements of a tonal resolution (F sharp to B in the bass) to a less stable association between an F minor triad and Davies's archetypal symphonic model, the symmetric D,F,A♭,B sonority (see Ex. 8.3b), a form of closure that combines focus with multivalence, convergence with divergence in a manner analogous to the concluding ritual of sacrifice in *The Rite of Spring*. As suggested earlier, there is little sense in *The Beltane Fire* of a 'victory' for the Kirk and a defeat for the spirit of paganism, rather a feeling that while it is difficult for the realist, the sceptic, to decide the truth of the matter, it is nevertheless vital for a sense of accommodation, a *modus vivendi*, to be worked out.

It is the difficulty of achieving social and spiritual harmony which is suggested at the end of *The Beltane Fire*, recalling the atmosphere of Arthur Miller's play *The Crucible*, with its comparable exploration of the devastating conflict between religion and what is perceived as witchcraft. Another more direct association, perhaps, is with the ending of *Petrushka*, where the opposition between the magical and the mundane is reinforced to chilling effect in what is arguably Stravinsky's most explicitly modernist ending. This was not the kind of effect that Stravinsky sought to sustain in his later works where, if anything, the sense that Apollonian and Dionysian tendencies share an impulse towards the transcendent in art and life was the prime motivation for his development. The result was a rich dialogue within his later compositions between these divergent yet comparable impulses, as the purely artistic possibility of balancing aspirations to ecstatic transcendence is set against the need for the composer's 'full consciousness', self-awareness as the main means of ensuring a legitimate form of communicative self-expression. For Davies, with his inescapable legacy from early twentieth-century expressionism, transcendence is a more elusive entity, and so is classicism – even that 'modern classicism' that seeks to re-establish synthesis as the fundamental technical and structural factor in music. So, in his own very different yet no less persuasive fashion, Davies has continued to explore the implications of the most potent contemporary dialogues – magical and mundane, spiritual and secular, pagan and puritan, modernist and classical. They all have contributions to make to *The Beltane Fire*, and between them they help to ensure that this score is one of the composer's most powerful demonstrations of his own very personal blend of certainty and scepticism.

# Appendix 1: *Alma Redemptoris Mater* first movement (Ex. 1.6)

a)   bars 7–9
b)   bars 10–12
c)   bar 18
d)   bar 25
e)   bars 31–2
f)   bars 36–7
g)   bar 40
h)   bar 46

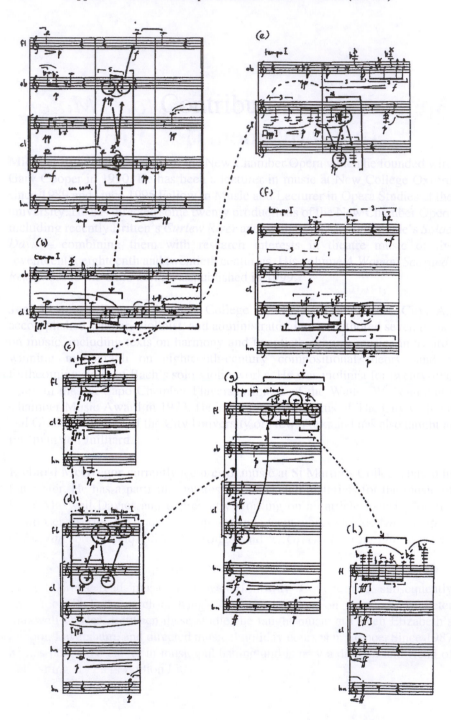

# Appendix 2: *Alma Redemptoris Mater*
## third movement
## with simplified notation (Ex. 1.7)

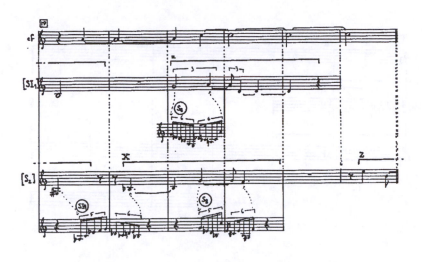

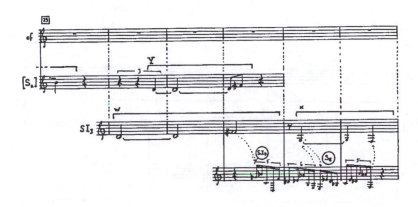

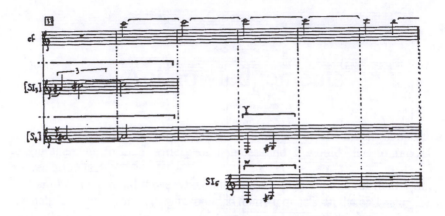

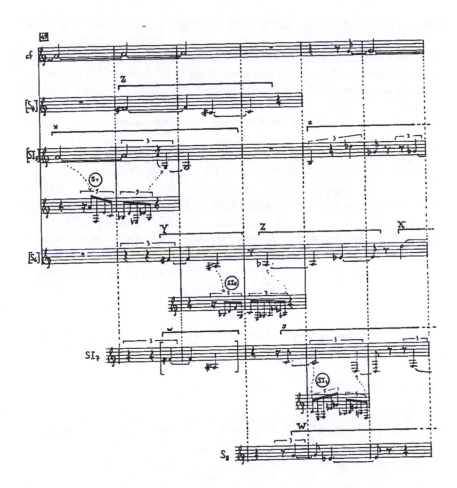

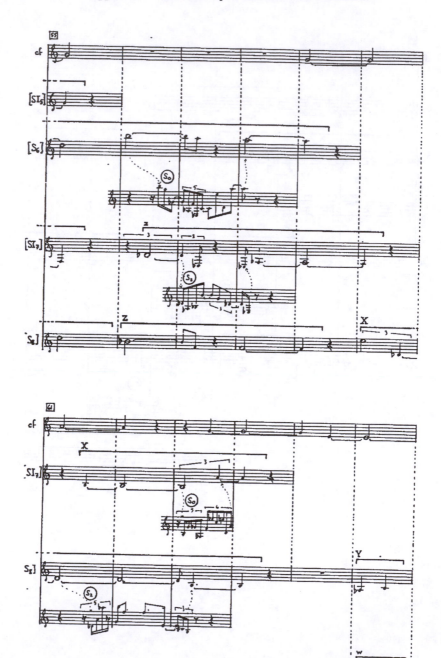

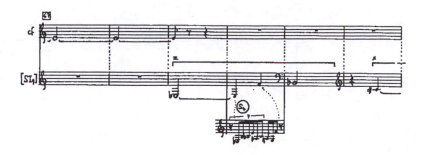

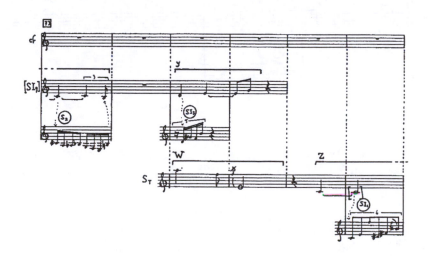

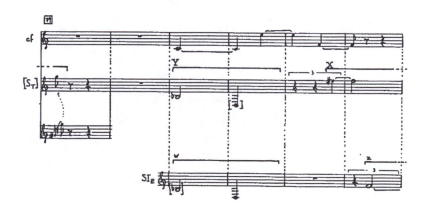

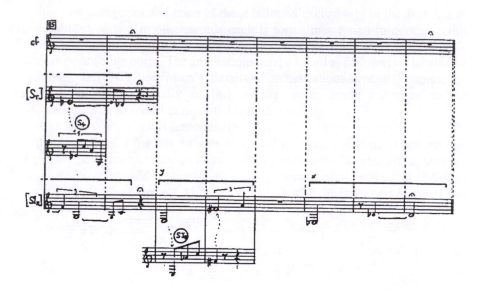

# Appendix 3: *Alma Redemptoris Mater* second movement (annotated) (Ex. 1.15)

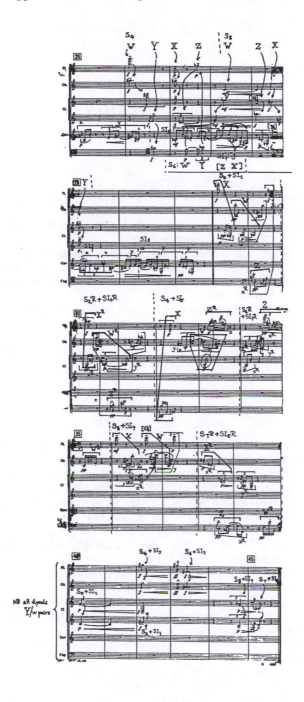

# Bibliography

## Theses

Basford, John, 'Analytical Study of the Works of Birtwistle, Davies and Goehr' (Ph.D., Sheffield, n.d.).

Davies, W.L., 'Astudiaeth o waith Peter Maxwell Davies (o'r *Sonata Op. 1* hyd *Le Jongleur de Notre Dame*, 1978)' (Ph.D., Aberystwyth, 1983).

Grossman, Orin, 'Thirteen Essays from the Three Yearbooks *Das Meisterwerk in der Musik* by Heinrich Schenker: An Annotated Translation' (Ph.D., Northwestern University, 1973).

Roberts, David, 'Techniques of Composition in the Music of Peter Maxwell Davies' (Ph.D., Birmingham University, 1985).

Rossberg, Stefan, 'Die Monodramen von Peter Maxwell Davies' (Ph.D., Hamburg, 1993).

Sisbee, Ann Loomis, 'Peter Maxwell Davies' *Stone Litany*: Integration and Dynamic Process' (D.M.A., Cornell, 1979).

Warnaby, John, 'The Music of Peter Maxwell Davies based on the Writings of George Mackay Brown' (Ph.D., Open University, 1990).

## Books

Adkins, Cecil, and Dickinson, Alis, *Doctoral Dissertations in Musicology*, (American Musicological Society International Music Society, 1977, 1990, 1996).

Bartlett, Ian, and Sarnaker, Benedict, 'Register of Dissertations and Theses on Music in Britain and Ireland', *Research Chronicle* 25 (1992), ed. Simon McVeigh.

Baker, James, Beach, David W. and Bernard, Jonathan W. (eds), *Music Theory in Concept and Practice* (Rochester: University of Rochester Press, 1997).

Bayliss, Colin, *The Music of Sir Peter Maxwell Davies* (London: Highgate, 1991).

Cammann, Schuyler van Renssalaer, 'Magic Square', *Encyclopaedia Britannica* (Chicago: William Benton, c.1971) vol. 14, pp. 573–5.

Connelly, Joseph, *Hymns of the Roman Liturgy* (London: Longmans, Green and Co., 1957).

Cook, Nicholas, *A Guide to Musical Analysis* (London: Dent, 1987).

Coulston Report 1962: Music in Education – Proceedings of the 14th Symposium of the Coulston Research Society ('Music Composition for Children' pp. 108–15 and discussion pp. 116–24) (London: Butterworths, 1963).

Danuser, Hermann (ed.), *Die klassizistische Moderne in der Musik der 20. Jahrhunderts* (Basel: Amadeus Verlag, 1997).

Dufallo, Richard, *Trackings* (New York: OUP, 1989).

Dunsby, Jonathan, *Pierrot Lunaire* (Cambridge: CUP, 1992).

Dunsby, J. and Whittall, A. *Music Analysis in Theory and Practice* (London: Faber, 1988).

Dunstable: John Dunstable Complete works, ed. Manfred F. Bukofzer, *Musica Britannica*, vol. 8, rev. Margaret Bent, Ian Bent and Brian Trowell (London: Stainer and Bell, 2nd revised edition, 1970).

Foreman, Lewis (ed.), *British Music Now* (London: Elek, 1975).

Gardner, Martin, 'Magic Squares', *More Mathematical Puzzles and Diversions*, (Harmondsworth: Penguin Books, 1966).

Goehr, Alexander, *Finding the Key* (London: Faber and Faber, 1998).

Griffiths, Paul, *Modern Music: the Avant-Garde Since 1945* (London: Dent, 1981).

Griffiths, Paul, *Peter Maxwell Davies* (London: Robson, 1982).

Griffiths, Paul, *New Sounds, New Personalities* (London: Faber, 1985).

Griffiths, Paul, *Modern Music and After: Directions Since 1945* (Oxford: Oxford University Press, 1995).

Hall, Michael, *Birtwistle* (London: Robson, 1984).

Jeutner, Renate, *Peter Maxwell Davies: Ein Komponistenporträt*, Musik der Zeit Dokumentation und Studien 3 (Bonn: Boosey and Hawkes, 1983).

Lester, Joel, *Analytical Approaches to Twentieth-Century Music* (New York: Norton, 1989).

Lewis, Geraint (ed.), *Michael Tippett. A Celebration* (Tunbridge Wells: The Baton Press, 1985).

Macqueen, John, *Numerology* (Edinburgh: Edinburgh University Press, 1985).

Mann, Thomas, *Doktor Faustus* (Stockholm: Bermann-Fischer, 1947); translated Helen T. Lowe-Porter (New York: Knopf, 1948).

Moldenhauer, Hans and Rosaleen, *Anton von Webern: A Chronicle of his Life and Work* (New York: Knopf, 1979).

Northcott, Bayan, *The Music Theatre of Alexander Goehr* (London: Schott and Co., 1980).

Paddison, Max, *Adorno's Aesthetics of Music* (Cambridge: CUP, 1993).

Pruslin, Stephen, *Peter Maxwell Davies: Studies from Two Decades*, Tempo Booklet no. 2 (London: Boosey and Hawkes, 1979).

Reese, Gustave, *Music in the Middle Ages* (London: J.M. Dent and Sons, 1941).

Schafer, R. Murray, *British Composers in Interview* (London: Faber and Faber, 1963).

Schenker, Heinrich, *Das Meisterwerk in der Musik*, vols 1–3 (Munich: Drei Masken Verlag, 1925–30); facsimile edition (Hildesheim: Georg Olms, 1974).

Schools Music Association, *Music in Schools, A Personal View*, presidential address by Peter Maxwell Davies CBE at the North of England Education Conference (London: Boosey and Hawkes, 1985) (booklet).

Seabrook, Mike, *Max* (London: Gollancz, 1994).

Smith, Carolyn, *Peter Maxwell Davies: Bio-Bibliography* (Westport, Conn.: Greenwood, 1995).

Stern, J.P., *Nietzsche* (London: Fontana/Collins, 1978).

Stravinsky, Igor (translated anon.), *An Autobiography* (New York: M.J. Steuer, 1958).

Stuckenschmidt, Heinrich, *Arnold Schoenberg* (London: Calder, 1955).

Taruskin, Richard, *Stravinsky and the Russian Traditions: A Biography of the Works through 'Mavra'* (Berkeley and Los Angeles: University of California Press, 1996).

Taruskin, Richard, *Defining Russia Musically* (Princeton: Princeton University Press, 1997).

Williams, Alastair, *New Music and the Claims of Modernity* (Aldershot: Ashgate, 1997).

## Articles

Andrews, John, 'Maxwell Davies's *The Shepherd's Calendar*', *Tempo* 87 (Winter 1968–9), pp. 6–9.

Arnold, Stephen, 'The Music of *Taverner*', *Tempo* 101 (1972), pp. 20–39.

Beecroft, Julian, 'Maxwell Davies's Fifth Symphony', *Tempo* 191 (December 1994), pp. 2–5.

Chanan, Michael, 'Dialectics in Peter Maxwell Davies', *Tempo* 90 (Autumn 1969), pp. 12–22.

Clements, Andrew, 'The Festival of St Magnus', *Music and Musicians*, 25/10 (June 1977), pp. 42–4.

Clements, Andrew, 'Maxwell Davies's New Symphony', *Music and Musicians*, 26/6 (February 1978), pp. 24–5.

Clements, Andrew, 'Peter Maxwell Davies' in *New Grove Dictionary of Opera*, vol. III, ed. Stanley Sadie (London: Macmillan, 1992).

Cole, Bruce, '*The Blind Fiddler*', *Tempo* 117 (June 1976), pp. 32–3.

Conway, Paul, 'Recent Maxwell Davies Premieres', *Tempo* 204 (April 1998), pp. 36–7.

Davies, Lyn, 'Maxwell Davies' Organ Music', *Musical Times*, 125/1699 (September 1984), pp. 525–7.

Davies, Peter Maxwell, 'The Young British Composer', *Score* (1956), p. 84.

Davies, Peter Maxwell, 'Problems of a British Composer Today', *The Listener*, 62 (8 October 1959), pp. 563–4.

Davies, Peter Maxwell, 'Composing Music for School Use', *Making Music* 46 (Summer 1961), pp. 7–8.

Davies, Peter Maxwell, 'Music Composition for Children', in W. Grant (ed.), *Music in Education*, Colston Papers 14 (London: Butterworths, 1963), p. 108.

Davies, Peter Maxwell, 'The Young Composer in America', *Tempo* 72 (Spring 1965), pp. 2–6.

Davies, Peter Maxwell, 'Where our Colleges Fail', *Times Educational Supplement* 2699 (1967), p. 4.

Davies, Peter Maxwell, 'Sets or Series', *The Listener*, 79 (22 February 1968), p. 250.

Davies, Peter Maxwell, 'Peter Maxwell Davies on some of his Recent Work', *The Listener*, 81 (23 January 1969), p. 121.

Davies, Peter Maxwell, 'The orchestra is becoming a Museum' in 'The Symphony Orchestra – Has it a Future?', *Composer* 37 (Autumn 1970), pp. 6–8.

Davies, Peter Maxwell, '*Taverner*: Synopsis and Documentation', *Tempo* 101 (1972), p. 4.

Davies, Peter Maxwell, 'Pax Orcadiensis', *Tempo* 119 (December 1976), pp. 20–2.

Davies, Peter Maxwell, 'Symphony', *Tempo* 124 (March 1978), pp. 2–5.

Griffiths, Paul, 'Maxwell Davies's Piano Sonata', *Tempo* 140 (March 1982), pp. 5–9.

Harbinson, John, 'Peter Maxwell Davies' *Taverner*', *Perspectives of New Music*, 11/1 (Fall–Winter 1972), pp. 233–40.

Harvey, David, '*Hill Runes*', *Tempo* 149 (June 1984), pp. 14–18.

Harvey, Jonathan, 'Maxwell Davies's *Songs for a Mad King*', *Tempo* 89 (Summer 1969), pp. 2–6.

Henderson, Robert, 'Peter Maxwell Davies', *Musical Times*, 102/1424 (October 1961), pp. 624–6.

Henderson, Robert, 'Peter Maxwell Davies's *Shakespeare Music*', *Tempo* 72 (Spring 1965), pp. 15–18.

Henning, Lohner, 'Komponieren wider die Indifferenz: Der englishe Komponist Peter Maxwell Davies in Gespräch', *Neue Zeitschrift für Musik* CXL, VII/2 (February 1986), pp. 21–4.

Jones, Nicholas, '"Preliminary Workings": The Precompositional Process in Maxwell Davies's Third Symphony', *Tempo* 204 (April 1998), pp. 14–22.

Josipovici, Gabriel, '*Taverner*: Thoughts on the Libretto', *Tempo* 101 (1972), p. 12.

Keller, Hans, 'The State of the Symphony, not only Maxwell Davies's', *Tempo* 125 (June 1978), pp. 6–11.

Kerman, Joseph, 'Popish Ditties', *Tempo* 102 (1972), pp. 20–4.

Lawson, Peter, 'Maxwell Davies's *Worldes Blis*', *Tempo* 90 (Autumn 1969), pp. 23–27.

McGregor, Richard, 'The Early Music of Peter Maxwell Davies', *Tempo* 160 (March 1986), pp. 2–5.

McGregor, Richard, 'The Maxwell Davies Sketch Material in the British Library', *Tempo* 196 (April 1996), pp. 9–19 and 197 (July 1996), pp. 20–2.

Meph, Johannes, 'Past or Future? Peter Maxwell Davies: Symphony No. 6', *Musical Times* 137/1842 (August 1996), p. 33.

Milnes, Rodney, 'Towards Music Theatre', *Opera* 23/12 (1972) p. 1067.

Northcott, Bayan, 'Peter Maxwell Davies', *Music and Musicians* 17/8 (April 1969), pp. 36–41, 80, 82.

Owens, Peter, 'Revelation and Fallacy: Observations on Compositional Technique in the Music of Peter Maxwell Davies', *Music Analysis*, 13 2/3 (October 1994), pp. 161–202.

Payne, Anthony, 'Maxwell Davies's *Veni Sancte Spiritus*', *Tempo* 70 (Autumn 1964), pp. 15–18.

Payne, Anthony, 'Peter Maxwell Davies's *Five Motets*', *Tempo* 72 (Spring 1965), pp. 2–11.

Pinzauti, Leonardo, 'A Colloquio con Peter Maxwell Davies', *Nuova RM Italiana* VI/I, (Jan.–Mar. 1972), pp. 87–92.

Pruslin, Stephen, '*Second Taverner Fantasia*', *Tempo* 73 (Summer 1965), pp. 2–11.

Pruslin, Stephen, 'An Anatomy of Betrayal', *Music and Musicians* 20/11 (July 1972), p. 28.

Pruslin, Stephen, 'Returns and Departures: Recent Maxwell Davies', *Tempo* 113 (June 1975), pp. 22–8.

Pruslin, Stephen, 'The Triangular Space: Davies's *Ave Maris Stella*', *Tempo* 120 (March 1977), pp. 16–22.

Pruslin, Stephen, 'Maxwell Davies's Symphony: An Introduction', *Tempo* 124 (March 1978), pp. 6–9.

Pruslin, Stephen, '"One if by Land, Two if by Sea" – Maxwell Davies the Symphonist', *Tempo* 153 (June 1985), pp. 2–6.

Pruslin, Stephen, 'Peter Maxwell Davies's Symphony no 4', *Musical Times* 130 (September 1989), pp. 520–3 and reprinted on the website <http://www.maxopus.com>.

Roberts, David, 'Maxwell Davies in Orkney: *The Martyrdom of St Magnus*', *Musical Times* 118/1614 (1977), pp. 633–5.

Roberts, David, review of scores by Peter Maxwell Davies in *Contact* 19 (Summer 1978), pp. 26–9; *Contact* 23 (Winter 1981), pp. 26–9; review of Griffiths, *Peter Maxwell Davies*, in *Contact* 24 (1982), pp. 23–5.

Schotel, Brian, 'Peter Maxwell Davies's Music for Young People', *Music Teacher* 52 (September 1973), pp. 13–14.

Smalley, Roger, 'Some Recent Works of Peter Maxwell Davies', *Tempo* 84 (Spring 1968), pp. 2–5.

Sonntag, Brunhilde, 'Interview mit Peter Maxwell Davies', *ZM Pädagogik* VIII/21 (1983), pp. 3–17.

Sutcliffe, Tom, 'The Origins of Vesalius', *Music and Musicians* 18/4 (December 1969), pp. 24, 74.

Sutcliffe, Tom, 'A Question of Identity: *Blind Man's Buff* and *Taverner*', *Music and Musicans* 20/10 (June 1972), p. 26.

Swan, Annalyn, 'A Visionary Composer', *Atlantic* CCLV (March 1985), pp. 105–7.

Sweeney-Turner, Steve, 'Resurrecting the Antichrist: Maxwell Davies and Parody – Dialectics or Deconstruction', *Tempo* 191 (December 1994), pp. 14–20.

Taylor, Michael, 'Maxwell Davies's *Vesalii Icones*', *Tempo* 92 (Spring 1970), pp. 22–7.

Trowell, Brian, 'Proportion in the Music of Dunstable', *Proceedings of the Royal Musical Association* 105 (1978–9).

Walsh, Stephen, 'Taverner', *Musical Times* 113/1553 (1972), pp. 653–55.

Walsh, Stephen, with Roberts, David, 'Davies, Peter Maxwell', *The New Grove Dictionary of Music and Musicians*, ed. Stanley Sadie (London: Macmillan, 1980), vol. 5, pp. 275–9.

Warnaby, John, '*Westerlings* – a Study in Symphonic Form', *Tempo* 147 (December 1983), pp. 15–22.

Warnaby, John, 'Peter Maxwell Davies' Orchestral Music', *Music and Musicians* 33/4 (December 1984), pp. 6–8.

Warnaby, John, 'Peter Maxwell Davies' Educational Music: The Orkney Years', *Music Teacher* 64/4 (April 1985), pp. 10–11.

Warnaby, John, 'Resurrection: Origins, Themes, Symbolism', *Tempo* 191 (December 1994), pp. 2–5.

Waterhouse, John C.G., 'Peter Maxwell Davies: Towards an Opera', *Tempo* 69 (Summer 1964), pp. 18–25.

Waterhouse, John C.G., 'Meeting Point', *Music and Musicians* 13/2 (October 1964), pp. 24–6.

Whittall, Arnold, 'Music Analysis as Human Science? *Le Sacre du Printemps* in Theory and Practice', *Music Analysis* 1/1 (March 1982), pp. 33–53.

Whittall, Arnold, review of 'Peter Maxwell Davies Symphony No. 2', *Music and Letters* 64 (1983), pp. 318–29.

Whittall, Arnold, 'The Bottom Line', *Musical Times* 135/1819 (September 1994), pp. 544–50.

Whittall, Arnold, 'Comparatively Complex: Birtwistle, Maxwell Davies and Modernist Analysis', *Musical Analysis* 13 2/3 (October 1994), pp. 139–59.

Whittall, Arnold, 'Cross-currents and Convergencies: Britten, Maxwell Davies and the Sense of Place', *Tempo* 204 (April 1998), pp. 5–11.

Whitall, Arnold, 'Peter Maxwell Davies and the Problem of Classicizing Modernism', in Hermann Danuser (ed.), *Die Klassizistische Moderne in der Musik den 20. Jahrhunderts* (Basel: Amadeus Verlag, 1997), pp. 143–51.

## Other

Cox, John, staging note in *Naboth's Vineyard* (London: Schott and Co., 1973).

Graham, Colin, production note in *Curlew River* (London: Faber Music, 1965).

Note: This bibliography contains cited or substantive *Tempo* articles about Davies's music. A complete list of *Tempo* articles including reviews etc., programme notes for most works, spoken introductions for selected pieces and a collection of general essays can be found at the Maxopus webpage: <http://www.maxopus.com>.

# Index

In the light of Davies's later practice, it is natural to seek some systematic means of transforming the plainchant into the set, but I have had no success in finding one. It is perhaps more productive to observe that the set and the opening of the plainchant are unified by four ordered trichords held in common – one of these is the same as the final isolated trichord of the oboe (Ex. 1.14). These correspond to the four trichordal divisions of the partitioning of S and SI in this movement (compare this with Ex. 1.3).

Ex. 1.14: *Ave Redemptoris Mater* – set trichords

The juxtaposition of the oboe line and the material derived from S seems to have been carried out with an eye to interfusion and harmonic interaction. For example

- the opening C–F of bars 9–13 interfuses with S₀ 6–7 and I-SI 0–1
- the C of bars 18–12 combines with the interfused S₀ 6–7 and SI 0–1 (D–G♯ I of bar 40) to form a (0,4,8) trichord
- the B–E of bars 65–9 combines with the interfused S₀ 6–7 and SI₁ 0–1 (B♯–C of bar 66) to form another (0,4,8) trichord

**Conclusion**

The discussion of the first movement doesn't do full justice to the variety of transformations the set undergoes, nor does it explain the more rarified structural procedures of the second and third movements, the double bass chaconne which combines permuted set material.

neither content X of the primes is associated with Y but is accompanied by
all five now, in segments of the primes are state (accompanied by the remaining
instruments). X is again are therefore

The same features are articulated on a different basis. On essence the first
section, bars 1–15, creating the six spaces, giving intervals and within those units
dynamics, dynamics, etc are superimposed. On the rhythm and so on the
X, Y, Z, are superimposed are of YZ, on each beginning point begin to
grow into how subtly indicate subtle a removal of the other segments and form as
and one every as the series sum there to is sung as parts

X ... is superimposed with
Y ... associated with
Z ... blended with

and in addition the primes segments have, out not pitch classes in common (for
instance)

Ex. 1. from *Allan Ridout*'s series on pitch class correspondence

The third section, bars 28–45, is a reworking of the first. The six are designated
(Y + W) verticals are extracted from their proper places and placed at the end. The
remaining interposed segments appear in a more condensed form than in the first
section, with a great deal of elision; for example, X and Y are always combined
so that the two notes of x are assigned to one instrument and the additional note
that converts x into X as assigned to a second.

Decoration in this movement is restricted to non-serial mordents, trills, and
single grace notes fixed at a distance of scalar interval 11 or 13 from the note they
decorate.